# Balakirev

1. Balakirev in 1866

# BALAKIREV

*A critical study
of his life and music*

*by*

EDWARD GARDEN

ST. MARTIN'S PRESS
NEW YORK

*Printed in Great Britain*

*First published in the United States 1967*
*by St. Martin's Press, Inc.*
*Library of Congress Catalog Card Number*
*67–18825*

# CONTENTS

# Contents

# ILLUSTRATIONS

# A NOTE ON THE BIBLIOGRAPHY

Most of the important bibliography on Balakirev is in Russian. One of the most useful articles is by G. I. Timofeyev in *Russkaya Mysl* (1912), Nos vi and vii, supplemented by S. M. Lyapunov's article in *Ezhegodnik imperatorskikh teatrov* (*Year Book of the Imperial Theatres*), Nos vii and viii (1910).

Amongst the published volumes of correspondence are those between Balakirev and V. V. Stassov, *Perepiska M. A. Balakireva s V. V. Stasovym*, Vol. I, 1858–69 (Moscow, 1935); between Balakirev and Tchaikovsky, *Perepiska M. A. Balakireva s P. I. Chaikovskim*, (St Petersburg, 1912); Balakirev's correspondence from Prague in 1866–67, published in *Sovremenny Mir*, (1911), No. 6, by Timofeyev.

All the above are in Russian, and, except for the Tchaikovsky correspondence, were lent to me by Dr Gerald Abraham, together with many other useful volumes and scores. Dr Abraham also let me see the original letters between Balakirev and M. D. Calvocoressi in his possession.

For many of the other volumes in my possession I am indebted to N. T. H. Jones of Clifton College, Bristol, and M. Lester-Cribb of Fettes College, Edinburgh. Particularly useful were some early songs, the Tchaikovsky–Balakirev correspondence, and the complete piano works of Balakirev edited by K. S. Sorokin (Moscow–Leningrad, 1949–54).

A recent book of interest is *M. A. Balakirev: Issledovaniya i stati*: (*M. A. Balakirev: Analyses and Articles*), published in Leningrad in 1961. This is by various authors and includes much hitherto unpublished information. It does not pretend, however, to be a co-ordinated book; the articles are quite separate and are

# A Note on the Bibliography

given in the bibliography (Appendix I) under separate headings to avoid confusion. Another recent volume containing documents is *M. A. Balakirev: Vospominaniya i pisma* (Leningrad, 1962). A list of the Recollections of Balakirev and the correspondence contained in this book is given in the bibliography.

Articles on Balakirev in languages other than Russian are few and for the most part of negligible value, except for those by Gerald Abraham in English. Dr Abraham's short article in the fifth edition of Grove's *Dictionary of Music and Musicians* (London, 1954), p. 362, is masterly in its concise appraisal and summary of Balakirev's life and importance, and only a few minor facts in this article have been proved to be inaccurate in the light of more recently available documents and books. The same author's other articles, particularly those on the *King Lear* music, the piano sonata and the symphonies (in *On Russian Music*, pp. 193, 204 and 179) show insight into the composer's mind. It is these articles which first inspired me to probe deeper into the works and life of Balakirev.

A complete list of the main bibliography used in the present work is given in Appendix I, together with the reference letters used for the various volumes in the footnotes, which also contain all references to other volumes and documents. All quotations in the main body of the book are from the original Russian, and are translated by me unless the contrary is stated.

I should like to thank Dr Abraham for putting all the invaluable and otherwise unobtainable material in his possession at my disposal. I should also like to thank for their help with documents and illustrations: N. T. H. Jones; Mrs E. N. Alexeyeva—Director of the Central Museum of Music in Moscow; the Society for Cultural Relations with the U.S.S.R.; the Novosti Press Agency; and in particular Miss A. S. Lyapunova of Leningrad and Mr V. A. Kiselev of Moscow.

EDINBURGH, 1966                                                       E.G.

# A NOTE ON THE SPELLING

The transliteration of Russian names into the English equivalent has been done on the following basis:

1. In names, such as Tchaikovsky, which have a generally accepted spelling, that spelling has been retained.
2. The pronunciation in *English* only, has been taken into account. Thus, a 'j' as pronounced in English does not occur in Russian, and is therefore not used. The French 'j', as in *jamais*, has been spelt 'zh'.
3. A hard 'i' and endings in 'ii' have been changed to a 'y' (vowel), as is common practice; 'y' has also been used extensively as a consonant (as in 'yes') rather than 'i', which is not used as a consonant in English.

(In Balakirev's patronymic 'Alexeyevich', the English 'x'—associated in our minds with the name—rather than the Russian 'ks' has been used.)

Any transliteration can only be a rough guide.

# INTRODUCTION

Tchaikovsky:

Balakirev's personality is the strongest in the whole group . . .
His talent is amazing, but various fatal draw-backs have helped
to extinguish it . . . In spite of his wonderful gifts, he has done
a lot of harm . . . He is the inventor of all the theories of this
extraordinary circle, in which are to be found so many undeveloped, incorrectly developed, or prematurely decayed
talents.[1]

Rimsky-Korsakov:

Balakirev made a great impression on me from the very beginning. He was an excellent pianist, and his capacity for playing
at sight and extemporizing was boundless . . . He had a wide
knowledge of music of all kinds and was able to call to mind,
at any moment, every bar he had ever heard or read . . . We
were completely bewitched by his talents, his authority, his
magnetism . . .[2]

Lyapunov:

The part he played in the development of Russian Music is
incomparably important, and after Glinka first place in the
history of Russian music should be allotted to Mily Alexeyevich Balakirev.[3]

Cui:

I am of the opinion that he could have achieved much more
than he did achieve. At one time he had all music in his hands.
He could have been at the head of the Conservatoire and also

15

at the head of the Imperial Opera. He conducted the symphony concerts and made much of the Free School of Music. The musical powers-that-be were ready to patronize him. But Mily Alexeyevich found it difficult to get on with people. He was a man of independent nature, not a good mixer, perhaps rather disobliging. He was not in the habit of paying compliments. Balakirev undertook much, but, thanks to his disposition, soon had to give up.[4]

Borodin:

Liszt is a real Balakirev, a great-hearted man indeed—such friends are really 'friendly friends'.[5]

Ludmila Shestakova (Glinka's sister):

Towards Balakirev his [Mussorgsky's] behaviour was invariably one of deep respect, testifying to his admiration for his teacher's great talent and wonderful memory.[6]

These are the sort of remarks about Balakirev that it is possible to read in the course of works about other composers, and if we know anything about him at all, it is usually by reading such isolated paragraphs on him, sometimes bigoted and untrustworthy, sometimes fair and reasonably accurate. There is not a single full-length study of his life and works in any language, and it is this gap in our knowledge of a composer who at last is slowly gaining the recognition he deserves, that the present critical study is intended to fill.

This extraordinary character is as contradictory a figure as can be found anywhere in the history of music: selfless and autocratic, helpful and domineering, thoroughly sincere and remarkably tactless. But does he deserve more than his place in history as the leader and mentor of the Russian national group of composers known erroneously in English speaking countries as 'The Five'? We know that Tchaikovsky was wrong about 'so many undeveloped, incorrectly developed, or prematurely decayed talents'. Our knowledge of Borodin, if it goes no further than the second

## Introduction

symphony, the second string quartet and *Prince Igor*; of Rimsky-Korsakov, if only in *Sheherazade* and an opera or two; and of Mussorgsky, perhaps particularly in *Boris Godunov*, a few songs and *Pictures from an Exhibition*, should preclude our taking Tchaikovsky's letter too seriously. But what were the 'drawbacks' (if any) in Balakirev's talent to which he referred, and were they 'fatal'? Are we to agree with César Cui, his one-time collaborator and a member of 'The Five', that 'he could have achieved more than he did achieve'? Was he 'rather disobliging' or a 'great-hearted man indeed'? The present enquiry endeavours to throw more light on such questions as these, light which it is hoped will not be thought unnecessary if only because the literature dealing with this subject is so scanty and often erroneous.

### NOTES ON THE INTRODUCTION

1. Much-quoted letter from Tchaikovsky to Madame von Meck, written in 1877.
2. Rimsky-Korsakov: *Record of my Musical Life* (*Letopis moei Muzykalnoi Zhizni*), Moscow, 1955, p. 18, quoted by S. Lyapunov, L(2)A, No. vii, pp. 52–53.
3. L(2)A, No. viii, p. 53.
4. Cui in his *Recollections* (*Vospominaniya*) quoted by Grodsky G(3)A, p. 16.
5. Borodin, after meeting Liszt in 1881; quoted by M. D. Calvocoressi in his article on Borodin in *Masters of Russian Music*, p. 168.
6. CB, p. 65.

# His Life and Character

# CHAPTER 1

*1837–1857: Birth – early precocity – piano lessons with Dubuque – introduction to Ulybyshev – conducts Ulybyshev's orchestra – teaches himself from the works in Ulybyshev's library – Ulybyshev's fatherly feelings towards him – septet, octet, Grand Fantasia on Russian folk tunes – enters university of Kazan with Boborykin –* Fantasia on Glinka's A Life for the Tsar *– string quartet – concerto movement in F sharp minor – three songs – Ulybyshev takes him to St Petersburg – musical life in St Petersburg – introduced to Glinka and Ludmila Shestakova – effects of Glinka's death – plays* Fantasia *to Glinka – Spanish March Theme – first public appearances – meets other influential musical figures including Cui, Dargomyzhsky and the Stassov brothers – early pianoforte music.*

Mily Alexeyevich Balakirev was born on 21 December 1836/2 January 1837,[1] in Nizhny-Novgorod,[2] a city on the Eastern frontier of ancient Muscovy first built in the thirteenth century as a stronghold against the invasions of tribes from the East. For many hundreds of years an annual fair had been held there, which attracted a very mixed group of races, Slavonic, Tartar and even Mongol.[3] The folk music of these people must have impressed the boy, but otherwise there was no music to speak of in the rather drowsy town, which had a population of about seventy thousand in the 1880s. When the young Balakirev returned to his native town in the early 'seventies to give a concert—by this time he was well known in both St Petersburg and Moscow—the hall remained more than half empty; Nizhny-Novgorod was not interested.

It is therefore more than likely that if his mother had not given him early music lessons and taken him, during his summer holidays from the local *gymnasium*, for a course of ten piano lessons with Field's pupil, Alexandre Dubuque, in Moscow, and generally encouraged his music, his talents might have remained hidden and unacknowledged. His father does not appear to have been very interested, though Balakirev recalled in his late life how he played, in those far-off days, a pianoforte trio of Schubert of which his father was fond.[4]

Mily showed himself to be musical at a very early age, with a good ear and an excellent memory. He could reproduce tunes by ear on the pianoforte at the age of four, though it is doubtful if he showed such a predilection for the keys which were later almost to haunt him—B flat minor, D major and their relatives. It would be tempting, but unwise, to imagine Mily haunted as a child by five flats and two sharps as other children are haunted by giants or ghosts.

Balakirev, as an old man (on 16/29 March 1907), wrote to N. F. Findeisen ,editor of the *Russian Musical Gazette*, about his youth:

I have only a very vague recollection of my musical development in the period of my infancy. As far as I can remember, from the age of eight I seldom left my piano, endeavouring to play any music which I heard. I recall very well having had, from my infancy, a very well-developed sense of sound, for, when visiting the house of my uncle, Vassily Yasherov, I reckoned that his piano was tuned a tone lower than ours.[5]

Balakirev's father could trace his descent back to one Andrei Simonovich Balakirev, who lived in the early seventeenth century. In the eighteenth century Ivan Ivanovich Balakirev received from his wife as a dowry estates in the Nizhny-Novgorod area which their grandson Stepan Vassilevich Balakirev inherited in 1762.[6] S. V. Balakirev was an officer in the household troops; in 1781 he married, and the elder of his two sons, Konstantin Stepanovich, born in 1783, was Balakirev's grandfather. He had four sons and four daughters. K. S. Balakirev died in 1861, leaving his estates—heavily burdened with debts—to Balakirev's father, Alexei Konstantinovich, who was born in 1809 and married Elizabeth Ivanovna Yasherova in 1834.[7] The Yasherovs were of the minor nobility in the Nizhny-Novgorod district, and as far as Balakirev's talent can be ascribed to either of his parents, it should be ascribed to his mother's side of the family. His father's career was a failure. From 1827 he held a minor post as a government official until a year or two after his wife's death in 1847. From 1851 to 1857 he was assistant to the head of the department of state property; after this he was unable to hold down a job for more than a year or two at a time. Both he and his family were poverty-stricken; he was a man totally without initiative.[8]

Mily was the eldest of four children and the only son in the family. His sisters were Anna (b. 1838), Maria (b. 1843) and Varvara (b. 1845). Mily was transferred from the *gymnasium* to the Alexandrovsky Institute as a boarder after his mother's death. The only lessons in music from which he would later acknowledge that he had gained any benefit were those given to him by Dubuque, who made him learn Hummel's A minor piano concerto with Field's fingering. Balakirev later used to say: 'If I have any technical ability at all, I am indebted for this to A. I. Dubuque, who taught me the principles of correct technique and fingering on the pianoforte.'[9]

A certain Karl Eisrich, who was known locally as a teacher and conductor, continued his musical education. Eisrich was conductor of the local theatre orchestra which played at musical evenings at the house of a local landowner named Alexander Dmitriyevich Ulybyshev. Besides being a keen amateur musician, Ulybyshev had written a book on Mozart in 1844 and later wrote one on Beethoven (1857). Chamber music and piano music were also played at these musical evenings. Eisrich arranged the music, and it was through him that Balakirev first heard Chopin's E minor piano concerto, for which he was to have lasting affection. In old age he re-orchestrated it for a concert on the occasion of the centenary of Chopin's birth in February 1910.

Once the boy was taken specially from school and was driven to the house of a friend of his father's in order to hear the pianist and composer Ivan Feodorovich Laskovsky who was visiting Nizhny. Laskovsky played, amongst other things, the first movement of Chopin's B minor sonata.[10]

Eisrich also introduced to him the **Grand Trio** from Glinka's *A Life for the Tsar,* and it must have been as a result of the profound impression these and other works of the same composers made upon him that Balakirev admired Chopin and Glinka as much as any other composer for the rest of his life. It is perhaps from this period too (the early 1850s) that his absorption with the keys of B flat minor, D major and their relative keys began—probably unconsciously at first. Both Chopin and Glinka were fond of these keys but not to the same extent as Balakirev was later to become.

Soon after Eisrich had introduced him to Ulybyshev he was made Eisrich's assistant and widened his musical experience by taking part in chamber music and the conducting of various music, including, in 1852, Beethoven's first, fourth and eighth symphonies.[11] A year or two later Ulybyshev required him to play through Beethoven's piano sonatas to him in connection with his work on that composer, *Beethoven, ses critiques et glossateurs,* and probably also the concertos, as Balakirev was clearly acquainted with these on his arrival in St Petersburg in 1855 and played the solo part in the E flat concerto in the presence of the Tsar and the whole Imperial family in 1858.

It was due also to the excellent musical library of Ulybyshev that he became acquainted with Beethoven's late string quartets, which he appreciated and admired when they were still imperfectly understood by many Western musicians. One of his first published transcriptions for piano was an arrangement of the Cavatina from Beethoven's quartet Op. 130, in 1859.

Ulybyshev's feelings towards Balakirev may be judged from a letter he wrote to him when he was dying (7/19 January 1858): 'You know that I am not a sentimental sort of person, but I must tell you now that I love you as a son and would have indeed thanked God if you had really been my son.'[12]

Many other composers were represented in the concerts given at Ulybyshev's house, including Mendelssohn, Hummel and Mozart. Balakirev helped Eisrich to prepare a performance of

Mozart's *Requiem* in 1851.[13] He derived great advantage from the knowledge and experience he gained both from these concerts and from the music library. The library was well stocked with a great variety of music which Balakirev made use of and studied extensively, learning to compose at as early an age as fifteen from the actual works of other composers.[14] His keen musical intelligence must soon have absorbed what he wanted from the compositions, noting interesting harmonic progressions for future use, and his phenomenal memory and also his extemporising ability would ensure that he understood and was able to make use of whatever music he came in contact with.

His first compositions, which appeared in 1852, show what he had been able to teach himself. The first, a movement of a septet for strings, flute, clarinet and piano, was written in imitation of Henselt's piano concerto, according to Timofeyev. This was probably arranged later as an octet, of which the first movement, an allegro in C minor, and sixty-nine bars of a scherzo were written in 1855–56. (The scherzo was not scored.) The date of completion of the allegro on the score is March 3, but no year is given. The octet is scored for piano, flute, oboe, horn, violin, viola, cello and double bass, and it is numbered Op. 3.[15] It is for this reason that it is likely to be an arrangement of the septet, as his Op. 4, finished on 12/24 December 1852, was a Grand Fantasia on Russian Folk Tunes for piano and orchestra. The title and inscription at the head of the manuscript reads: 'Grande Fantaisie sur airs nationales (*sic*) russes pour le pianoforte avec accompagnement d'orchestre composée et dédiée à son maître Monsieur Charles Eisrich par Mily Balakireff, Op. 4.'[16] At the end of the manuscript appears the following inscription: 'Finis del prima parte Auctor Milius Balakireff.' Mily was clearly a normally exuberant boy.

At the age of sixteen, in 1853, he left the Alexandrovsky Institute and entered the University of Kazan as a mathematics student. The novelist Peter Dmitriyevich Boborykin, who had been at the Institute with him, went to Kazan at the same time. They shared a flat, and Boborykin wrote of their life in Kazan in his recollections, published in *Russkaya Mysl* in 1907.[17]

The musical life at Kazan was almost as restricted as at Nizhny-Novgorod. Visiting artists occasionally gave recitals. He was introduced to two such artists of note, both of them pianists: Seymour Sheath and Anton Kątski.[18] According to Boborykin, Kątski visited them in their flat and gave Balakirev a few piano lessons; and he again met Laskovsky. He admired Laskovsky's piano compositions and in later life tried to have some of them published again, but with little success. He planned to have further lessons in St Petersburg with Kątski, but when he went there decided against it.

Balakirev's father's income was so small that he could not afford to pay the fee for Mily's matriculation at the University, so he studied as an unmatriculated student. His means were consequently very slender and he eked them out by giving music lessons. He lived in the hope that he might be able to go to St Petersburg and take up music as a career, but his father's straitened circumstances did not seem to promise much in this direction. In all, he spent two years in Kazan but apparently only one year at the University. Balakirev's application for admission as an external student is dated '3 September 1853', and on '10 May 1854' he applied to the Rector for the return of his documents. Although he lived in Kazan during the winter of 1854–55, he had no connection with the University.[19] During the summers of 1854 and 1855 Balakirev spent his holidays with Ulybyshev, and Philippe Valier, who heard him playing the piano in 1854, testifies to his virtuosity.[20] Apparently, during the latter part of his time at Kazan, Balakirev lived with Valier in his flat; Valier taught music at the Rodionovsky Institute for Girls in Kazan, the headmistress of which was Mrs Zagoskina. This admirable lady invited Balakirev to her 'evenings' at which he met many young people, even, so the gossips said, falling in love with her daughter.[21] While he was at Kazan, Balakirev composed a pianoforte Fantasia on themes from Glinka's *A life for the Tsar* and attempted a String Quartet (the linguistic acrobatics had not yet disappeared from manuscripts; this was called 'Quatuor Original Russe'). It may be that this work was started earlier and was intended to be Op. 2, but it was never completed. Boborykin recalled that he was working on it at this time, and confirmed that Balakirev had no books on harmony, orchestration or the theory of music.

The piano Fantasia shows considerable development and is in the nature of a written-down extemporisation. It is a quite brilliant and fairly effective work, and is mentioned by Balakirev in a letter to Ulybyshev of February 1855. It was later revised and published by Zimmermann in July 1899. The first movement of a piano concerto in F sharp minor was also started in 1855. On the autograph manuscript of the work it is called First Concerto, Op. 1, and is probably a revision of one of his earliest compositions.

Three songs also date from the year 1855. They were published by Zimmermann in 1908 as *Three Forgotten Songs*; these show the influence of Glinka and the first in the group, 'Thou Art so Captivating', simple, short and lyrical, is a worthy predecessor to his great songs. Stylistically it reveals traits which were later to appear constantly in his songs and melodies. Already, at the age of eighteen, his ideas and outlook on music as well as his likes and dislikes and his general musical taste were well on the way to being decided. Add Schumann, Berlioz and Liszt to the composers already mentioned, and nearly all the composers he really admired are accounted for.

Towards the end of 1855 Ulybyshev offered to take Balakirev to St Petersburg. He naturally accepted gladly, and the final decision to follow a musical career was taken.

During the eighteenth century, and the early nineteenth century too, it was the Imperial Court which mainly controlled musical activities in St Petersburg. If the court and society approved, then a man would be accepted as part of society, in his capacity of musician. So it was for John Field, who spent the latter part of his life in Russia. He was taken up by Petersburg society, and became their 'darling'. His sophisticated style of composition—he invented the pianoforte 'Nocturne'—and its very simplicity appealed greatly to an aristocracy who appreciated to the full anything which came from the civilised West.

Field died in Moscow in 1837. Visiting artists from the West—particularly Frenchmen, Italians and also Germans, were usually

27

well received and many of them included St Petersburg in their travels. The only other music was the opera at the Imperial Theatre, which was very much in vogue for similar reasons. A list of operas and plays performed there *in a Russian translation* in the 1790s includes Gluck's *Alceste, Armide, Echo et Narcisse* and *Iphigenia in Tauris*, and works by Grétry, Monsigny, Piccini and Salieri.[22]

The permanent opera had been founded as far back as 1734 by the Empress Anna, who imported a complete Italian company under Araja. In Russia, as in other countries, opera was for many years considered to be an art suited only to classical subjects. Both singers and composers constantly travelled between Italy and St Petersburg and many Italians held lucrative court posts, including Galuppi, Sarti, Paesiello and Cimarosa. Russian composers were sent to Italy for training, to write operas in the Italian style. By the beginning of the nineteenth century there were as many as three opera companies, Italian, French and Russian, but all under the direction of an Italian. In 1823, however, a Russian, Verstovsky by name, became Director of the Moscow opera and composed a certain number of Russian operas, and Glinka's first opera, *A Life for the Tsar*, was produced in St Petersburg in 1836.

A certain national influence may be felt in this opera, performed in the year before Balakirev was born. The national feeling in Russia was engendered not only by the Napoleonic wars, but by the literary upsurge initiated by Pushkin (1799–1837), whose works were used both as the basis of libretti and for numerous songs by Russian composers. A great deal of folk-melody was introduced in serious Russian music before Glinka, but by composers vastly his inferiors in technique and every other respect.

Glinka, born in 1804 in the government of Smolensk, had known Bellini and Donizetti in Italy, and at the age of twenty-nine had studied harmony and counterpoint with the great German teacher, Dehn; he was anxious to write a Russian opera. The result was *A Life for the Tsar*, which enjoyed a measure of success, not least for the Polish dances, Mazurkas and Polonaises, which are used in some of the scenes. But it is still very much in the Italian style; in his second opera, *Russlan and Ludmila*, however, produced in 1842 and based on a poem by Pushkin, it is otherwise. This first really national opera was a failure as, indeed, taking into account the taste of the society who patronised it, it was bound to be. It nevertheless had a profound influence on Balakirev, particularly Ratmir's Romance in Act V and the Turkish dance in Act IV (in D flat and D major respectively) and the orchestral accompaniment to the Persian chorus (in triplets).

It was not until 1862 that the St Petersburg Conservatoire of Music was founded by Anton Rubinstein, and before then the only orchestral concerts (as distinct from operas or recitals) were those of the Russian Concert Society, founded in 1850 by A. F. Lvov, which gave three concerts every year during Lent (when opera was not allowed), and the University Concerts founded by A. F. von Eckstedt. It was only at the University concerts that any new work was ever performed. Dargomyzhsky's opera *Rusalka* failed in 1856, though a concert of his works in 1853 had been well received. (*Rusalka* was later to achieve some popularity.)

Such was the musical life of the Petersburg to which Ulybyshev took Balakirev in the late autumn of 1855. He introduced the young man to Glinka. This introduction had a lasting effect on Balakirev, who was willing to take advice from Glinka as he would from no other man. When Glinka died in 1857, Balakirev himself was the only man to lead, guide and educate the other Russian composers who gathered round him. In this way he became used to being an undisputed authority at as early an age as twenty. He was well fitted to be the mentor of this small group of men, but it would have been better, from the point of view of his own character, if there had been just *one* man whose advice he himself considered worth taking, whose mild rebukes he would have countenanced, and who would have taken some of the self-imposed burden off his shoulders.

As it was, he was accustomed, with all his magnificent talent and infectious energy, to being agreed with on almost every point, initially at any rate, by his own circle, which, including Mussorgsky, Rimsky-Korsakov and Borodin, was a mighty one indeed in the 'sixties. He certainly realised that once these composers had gained all they could from him, they would have little further use for his advice. Their desire for artistic freedom and increasing intolerance of his despotism, however benevolent, were additional irritations to the main causes of the mental illness and lethargy which almost overcame him by 1872, but which he was successfully throwing off three or four years later. Although a rather changed man emerged from the crisis, he soon had about him again a group of composers who relied on him as much as his former pupils had done. What a changed list of names in the later group! But Lyapunov, Tchernov, Olenin and the others seemed to satisfy him although he never gained first place in the Russian musical world again.

How differently it might have turned out, had he been able to rely on Glinka for occasional advice; for even if it is certain that Glinka would never have come to the forefront of any battle, he might all the same have been able to stop Balakirev making so many tactless and thoughtless remarks which very nearly alienated even his closest friends particularly in the early 'seventies. There was nobody else whose help he could, or rather would, take. He imagined that the cause of 'true art', as he called it, was in his own hands in Russia, and it could only be that to disagree with him fundamentally was to be wrong. Once Mussorgsky had stopped taking his advice, Balakirev had no further use for him— he ignored most of *Boris Godunov*. The same happened with Rimsky-Korsakov. The latter has rather maligned him in his *Record of my Musical Life*, but Balakirev seems to be the sort of man who *was* maligned, and the fault could not have been all on one side.

But, in spite of this, it will also be seen how kind, helpful and disinterested he was in dealing with his pupils and music in general. He stuck to his ideals and never turned aside from them for any reason, even at great cost to himself. It is a pity, however, that a man who thought similarly on musical matters to Balakirev, an older man, should not have survived to guide the 'guide', to help the 'helper', even to teach the 'teacher'.

Glinka would have been such a man. Balakirev considered his

advice to be valuable and made use of it in the scoring of his octet and other early works. In an article on 'Glinka and Balakirev' in *Soviet Music*, 1953,[23] A. Lyapunova quotes from a recollection of Balakirev:

> Glinka was amiably disposed towards me, and I would come to him mostly in the mornings to show him my latest works, among which was also the allegro from the Octet . . . Glinka appraised them favourably and gave me valuable advice about the instrumentation . . . And so it was until his departure for Berlin on 27 April/9 May 1856,[24] never to return.

Balakirev also met Ludmila Ivanovna Shestakova, Glinka's sister, who was to be a lifelong friend. She recorded of Balakirev's meetings with her brother that 'my brother was delighted with Balakirev's Fantasia on themes from *A Life for the Tsar*'. Balakirev was invited to call as often as possible and Glinka insisted that he play the Fantasia each time.[25] Although he thought highly of Balakirev's compositions, he realised that the latter's technique was still immature, and defective from the text-book point of view. Glinka gave instructions that Ludmila Shestakova's little daughter Olia was to be taught by Balakirev and no one else, if he himself did not survive to supervise her musical education, as Balakirev was the only man who shared his views on music. 'You can trust him completely,' he is reported as saying, 'and believe me, in time he will be a second Glinka.'[26]

Glinka had made a collection of Spanish themes on his two-year visit to Spain from 1845 to 1847; he gave Balakirev some themes from his collection, one of them is used in a 'Fandango-Étude' which was later revised as *Spanish Serenade*.[27] Another melody which Glinka gave to Balakirev, just before leaving for Berlin, was a march which Balakirev used as the main subject in an Overture on a Spanish March Theme composed in 1857.

One or two other piano works were also being written at this time. A Nocturne and Scherzo, together with the Glinka Fantasia and the Octet movement, were performed by him at a concert on 22 March/3 April 1856. In later life he considered the Nocturne to be good, but the Scherzo feeble. He also played works by Glinka, Dargomyzhsky and Laskovsky. Two months earlier he had appeared as pianist in a concert at Kronstadt—his first public appearance outside his home town, and on 12/24 February, he had made his Petersburg début at a University concert where he played the first movement of his F sharp minor concerto with an orchestra under the direction of Karl Schubert. The audience was enthusiastic and the music critic A. Serov, later to become so hostile to Balakirev, wrote in glowing terms of the work.[28] His compositions were undoubtedly successful, immature as they were, and his success as a pianist was unquestionable.

During his first months in St Petersburg Balakirev stayed with Ulybyshev's friend V. A. Kologrivov, by whose influence these concerts had been arranged. Kologrivov was a cellist, and Balakirev dedicated to him a *Romance for Violoncello* which was finished on '3 November 1856' according to a note on the score.[29]

In 1856 he also met César Cui, the Stassov brothers, Serov, Lvov, Dargomyzhsky and various influential nobles including Prince Odoyevsky, whose Berceuse he later arranged, and Count M. V. Vyelgorsky. All these men were older than Balakirev (though Cui, an army officer, only by two years), Vladimir Stassov having been born in 1824, Serov in 1820, Lvov in 1798 and Dargomyzhsky in 1813; but none of them had anything to teach Balakirev. Lvov had composed the Russian National Anthem (God save the Tsar) in 1833, and was therefore well known. Lvov and Vyelgorsky, both of them very much amateurs, thought that *Russlan and Ludmila* was cheap.

On 10/22 December 1857, Ulybyshev wrote to Balakirev that Lvov was worth cultivating—'No one can be more useful to you than he.'[30] Unfortunately Balakirev was not good at cultivating the right people. Of the others mentioned Serov wrote enthusiastically about his early works, but was later to write violently adverse criticisms of the 'National' group, and Dargomyzhsky was too egocentric really to care about a younger man, especially one who was likely to become a rival to himself. He was jealous of Glinka's success. There was, then, nobody amongst these people to advise him *as an older man*, except Stassov in a mild way.

2. The house in Nizhny-Novgorod in which the Balakirevs lived from 1842 to 1848

3. Balakirev's father A. K. Balakirev and his sisters Maria and Varvara

The Stassov brothers, particularly Vladimir, played a very important part in furthering the cause of Russian music. Vladimir became acquainted with Glinka in the early 'fifties. He believed *Russlan and Ludmila* to be a great work when it had been a failure. His faith in the greatness of contemporary Russian composers was a source of constant inspiration to them, and his judicious propaganda on their behalf made steady, if slow, progress in the face of continual opposition from those who thought that 'national' music was bound to fail, and was barbaric and tasteless. Indeed in 1855 Anton Rubinstein had published an article in a German magazine in which he wrote that passions were not national and that there could be no national opera. Attempts to write national music were doomed to failure, he asserted, citing the failure of Glinka's operas as an example.[31] Glinka's own teacher in Berlin, Siegfried Dehn, had not been so narrow in his outlook, sending him back to Russia with the words, 'Go and write *Russian* music.' But Dehn was a great teacher.

The Russian composers, therefore, needed someone to espouse their cause, since men like Rubinstein, later Serov, and a host of others were sincerely hostile to this new music. As late as 1870, a Russian critic could still write of the harshness, dissonance and proclivity to ugliness of Borodin's songs.[32]

Whereas Cui's propaganda was rather violent and bigoted, it was otherwise with the influential Vladimir Stassov. Though not a composer himself, he had many ideas which he passed on to Balakirev, Mussorgsky, Borodin, Rimsky-Korsakov and Tchaikovsky, about opera libretti, descriptive symphonic works or the use of folk-tunes. They always valued his advice. The inspiration of many of their works originated with him. A tone poem based on *Sadko* was suggested to Balakirev in 1861. It was passed to Mussorgsky and then to Rimsky-Korsakov, who made use of it in a way which pleased Balakirev. His was the idea for *Prince Igor* and *Khovanshchina*. He suggested, too, English themes for Balakirev's *King Lear* music, and this nearly half a century before the English themselves were to think of using their own folk themes. The stultifying German influence was thrown off later in England than in Russia.

A list of Balakirev's early piano music is appended. In later life Balakirev used to say that he created an impression when he played his own early piano compositions of the 'feminine nocturnes of Chopin', hastening to add, however, '*I am not calling Chopin a feminine composer . . .*'[33] The salon element in his own earlier compositions clearly did not please him. It was this very salon element in the piano music of Anton Rubinstein and the Conservatoire group of composers that he abhorred. Nevertheless, it seems that he cannot really rid himself entirely of this element in all his own music, since some of Balakirev's late piano music could be accused of this very failing, lacking as it sometimes does a feeling for really beautiful melody. In spite of his own feelings towards his earlier piano music, it shows great promise and reveals an original if rather untutored mind at work.

## APPENDIX TO CHAPTER 1

*Early piano music*[34] (and music for piano and orchestra).

1. *Grande Fantaisie* on Russian Folk Songs for piano and orchestra, Op. 4, completed on 12/24 December 1852. First published, Moscow, 1954.
2. Fantasia on themes from the opera *A Life for the Tsar* by Glinka, written in 1854–5, published by Zimmermann in 1899.
3. 'Witches' Dance'—1 February 1854, on the autograph. Unfinished and unpublished. (Now in the State Public Library, Leningrad.)
4. Piano Concerto in F sharp minor, first movement only written in 1855–6, and definitely completed by 12/24 February 1856, when Balakirev performed it at a University Concert. It is probably an arrangement of earlier ideas and is called 'Op. 1' on the title page. First published, Moscow, 1954.
5. Scherzo No. 1 in B minor, completed by 22 March/3 April 1856, when Balakirev performed it at a recital in St Peters-

burg. First published by Stellovsky in the 1860s. There is no reason to suppose that this scherzo was originally intended for the piano concerto, and that it is the one mentioned by Ulybyshev in a letter to Balakirev of 16/28 February 1855, asking why he had not sent the 'Fantasia on Themes by Glinka' and the scherzo of the piano concerto.[35] It is probable that Ulybyshev had confused the concerto with the octet, of which 69 bars of a scherzo were written in a piano version at about this time (the octet was numbered Op. 3.) This latter scherzo, however, eventually became Scherzo No. 2.

6. Nocturne No. 1 in G sharp minor, finished by 22 March/ 3 April 1856. Published in revised form by Gutheil in 1898, and subsequently by Schott in 1901, in B flat minor.

7. Sonata No. 1 in B flat minor, written as Op. 5. Three movements only were completed.

*First movement, Andante—Allegro assai feroce—Maestoso.* The *meno mosso* D flat major version of the Maestoso subject was later used as the second subject of his Scherzo No. 2 in B flat minor.

*Second movement*, Mazurka in D major, to be used as a basis of the second movement of his later piano sonata and for the fifth mazurka, published by Zimmermann in 1905 and 1900 respectively. The later mazurka and later sonata movement are identical.

*Third Movement, Andante*. The date of this work is doubtful. It is a revision of a *still earlier* attempt in 1855, when all four movements were completed, and judging by the dedication: 'To my dear friend César Antonovich Cui', it was written between 1856 and 1857, the period of the closest friendship of the two composers.

8. Polka in F sharp minor. This was the first piano work of Balakirev to appear in print. It was published by Denotkin who published Balakirev's first songs in 1859.[36] As Balakirev sold nothing to Denotkin after 1859, this polka must have been composed by then.

9. Transcription for piano solo of the Cavatina from Beethoven's string quartet Op. 130, published as a supplement to

the journal *Musical and Theatrical Herald* by Stellovsky in May 1859.

10. Mazurka No. 1 in A flat major, first published by Stellovsky between 1859 and 1861. A subsequent edition by Gutheil (who eventually took over Stellovsky's business) shows some slight alterations.

11. Mazurka No. 2 in B minor, published by Stellovsky as a supplement to the *Russian World*, No. 50, in 1861—composed probably in 1860. In two later editions by Gutheil the work has been transposed into C sharp minor and slightly altered.

12. Scherzo No. 2 in B flat minor, first published by Zimmermann in 1900. The history of this scherzo is fascinating and complicated. The first subject is taken from the scherzo of the Octet, Op. 3, the first 69 bars of which were written in 1855–6. The autograph of this (written for piano solo) is dated 'Kazan, 6 March 1855'. The theme of the middle section Balakirev adapts from the second subject of the first movement of his early piano sonata, Op. 5 (*c.* 1856–7). It is included here for these reasons.

13. Polonaise in D major, unfinished and unpublished (now in the State Public Library, Leningrad).

14. *Fandango-Étude*, later revised as *Spanish Serenade*.

15. Two transcriptions for piano which date from 1862, a third from 1864 and a fourth which also dates from the 'sixties are mentioned in the next chapters. They are transcriptions of works by Glinka, Berlioz and Beethoven.

### NOTES ON CHAPTER 1

1. For a note on the dates see the introduction to the Chronology (Appendix II).
2. Now known as Gorky after the author of that name.
3. CA, p. 100.
4. TA, No. vi, p. 39.
5. Obituary on Balakirev (in French) in *Société Internationale de Musique, revue musicale mensuelle*, July 1910, p. 416.
6. FC (i) (*Balakirev's early years*), p. 10.
7. ibid, p. 11.

8. FC (ii) (Commentary on Balakirev's letters to his father), p. 72.
9. L(2)A, No. vii, p. 44.
10. TA, No. vi, p. 40.
11. L(2)A, No. vii, p. 46.
12. ibid, p. 46; and TA, No. vi, p. 50.
13. TA, No. vi, p. 41.
14. L(2)A, No. vii, p. 49.
15. First published, Moscow, 1959.
16. SA, Vol. III, pt 2, p. 273.
17. TA, No. vi, p. 43 et seq.
18. TA. See note 4.
19. FC (i), p. 31.
20. FC (i), p. 43. Valier wrote: 'Durant mon séjour à Nijny-Novgorod me trouvant dans une soirée donnée par le général Oulibicheff, quelqu'un m'a dit: "Nous possédons ici un prodige de talent musical. Vous allez l'entendre". Je dois avouer que dans maintes occasions déjà, j'avais été déçu par de fausses apparences. Par ces entrefaites le général me présenta un jeune garçon d'un embonpoint et comptant à peine 17 ans. On ouvrit un paquet de musique reçu la veille de Pétersbourg et, prenant un Quintuor de Hummel, pièce d'une difficulté connue, l'enfant le joua d'un bout à l'autre sans reprendre haleine; c'était connue une cataracte, un torrent. Dès les premières strophes je demeurais étonné, ébahi par ce jeu fulminant et par trop brillant et je m'écriais: je ne me tromperai pas, car voilà un véritable prodige de génie!'
21. FC (i), p. 44.
22. *Annales de la Musique et des Musiciens en Russie au XVIII siècle* by R. Aloys Mooser, Vol. III, p. 853.
23. *Sovyetskaya Muzyka*, No. 2, 1953: quoted in K(3)A, p. 193.
24. Timofeyev (TA, No. vi, p. 47) gives this date, incorrectly, as 26 April (old style).
25. TA, No. vi, p. 46.
26. ibid., p. 47.
27. According to Timofeyev (TA, No. vi, p. 47) Balakirev turned to this theme again 'in the 1890's' but '24 May 1902' is written at the end of the manuscript (SA, Vol. III, pt. 1, p. 321).
28. TA, No. vi, p. 48.
29. FC (i), p. 58. Manuscript is to be found in the State Public Library, Leningrad, F.41.
30. TA, No. vi, p. 49.
31. TA, No. vi, p. 58.
32. Article on 'Alexander Borodin' by M. D. Calvocoressi in *Masters of Russian Music*, p. 165.
33. L(2)A, No. vii, p. 55.
34. The information for this list has been mainly taken from SA, Vols I, II and III; and K(4)A, p. 205 et seq.
35. TA, No. vi, p. 44.
36. K(3)B, p. 6.

# CHAPTER 2

*1858–1861: Plays as soloist in Beethoven's E flat pianoforte concerto in the presence of the Tsar – gives up career as pianist – views on public performance – poverty – support of his father – Illness (inflammation of the brain) – Overture on the themes of three Russian songs – Serov's praise – death of Ulybyshev – King Lear music – overture performed – songs – pianoforte concerto in E flat and projected* Requiem.

At the age of twenty-one Balakirev was equally well-known as pianist and composer. He had been praised by Serov in both capacities, and Dargomyzhsky described him as 'eagle-like'. He was engaged, early in 1858, to play as soloist in Beethoven's E flat piano concerto at a concert of the Petersburg 'Concert Society'. This concert was a splendid occasion. It was one of the musical events of the year; the Tsar and the whole Imperial family attended. Imagine the English Royal St Cecilia's day concert taking place in pre-revolution Paris, with the whole royal family and all society present, and something of the atmosphere will be appreciated.

On the 28th February/11 March, Balakirev wrote to his father:

I am writing this letter directly after a concert in which I played. The public appeared to be pleased with me, and I even earned the applause of the Grand Duke Constantine Nicolayevich, who was at the concert with the Emperor and the young Empress.

Perhaps this will result in something good for us . . . Apart

38

from the Grand Duke's applause, so flattering to me, I shall receive 100 rubles for this concert. Tomorrow I am playing at a musical evening at the house of the General-Adjutant Count Sumarokov, where Constantine Nicolayevich will again be present! If I have the good fortune to please him once more, perhaps Varenka [Varvara] really will get a place at one of the institutes here.[1]

Had Balakirev wanted to make his career as a pianist, it seems that nothing would have been easier. But the career of a soloist did not hold any attraction for him. On 19 February/3 March 1857,[2] he had written to the Moscow doctor N. Zatkevich: 'B [oborykin] tells me that ignorance of French will harm me a great deal in the society of artists *which is so useful for me* (?) All virtuosos are the most unmusical of people. For them money comes first, not art (it is not for nothing that I went to Kronstadt with *Serve*[3] to give a concert).'

The following letter to Stassov is also very revealing about his views on public performance.[4]

> . . . it is especially repulsive to me to appear before our public audiences; my fingers are paralysed when you make me play *Lear*[5] or something else about which, to tell the truth, our society does not care at all. I have to force myself to play in public or conduct an orchestra, and I cannot, of course, do this without harming my nature. It has always been a terrible thing for me that if you compose something there is no means of hearing it other than at a concert. This is like relating the most precious secrets of one's soul to police officials. After each public appearance I feel morally strained . . . In Petersburg I was forced into this by something near hunger . . .

He was still very poor, but it does *not* seem that he gave many lessons in his early days in St. Petersburg, as M. D. Calvocoressi supposes in *Masters of Russian Music*.[6] In an undated—but much later—letter to the pianist V. Adamovsky (preserved in the Institute of Russian literature)[7] Balakirev wrote: 'As soon as I appeared in Petersburg I was noticed by the public, and my name was soon fairly well known, but I gave very few lessons. People went more to old and experienced teachers, chief among whom was Henselt. Hoping for lessons in the future, I ran into debt, but no lessons came.' But he was able to comfort himself in this way: 'Apart from this, I felt that a large number of lessons would be destructive to me as a musician, would deaden my aesthetic feeling and eventually make me completely indifferent and apathetic to music itself.'

Because of his extreme poverty during these years he was forced to take whatever work he could find, and this included assisting the publisher Stellovsky with the preparation of the works of Glinka, Chopin and other composers for publication. He wrote to his father on 2/14 April 1858 that he was 'very busy' preparing for publication the piano compositions of Laskovsky.[8] In the previous year Balakirev's father resigned from his post as assistant to the head of department of state property. During the next few years Balakirev was constantly trying to find him a suitable job with a reasonable salary, through his Petersburg acquaintances. (In this connection he met V. M. Zhemchuzhnikov, who was to become one of his closest friends.) Attempts to get his father the post of agent of the steamship company 'Caucasus and Mercury' succeeded only in 1860. In 1862 he obtained a more satisfactory clerical post in Yaroslavl. From time to time Balakirev's sister Anna, although she was already married, sent him money. In 1859 Balakirev was having to support his father and his two youngest sisters Maria and Varvara, as well as to provide for himself; his letters to his father show that he sent the latter a monthly allowance.[9]

Early in April 1858,[10] Balakirev fell ill with inflammation of the brain. During the worst part of his illness, in April and May, he was looked after by Dmitri Stassov and the young Mussorgsky.[11] By the end of May he had sufficiently recovered to be able to travel with Ludmila Shestakova to her country cottage at Zamanilovka, where he spent a fortnight recuperating. As a result of this illness, he was subject to headaches and to other nervous disorders for the rest of his life.

On 26 June/8 July at Zamanilovka Balakirev finished an Overture on Three Russian Themes which he had started the previous autumn (it was first performed at a University concert six months later).[12] This beautiful work and the Overture on a Spanish March Theme composed in the first six months of 1857 and performed soon afterwards, are Balakirev's first orchestral works (except for a Polonaise-Fantaisie on an episode from Gogol's *Taras Bulba* later used in a Suite for Piano Duet).

The Overture on Three Russian Themes shows great promise. Dedicated to Dmitri Stassov, it is a work of exciting originality, though it is only a rather simple ternary form that holds it together. It starts with a slow, soft introductory theme (preceded by eighteen vigorous bars of allegro), moves on to the main body of the allegro, and ends with the slow theme again, *pianissimo*, on muted first violins, divisi, over a pedal. The short energetic preface is probably influenced by Berlioz' *Carnaval Romain* overture. It is a form of preface he does not use much in later works. But the slow, soft introduction, or conclusion, or both, to a mainly fast movement, is a device he uses to great advantage in more mature works (opening of Symphonic Poem *Russia* and C major symphony, conclusion of the scherzo in the same work, and the opening and close of *Tamara*).

In this overture the themes are merely strung together. They do not appear to arise from one another, as in the more mature works. On the other hand, he handles them in masterly fashion, making them his own in a particularly individual way, while preserving their character tastefully. Both the allegro themes were to be used in simpler versions by later composers, the first by Tchaikovsky (fourth symphony) and the second by Stravinsky (*Petrushka*). The texture is clear and the orchestration is brilliant.

Though it uses Russian folk-tunes and clearly shows the way to Balakirev's future style, revealing the path his orchestral works were to follow, the critic Serov praised the overture in a notice, saying that Balakirev 'must be prepared for the indifference of the Russian public towards him since his name is Balakirev, not Balachirini or Balakirstein . . .'[13] But Serov's praise was not unreserved which displeased Balakirev. Serov recollected later that the atmosphere between him on the one hand, and

Stassov and Balakirev on the other, was already becoming chillier and chillier.

Early in 1858,[14] Ulybyshev had died. He left Balakirev his music library, two violins and a thousand rubles. Balakirev was always grateful to him for his kindness, and dedicated his second symphony to his memory. After his illness, Balakirev went on from Ludmila Shestakova's cottage to Nizhny-Novgorod, where he had great difficulty in collecting from Ulybyshev's sons the money which had been left to him. His letters to Stassov reveal ideas for a big choral symphony in honour of Glinka, and incidental music to Shakespeare's *King Lear*, which he had planned earlier in the year.[15] Stassov wrote him a long letter on 19/31 July 1858, including some English tunes taken from William Chappell's *Collection of National English Airs*.[16] Stassov had English connections, as his wife was related to a family named Clark who owned an iron foundry in St Petersburg.[17] Stassov wrote: 'I should like to know, more than anything, whether you are sticking to your intention to write music for *Lear*, and, if so, entr'actes and an overture or an overture only; and if you have in fact started working on all this, is it going well, and *how* and *what?'*[18] Stassov asks these questions because he would like to pass on officially to the Director of the Imperial Theatres that music on 'such-and-such' lines is being prepared which they would do well to bear in mind.

As far as his own compositions were concerned, however, Balakirev was not a man with an eye to the main chance—one cannot imagine Mozart or Bizet missing such an opportunity. Balakirev replied to Stassov on 25 July/6 August:[19]

> *King Lear* is now silent. I have started the last entr'acte and, but for a few bars, finished it. But it is impossible that anything more will be written during the summer. I am not even thinking about music at all—my head is so stuffed full of diverse petty nonsense, that somehow it seems odd to recollect that there is a Schumann quintet, Shakespeare and so on. It is impossible to write in Nizhny in these circumstances; however, I'll see what can be done.

But he could not possibly finish it all by September. The longer he takes to write it, the better it will be. 'I don't mind telling you that I'm extremely satisfied with the last entr'acte and even now I can see that, if I'm able to write all the entr'actes *well*, the overture may easily turn out *excellent* . . .'

It was only on return to St Petersburg, doubtless refreshed by his holiday in spite of the complaints, that he was able to start composing again. Inaction, time to think, does not seem to have helped him to compose. On the other hand he frequently averred that in order to compose properly he needed absolute freedom and peace of mind. He found composing to order difficult. But the 1858–9 period was very promising as far as composition was concerned.

He completed the *King Lear* Overture on 13/25 September 1859,[20] and orchestrated it in the next five days. He found no difficulty in orchestration, though he was not quite satisfied with the orchestration of this overture and would not allow it to be published. His knowledge of instrumental technique was in some respects faulty. In connection with his *Sadko*, Rimsky-Korsakov commented that, on Balakirev's instructions, he had written for natural horns and trumpets, and that it would have been beneath their dignity to have consulted a practical musician who could have corrected them. They were the comrades-in-arms of Berlioz, not of some talentless bandmaster.[21]

The *King Lear* Overture (and incidental music) was revised in 1902 and published in 1904. The Overture received much praise when it was first performed on 15/27 November 1859 at a University concert.[22] Considered to be outstanding, it was performed as frequently as any other work of Balakirev and was compared with Beethoven's *Egmont* and Schumann's *Manfred*.

Berlioz and Balakirev are probably the only two composers successfully to have attempted *King Lear* music. Balakirev's overture is perhaps worthier of Shakespeare than that of Berlioz. To those musicians who only know *Tamara* or *Islamey*, the thought of an Eastern Lear does not recommend itself, and the overture is never performed in England. But the *Lear* Overture is quite different from those works. It shows classical restraint, and a quality of epic heroism; it is full of power; the unnecessary is ruthlessly excluded—in fact, a comparison with Beethoven's overtures is apt. The storm which constitutes the development section is restrained, unromantic and desolate. Every semi-quaver at the opening of the *allegro moderato* tells; the design is perfect. There is no carelessness and laziness in interminable repetitions, as so often with Liszt and Tchaikovsky, but a classical and heroic poise almost on a par with Shakespeare which pro-mised as much as any overture by a twenty-two-year-old com-poser could promise.

The rest of the incidental music to *King Lear* was not finished till 1861. Only two entr'actes remained to be done in January 1860. Balakirev wrote to Stassov in February 1861 that he had just finished the 'Procession' (first entry of Lear), which is a grand Polonaise for double orchestra.[23]

In 1858 Balakirev wrote eleven songs,[24] in 1859 three, and in 1860 two; these sixteen songs are almost as great in their way as anything else he wrote, and together with four more, composed in 1863, make up his first group of Twenty Songs. They are not necessarily great as *songs* (just as Mussorgsky's *Pictures from an Exhibition* is not great as a *piano* piece), but they are great pieces of absolute music. The songs written in 1858–60 show the same classical poise as the *Lear* Overture. There is not an unessential note anywhere, and the greatest of them show almost no trace of romanticism, but a beautiful classicism quite remote from *Islamey*. A wonderfully telling and judicious use of allegro semi-quavers can be observed in 'Hebrew Melody' (No. 13), set to words by Lermontov after Byron. It is not quite true to say that two other Lermontov songs, 'Song of Selim' (No. 11) and 'Song of the Golden Fish' (No. 16), which show a classical restraint in quasi-orientalism, are mere precursors of Balakirev's mature oriental works. On the contrary, all these three songs, together with 'Cradle Song' (No. 4) are masterpieces in their own right. 'Cradle Song' has the same use of semiquavers, but slow moving and even more beautiful to the listener than in the faster works.[25]

Tchaikovsky considered these songs to be little masterpieces.

In a letter of 24 August/5 September 1881 to Madame von Meck, he declared himself to be passionately fond of them, particularly 'Song of Selim' and 'Song of the Golden Fish'.

The later songs never quite live up to the promise of the earlier ones. They gain in harmonic fluency, but on the whole lack the classical terseness of the younger man. Balakirev's next group of songs did not appear until 1895–6.

By 1861 Balakirev was planning two big works, but neither these nor others which he contemplated in the next year or two were completed. Within the next ten years he did not finish a single large scale work and only three medium length works were not left unfinished—the Second Overture on Russian Themes (revised in 1869 as *Musical Picture, 1000 years*), the Overture on Czech themes, and the piano Fantasy *Islamey*. Both the orchestral works were later revised as symphonic poems.

The two works he was considering in 1861 (thematically connected) were a *Requiem* for which he had already written one chorus (it may be remembered that one of his first musical experiences was Mozart's *Requiem* at Nizhny-Novgorod), and a pianoforte concerto in E flat major, which he began in the summer, seeing that he was now 'free' of the *Lear* music, as he wrote to Stassov. The first movement was completed in the autumn of 1862, but it was only constant pestering by the publisher Zimmermann which induced him to take up the work again in 1906–9 and it had to be completed by Lyapunov after his death.

### NOTES ON CHAPTER 2

1. FA, p. 15. Balakirev had been trying for some months to get a place, in a Petersburg institute for young ladies, for his sister Varvara. In a letter written two months previously Balakirev had been trying to get her into the Zamiatin's institute (FA, p. 14), 'but up to the present I have not achieved anything definite—nothing but obstacles'.
2. FA, p. 15, quoted from *Russian Musical Gazette* (*Russkaya Muzykalnaya Gazeta*), 1910, No. 30–31.
3. Adrian-Francis Serve, a 'cello virtuoso.
4. K(3)B, p. 192, letter of 3/15 June 1863, written while Balakirev was on holiday in the Caucasus.
5. Balakirev's incidental music to *King Lear*, written between 1858 and 1861.

6. p. 109, 'He depended for his daily bread on lessons (of which he gave, at times, as many as nine a day) . . . ' Perhaps this should refer to a later period.
7. F 162, quoted in FA, p. 16.
8. FC (ii), p. 77.
9. ibid, p. 72 et seq.
10. Balakirev's illness was *not* in the Summer of 1857, as Timofeyev states (TA, No. vi, p. 51). A. S. Lyapunova gives full details of Balakirev's illness in a letter to the present writer dated 19 July, 1965.
11. Balakirev's ability as teacher and leader is described in full in Chapter 4.
12. K(3)B, p. 16. Timofeyev incorrectly gives the date of the first performance as 29th March (old style), TA, No. vi, p. 51. The correct date of the first performance is 21 December 1858/2 January 1859.
13. TA, No. vi, p. 51.
14. ibid., p. 50.
15. K(3)B, p. 17 et seq.
16. *Collection of National English Airs* by William Chappell (1838–40). Enlarged and renamed *Popular Music of the Olden Time*, 2 vols (1855–59). Recast by H. E. Wooldridge, 2 vols (1893) and reissued New York (1961), together with Frank Kidson's supplement.
17. AC, p. 194 et seq.
18. K(3)B, p. 20.
19. ibid., p. 28 et seq.
20. TA, No. vi, p. 53.
21. AE, pp. 34–35.
22. M(2)A, p. 70.
23. K(3)B, p. 94. The *King Lear* music is analysed in full in Chapter 12.
24. TA, No. vi, p. 52; K(3)B, p. 56, etc.
25. This song was orchestrated by Sir Henry Wood for use in a promenade concert, and this orchestration, perhaps rather surprisingly, shows the same superb classical restraint as the song. The following is the orchestration:

> Muted divisi violas and cellos
> Double Basses
> 1 Oboe
> 1 Clarinet (which has the semiquavers)
> 2 Horns, muted towards the end

This exquisite miniature exists in Wood's manuscript only, and is preserved in the Royal Academy of Music Library, London.

# CHAPTER 3

*1862–1866: Foundation of Free School of Music – Free School Concerts – aims of the School – summer holidays in the Caucasus – views on Lermontov – last four songs in the first group of twenty – Second Overture on Russian Themes (1000 years, Russia) – Serov cold towards the overture – Stassov's contempt of Serov's opera* Judith *– projected opera,* The Fire-Bird *– Krylov and Ghinken as librettists and Rimsky-Korsakov's testimony – projected* Mtsyri *symphony –* Lezghinka *– C major symphony – first collection of 40 folk-songs – contempt of rules of harmony and melody at Prague Conservatoire, and of Anton Rubinstein's methods.*

Early in 1862 Balakirev submitted to Gabriel Lomakin, a natural son of Count Sheremetyev, and conductor of the latter's choir, an idea for a Free School of Music,[1] where both Russian and foreign music would be performed—to some extent in opposition to the Russian Music Society (founded in 1859 and directed by Anton Rubinstein). Singers and instrumentalists were to be educated free of charge (in contrast to the St Petersburg Conservatoire, which was to be founded by Rubinstein later in 1862). A concert was given on 11/23 March in aid of the scheme. Only classical music was performed (Haydn, Mozart, Méhul, Pergolesi, Mendelssohn). On 18/30 March the foundation of the school was announced, with Lomakin as Director and Balakirev as his assistant. Balakirev's first appearance as conductor was in 1863 at the age of twenty-six. The pupils at the school were a mixed lot, numbering some two-hundred at first, students of the medical/surgical academy, state officials,

47

apprentices and so on. The patrons of the school were the Tsarevich Nicholas and later Tsar Alexander. Lomakin dealt more with the choral side, Balakirev with the orchestral, and soon the tuition began to take effect.

The concerts became, as Balakirev had intended they should, an important platform for the works of the Western composers he particularly favoured, as well as for the compositions of himself and his own pupils, for the Russian Music Society sponsored mainly classical music. An average of two concerts a year were given—twelve between 1862 and 1867—and the more modern composers represented included Berlioz (*Te Deum* and other works), Schumann and Liszt, whose *Danse Macabre* was performed in 1866. Russian works included Balakirev's *Lear* Overture, both overtures on Russian themes, 'Song of the Golden Fish';[2] Rimsky-Korsakov's first symphony, Russian Overture; Glinka, Dargomyzhsky and Cui were represented and Mussorgsky's first version of *The Destruction of Sennacherib* (a choral work) was given in 1867.

On 5/17 April 1869, in an official letter to the heir to the throne, Balakirev (by then Director of the School) formulated the tasks as follows:

> The aim of the establishment of this school is to supply a free musical education to the needy, with the object of directing their aspirations and training them to a suitable standard for the proper church choirs which are so necessary for our parish churches and so important for our church services; and also to develop their special gifts through training them as soloists.[3]

The financial condition of the school was not satisfactory, and in this letter a request is made for permission to arrange lotteries to assist in the financial support of the school.[4]

In the periodical *Golos* of 1863,[5] a pamphlet appeared, in which it was stated that the Free School of Music 'encourages in the study and the practice of the arts those who would otherwise never have considered the idea'.

In 1862, instead of going to Nizhny-Novgorod for his summer holiday, Balakirev visited the Caucasus mountains, which were

4. M. I. Glinka in 1856

5. Autograph of 'Fandango-Étude' (14 February 1856)

becoming a favourite holiday resort. He spent most of the time in Essentuki, which, as he wrote in a letter to Stassov on 25 July/7 August,[6] was a large village 17 versts[7] from Piatigorsk. Balakirev's views on the poet Lermontov are expressed in this letter:

> I breathe Lermontov (I read *A Hero of our Time* in Piatigorsk). Walking in Piatigorsk by the grotto (the scene with Vera), in the gap by the Aeolian harp, I felt Lermontov's ghost—there he was floating before me. After re-reading all his works once more, I must say that, of all things Russian, Lermontov affects me most of all, in spite of his monotonousness and a certain superficiality (amateurishness). I have become shackled to him as a *strong nature*. (In Pushkin and Gogol, despite their genius, I do not see Lermontov's heroic strength.) Apart from this we are at one about many things. I like the same natural beauty as Lermontov, its effect upon me is equally powerful. The Circassians, beginning with their costume (I know no better dress than that of the Circassians) are as much to my taste as to his; and there are many other strings on which Lermontov plays which find an echo in me too. I could never feel so close to Pushkin, in spite of his mature genius. Had Lermontov lived 40 years he would have been our first poet and one of the first in the world.

(On his return journey he went to Yaroslavl, where his father had at last found a reasonable post).

He had enjoyed himself in the Caucasus so much, he was so enthralled by the folk music of the people, that he returned there next year.[8] He travelled up the Volga to Tsaritsyn, from there to Rostov-on-Don, and then on to Piatigorsk and Zheleznovodsk.[9] A letter to Rimsky-Korsakov[10] (then at sea) dated 4/16 June 1863 states that Balakirev arrived in Piatigorsk on 31 May (12 June).[11] Besides offering Korsakov advice on orchestration, he complains that he is getting on in years and writes that there may come a time when his present pupils will not accept the advice of someone who is 'dried up'. Balakirev was twenty-six! Rimsky-Korsakov, writing to Piatigorsk, rebukes Balakirev (whom he believes to be twenty-seven) for already, at this early age, being a hypochondriac.

Balakirev went on to Tiflis, where he noted down some delicate Georgian folk-songs with the aid of L. I. Karmalina. His friends, the Karmalins, were spending a holiday on the outskirts of the town. He went on to Baku,[12] where he recorded some Persian songs, before returning to St Petersburg.

Of Balakirev's next four songs, one was dedicated to L. I. Karmalina and one, the most important of the group, 'Song of Georgia' to N. N. Karmalin. This song, which Balakirev orchestrated, is something quite new in his music. The accompaniment, which has always been of subtle importance in the earlier songs, assumes more ascendency in 'Song of Georgia'. The lovely ritornello at the end seems to put into a few exquisite bars the whole beauty of the song, which for want of a better term may be called Balakirev's first 'oriental' composition; at any rate, it is the first result of his visits to the Caucasus.

The songs (Nos 17–20 in the Gutheil edition) were almost finished by December 1863, as a letter written to Stassov on 20 December/1 January shows: 'Come to a meal with me tomorrow. Tomorrow is the 21 December, i.e. my birthday, and on such a day I present myself with my new songs and the pleasure of spending the time with you, saying in the words of Ludmila Ivanovna, that I "shall be really grateful to you" if you will come. I'll expect you at 5 o'clock.'[13]

Earlier, on 14/26 December, he had written a long letter to Rimsky-Korsakov, mentioning 'four more songs' and saying that he had almost finished his Second Overture on Russian Themes.

It seems that this Overture started as a 'Russian Symphony' in four movements.[14] In the end, however, it was planned on similar lines to his first Overture on Three Russian Themes.

He wrote to Stassov on 29 December 1863/10 January 1864: ' ... I'm staying at home and successfully orchestrating my new overture'.[15] It was completed early in 1864, and performed at a Free School concert on 6/18 April.[16] This overture was published as a musical picture *1000 years* in 1869 by Johansen. In 1882,

Balakirev started to revise it and the revised version was sold to Bessel in 1887 and published two years later as the Symphonic Poem *Russia*.[17] The latter edition has the following prefatory note:

> The inauguration, at Novgorod, of the monument erected as a memorial of Russia's 1000th anniversary, in 1862, was the occasion of the composition of the present symphonic poem *Russ*, that in the first edition bore the title *1000 years*. The work is based on three motives borrowed from my collection of Russian folk songs. In it I have attempted to express the three principal elements in our history: paganism, the period of princes and popular government, that gave birth to the Cossack institutions, and the Muscovite Empire. The contest between these elements, that ended with the fatal blow struck against Russian national and religious tendencies by the reforms of Peter I, supplied the subject of this instrumental drama. In publishing a second edition, I found it necessary to remodel the orchestration and to emendate some passages.
>
> 11th May, 1887                                        M. A. Balakirev

Historically speaking, this note is rather misleading and there is no evidence that he started work on the composition until 1863; and even then, as has been made clear, it was called Second Overture on Russian Themes. The title *1000 years* did not occur to Balakirev until *after* this, and it is more than probable that this 'historical' idea only occurred to him after the work had been written!

But it does give a very good idea of Balakirev's view of folk-song and of how he absorbed the songs with the object of treating them symphonically. The three folk-songs used from his collection are: No. 1 'It was not the wind', a wedding song; No. 2, 'I'll go up' and No. 20 'Jolly Katya', both peasant dances with patter words. This work, though on the same structural basis as the earlier overture, is much more highly developed and closely interwoven. It seems that one of the themes was partially suggested by Stassov, who wrote to Balakirev in October 1869,[18] 'I

twice offered you themes for your compositions, and they proved
useful to you: once for *Lear*, the other time (though you shared
in this yourself) *1000 years*'; Balakirev dedicated a fourth,
original, theme to Stassov in a manuscript he sent to him on
19/31 March 1869.

Serov spoke in cold terms of the work after its first performance
'In the field of Russian music I bow down before the genius of our
Glinka, the inventor of national opera, but I can see nothing but
feeble mediocrity in Dargomyzhsky and I find only pale reflections of talent in the efforts of my young compatriots.'[19] But
Serov's position is more understandable if one considers Stassov's
and later Balakirev's contempt for his opera *Judith*, which had in
fact been very successful. Stassov had written to Balakirev in
Piatigorsk on 17/29 May 1863:

> Do you know what I now have to tell you? About Serov's
> opera—it was given for the first time yesterday, and it went
> down in such a way as could not possibly have been foreseen.
> At once, from the first note, Serov became the idol of Peters-
> burg . . . You can have no inkling of what yesterday was like
> . . . everybody was saying that we had never had anything
> like it, that here was our first composer since the creation of
> the world; and only two or three, I should think, somehow
> remembering Glinka, then quickly hastened to declare that
> after Glinka Serov was the first . . . [20]

Serov was apparently angry that Stassov had not gone to the
first rehearsals.

In October, when Ludmila Shestakova invited Balakirev and
Stassov to attend a performance of *Judith* in her box, Stassov
refused,[21] and in his letter to Rimsky-Korsakov of 14/26
December[22] Balakirev says that it is 'always leading up to a point
and never reaching it'.

Balakirev also mentions in this letter that he has in mind the
composition of an opera to be called *The Fire-Bird*. 'The outline
of the subject may be similar to *Russlan* but the scenes and
developments are quite different. Krylov has already started work
on the libretto and when you arrive something will no doubt

have been achieved. In my next letter I'll tell you in greater detail about the subject of my opera . . .'[23] Unfortunately this promise was not fulfilled, or else the letter was lost.

Cui wrote to Rimsky-Korsakov on the 27 December/8 January 1864:[24]

Balakirev and Modinka[25] are setting about writing operas . . . Balakirev needs spurring on. Whether he finishes it or not he will write a few excellent numbers. The subject is Russo-Georgian. He brought with him from the Caucasus an enormous wealth of Eastern music and this must not remain fruitless.

Cui had introduced the dramatist Victor Alexandrovich Krylov (1838–1906) to Balakirev in 1858 or 1859. Krylov wrote to Balakirev on 24 February/8 March 1864, promising 'to let you have the whole of the first act towards the end of the first week in Lent'.[26] On 2 April Krylov again wrote: 'The first act is written, copied out in an exercise book, and for a week at least has been ready for you. Name a day for the reading and summon old Stassov.'

It was apparently not successful. Stassov wrote on 28 July/9 August to Balakirev of 'that unfortunate first act which made us laugh so much that we almost split our sides'.[27] Stassov and Balakirev looked around for another librettist. Ivan Alexandrovich Rozhdestvensky[28] was thought of; nothing came of that, but in this letter, Stassov encloses *another* first act, this time by Alexander Antonovich Ghinken, which is much better.

Krylov, however, had apparently gone ahead and written a *second* act, which Stassov had enclosed in a previous letter. This letter had been sent to Yaroslavl. Stassov writes:

. . . the libretto of the second act of *The Fire-Bird* which Krylov sent to me for you from Lake Como . . . I hastened to send it to you quickly, as Krylov asked that you should send him an answer by 6 July . . . let me say this about your libretto and librettist: do me a favour. Do not behave the same as the time before. Send some enquiry to Yaroslavl about the letter which does not seem to have reached you. I very much want you to read Krylov's letter to you and his second act. This latter, indeed, is not at all bad. At any rate, it's a hundred times better than that unfortunate first act . . .[29]

But Balakirev had already received Krylov's second act and Stassov's previous letter. He replied to it:

I really don't know what pleases you. Maybe the beginning is not bad (the water-nymphs, Baba Yaga and the brothers) but why did Krylov take it into his head to send the brothers into the underworld for no reason at all? As regards the scenes among the fire worshippers, they are not fit for anything, and they are certainly not what I need. Find me some tolerable librettist. Krylov is nothing short of an idiot.[30]

It is uncertain what ideas Balakirev wished to put into his opera.[31] The liberation by the Russian hero of the Georgian queen from the power of King Saltan (clearly not the good-natured King of Pushkin's tale, but a Turkish King) and the wedding of Prince Ivan and Tamara—from Krylov's libretto—could symbolise the union of Russia and the Caucasus.

Rimsky-Korsakov, referring to *The Fire-Bird* as it stood in 1865–66, said:

He [Balakirev] had at this time a rather cold attitude towards his intended opera, *The Fire-Bird*, although he played many magnificent excerpts mainly based on oriental themes. The lions protecting the golden apples and the flight of the fire-bird were splendid. I also remember a few songs and the service of the fire-worshippers on a Persian theme.[32]

Balakirev planned another work on the Lermontov-Caucasus theme—a programme symphony *Mtsyri*, which remained un-written. It was to be in C sharp minor, with the following pro-gramme:[33]

1. Mtsyri's childhood impressions: the pastoral life of the Circassians, the Caucasus, Circassian song, a battle, confusion,

the Russians capture Mtsyri and carry him off, far away . . .
The second scene follows immediately.

2. *Adagio*: Mtsyri in the monastery, evening, he walks about the
   monastery, looks around and is sorrowful; out of the distant
   church, the singing of the monks' choir (traditional chants)
   floats over to him.
3. Mtsyri's flight, his inner torments, the image of a Georgian
   girl he has seen has imprinted itself on his soul (2nd theme).
   In the middle, in a faint, he hears the voice of the little fish
   (song of the little fish), he is carried into the monastery. He
   dies.

It seems that this idea progressed towards the thought of an
orchestral poem to be entitled *Lezghinka*. On 10/22 January 1867
Rimsky-Korsakov wrote to Balakirev in Prague:[34] 'When you
return here you will live as of old: you'll compose *Lezghinka* and
finish the Czech overture . . .' It was in 1867 that *Lezghinka*
changed its name to *Tamara*.

Balakirev started sketches of his C major symphony in May
1864, and had started the composition of the first movement in
August of the same year, but his hope, expressed in a letter to
Cui, that he would finish the movement by the time he had
returned to St Petersburg in the autumn[35] (he was on holiday in
central Russia) was not to be fulfilled. He did not finish it until
the 'nineties![36]

Nevertheless, there are two important ideas in what he did
write at this time. First, that a whole symphonic movement
should spring, as it were, from an initial *largo*, giving a unitary
form to the whole; and secondly, that the *largo* should be in the
style of the old Russian church chant (perhaps an advance from
the idea of Mtsyri in the monastery).

This ancient church chant flavour is not only used in other
works of his, but also by Rimsky-Korsakov in the *Maid of
Pskov*, by Borodin in *Prince Igor*, and by Mussorgsky in *Boris
Godunov* and *Khovanshchina*. His idea of using it therefore had
wide repercussions.

Besides the influence of church chants, it seems also that the influence of the late Beethoven quartets can be seen in the with-drawn classical restraint of the opening *largo*; and the influence of Berlioz is plain.

In January 1864 Stellovsky published Balakirev's solo piano-forte arrangement of the introduction to *La Fuite en Égypte*.[37] Three more transcriptions were made for piano solo about this time. An arrangement of the Allegretto from Beethoven's string quartet Op. 59, No. 2, was finished on 28 June/10 July 1862. The autograph of this is in the Institute of Russian Literature in Leningrad, but the autograph of neither of the other two arrange-ments is extant. Both are transcriptions of works by Glinka; *Jota Aragonesa* exists in two versions, the first of which was probably arranged in 1862, as the following letter from Cui to Rimsky-Korsakov stated:[38] 'Mily is arranging the Jota, and Kholmsky[39] for four hands [piano duet], the Jota for two hands [piano solo], in the concert manner and all this will be published.' Stellovsky published all these arrangements soon afterwards.

The other Glinka arrangement is the lovely transcription of the song 'The Lark', written in 1840 to words of N. Kukolnik as one of a group entitled *Farewell to Petersburg*. Stellovsky pub-lished the first edition of the arrangement; subsequent editions were by Gutheil and also, in France, by Ch. Hayet of Paris, and in England, by Augener. It clearly enjoyed popularity. It is most beautifully and delicately contrived (in B flat minor) and is probably one of the best examples of arrangements by Balakirev.

During his summer holidays between 1860 and 1863, Balakirev had been noting down songs on his expeditions up the Volga. On 19 November/1 December 1865, he wrote to Stassov: 'Please send me the collections of songs of Práč, Kashin and Kirsha Danilov. I must have them, and the quicker you send them, the better it will be.'[40]

Stassov wrote in pencil at the foot of the letter 'for an edition *Collection of Russian Songs* of Balakirev himself'. Again Balakirev wrote, on 22 November/4 December: 'Don't delay, dear Bach,[41] sending me the collections of Práč and Kashin. I must have them. You'll very likely find them in the Public Library.'

Balakirev used one or two folk-songs from these collections, as well as those he had noted down himself, in his collection. The poet N. F. Shcherbina was responsible for the words.[42] There are forty songs altogether (thirty-six and four variants). They were published by Johansen in 1866; Belyaev published a second edition in Leipzig in 1895, and one with a French translation in 1898. All three themes in Balakirev's Second Overture on Russian Themes (symphonic poem *Russia*) are taken from this collection. They are harmonized without any text-book preconceptions about what ought to be done, and are not forced unnaturally into alien Western keys. Anything which will not harmonise adequately is left alone in bare octaves. These harmonisations are quite different from those later to be published by Tchaikovsky and Rimsky-Korsakov (1877, Op. 24). Tchaikovsky strait-jackets the tunes; Korsakov tames them. (Korsakov used two unpublished songs from Balakirev's *Volga* collection, Nos 24 and 58 of his edition.)

The unique quality of the harmonisation of these songs, as well as Balakirev's views on text-book harmony, are very well illustrated in a story he told Mussorgsky in a letter from Prague (11/23 January 1867)[43] where he was putting on Glinka's operas *Russlan and Ludmila* and *A Life for the Tsar*:

A nephew of my landlady, studying music in this celebrated institution [the Conservatoire in Prague], seeing my collection [of folk songs] on the piano, became interested, got to know me, took the collection home, and played it with his friends. They were all in a high state of excitement and they could only cry, 'This is Slav music and we only have German music'; and to show you the daring of their action, I shall tell you that here, as in all Germany, every Conservatoire professor is as big a blockhead as our Rubinstein, and as impudent towards his pupils as the latter are reverential to him. In Petersburg protests are made against the immaculateness of Rubinstein, but here there are none. What happened? The professor waxed wroth and said it was all 'ganz falsch! . . .'[44] In the harmonic progressions there was an exposed fifth, which is strictly forbidden here, and the melodies were quite contrary to the rules which are to be found in their courses in melody. The pupils returned with hang-dog expressions and explained dejectedly that although all this is very exciting, none-the-less it is all 'ganz falsch', and they do not dare to disbelieve their professor; and they never have a sceptical thought in their heads concerning the immutability of all these foolish rules of harmony and melody.

## NOTES ON CHAPTER 3

1. TA, No. vi, p. 59; L(2)A, No. vii, p. 57; G(3)A, pp. 30–31; K(3)B, pp. 159–160.
2. Orchestrated version.
3. FA, pp. 28–29. Document, in the form of a clerk's copy, in the Russian State Public Library, Leningrad, where all the correspondence is preserved.
4. The state allowance was insufficient to cover the financial losses of the concerts, and the other expenses.
5. *Golos*, 1863, No. 284.
6. K(3)B, pp. 165–169.
7. One verst equals 3500 feet.
8. On 20 March/1 April he gave a chamber concert (with the violinist E. K. Albrecht and the cellist Karl Schubert) to help finance his second expedition to the Caucasus. Included in the programme was Beethoven's Piano Trio Op. 70.
9. TA, No. vi, p. 60.
10. Rimsky-Korsakov was introduced to Balakirev on 26 November/8 December 1861.
11. L(1)D, p. 61.
12. TA, No. vi, pp. 61–62.
13. K(3)B, p. 207. 'Old Man's Song', No. 17, was not finished until 1865.
14. FB, p. 131.
15. K(3)B, p. 207.
16. ibid., p. 212; TA, No. vii, pp. 57–58. It received a second performance on 3/15 May at a Russian Music Society Concert directed by A. Rubinstein.
17. Literally, symphonic poem *Russ*, the old name for Russia.
18. K(3)B, pp. 270, 260 and 206: also FB, p. 132 et seq., and TA, No. vii, p. 58.
19. TA, No. vii, p. 58.
20. K(3)B, pp. 179–180.
21. ibid., pp. 202–203.
22. L(1)D, p. 74.
23. ibid.
24. C. A. Cui, *Selected Letters (Izbrannye Pisma)*, Leningrad, 1955, p. 61.
25. Mussorgsky.
26. G(2)A, p. 370.

27. K(3)B, p. 221.
28. ibid., p. 214.
29. ibid., pp. 221–222.
30. ibid., p. 219.
31. G(2)A, p. 375.
32. Rimsky-Korsakov, *Record of my Musical Life*, (*Letopis moei Muzykalnoi Zhizni*), Moscow, 1955, pp. 39–40, quoted in G(2)A, p. 377.
33. FB, p. 156.
34. L(2)C, 1916, No. vii, p. 89. There is a 'Lezghinka' in Glinka's opera *Russlan and Ludmila*.
35. C. A. Cui, *Selected Letters* (*Izbrannye Pisma*), Leningrad, 1955, p. 499.
36. A Scherzo alla cosacca, which he intended for this symphony, was later used in his second symphony.
37. SA, Vol. III, pt. 1, p. 323.
38. ibid., p. 321, letter of 15/27 June 1862.
39. Glinka's incidental music for N. Kukolnik's tragedy, *Prince Kholmsky*.
40. K(3)B, p. 232.
41. Stassov's nick-name.
42. G(1)A, p. 7 and p. 197.
43. TB, No. vi, pp. 168–169.
44. Totally incorrect.

# CHAPTER 4

*Balakirev as teacher (1857–1869): Mussorgsky introduced –*
*Balakirev the only teacher in 1857 – Mussorgsky's lessons with*
*Balakirev – Mussorgsky and Borodin meet – Balakirev and Borodin*
*– meticulous overhauling of works – Borodin's first symphony –*
*Mussorgsky's D major symphony – Balakirev and Rimsky-*
*Korsakov – Korsakov's E flat minor symphony – correspondence*
*with Korsakov – performance of Borodin's first symphony –*
*Mussorgsky and Korsakov begin to tire of 'interference'.*

When Mussorgsky was first introduced to Balakirev
the only living Russian composer of any standing was
Dargomyzhsky,[1] and the Petersburg and Moscow
Conservatoires were not to be founded until 1862 and 1864
respectively. Dargomyzhsky's music did influence Mussorgsky—
they had the same ideal of realism and musical truth—and
Balakirev's early songs were to some extent influenced by him.
But the scant success of the operas *Esmeralda* and *Rusalka* had
made him rather susceptible to flattery, and the adulatory and
mediocre musicians who frequented his house provided a far
from stimulating atmosphere. It was from Balakirev that Mussorgsky, the young, rather precious and exceedingly hand-
some army officer, sought tuition. Balakirev himself was irritated
by Dargomyzhsky's jealousy of Glinka's fame and success;
Vladimir Stassov nick-named his circle 'The Russian Invalids'.
Mussorgsky declared to Balakirev that the part of a pasha '*à la*
Dargomyzhsky' did not suit him. It was not till 1868 and the
composition of the *The Stone Guest*, that Balakirev's group were
to become really excited by Dargomyzhsky's music.

Balakirev was one of the only men in St Petersburg at the time not merely capable of teaching composition, but eager to teach, to encourage, to lead. In anything he did he liked to be the leader and for him a number of really talented pupils seemed to provide a stimulus. Though lacking facilities for learning composition, he had fought his way through all the difficulties without the aid of text-books. He taught his pupils to compose in the same way. Not only had he no text-book knowledge of harmony and counterpoint, but he did not know even some of the simple names of ordinary chords. The result was a completely fresh outlook and he had an infallible instinct for the right thing in a given set of circumstances. His memory and ear were both outstanding. He did everything he could to help his pupils master every branch of their art. They had to study instrumental forms; Balakirev, in a letter of 22 July/4 August 1906, wrote to M. D. Calvocoressi about his teaching of Mussorgsky:

We played piano duet versions (he was an excellent pianist) of all the existing repertoire of classical music, ancient and modern: Bach, Handel, Mozart, Haydn, Beethoven, Schubert, Schumann, Berlioz and Liszt. He was already familiar, without my help, with the music of Glinka and Dargomyzhsky. I also explained to him form in composition, which resulted in his composing for piano duet an 'Allegro symphonique' in C major not devoid of merit; unfortunately the manuscript was lost and has not been found again after his death. Later on, when our lessons ceased (they were only continued for a short time), he went to live with Rimsky-Korsakov, who was not married then, and who had just been appointed professor of musical theory at the Conservatoire . . . I continued to be on good terms with Mussorgsky until the end of his life. I saw him for the last time, and chatted with him, the day before his death.[2]

In another letter, Balakirev wrote to Stassov in 1881:

I was unable to teach harmony or theory, for example, as Rimsky-Korsakov teaches it now . . . but I explained form in composition to him and in this connection we used to play together the symphonies of Beethoven and many others (Schumann, Schubert, Glinka) ... I explained their formal structure. So far as I can remember, I gave him few paid lessons. Somehow or other, they soon turned into friendly discussions.[3]

Balakirev, beset by financial difficulties though he was, was quite willing to teach a promising pupil, who could not afford to pay, for nothing. And for guidance Mussorgsky relied entirely on Balakirev, whose teaching encouraged impulsiveness rather than methodical discipline. He was a teacher, it has been not too unsuitably averred, for men of genius only.

Balakirev's mind, even in the earlier days, was perhaps rather inflexible and it may be that someone as wayward as Mussorgsky would have been served better by a teacher who was capable of seeing things from his pupil's point of view more. Nevertheless, no other teacher in Russia and few others, if any, in Europe would have been capable of teaching the new Russian school so ably as Balakirev. His stimulating effect was astonishing, even if it was only a stimulus to disagree with him! Mussorgsky, without saying a word about it to Balakirev, gave up his career in the army to compose; Rimsky-Korsakov later gave up his in the navy; and although Borodin remained in his career as a chemist, the few compositions of outstanding beauty composed by him are a direct result of the teaching of Balakirev. Other composers in Balakirev's group in the early days (now forgotten) were Gussakovsky and Borozdin with both of whom he was very friendly.

From the very first, Mussorgsky's letters show him to be on intimate terms with his teacher.[4] He worked set exercises for Balakirev, while at the same time composing according to his own plans. On 8/20 July 1858 he told Balakirev that in his leisure hours he was at work on practical exercises in harmony. He was eager to learn the art of correct part-writing. Mussorgsky suffered a minor mental illness in 1859, as a letter to Balakirev, who was then at Nizhny-Novgorod, shows, though he afterwards admitted that he had under-rated the crisis *to avoid distres-sing Balakirev*. In June, he described in detail, in a letter, his first impressions of Moscow, the Kremlin and so on. The two men were more than teacher and pupil. They were also intimate friends. Later (in 1861) Balakirev was so concerned with his welfare in Moscow, where he was staying with friends whom Balakirev considered to be undesirable, that he (Balakirev) wrote to Mussorgsky's brother Filaret to find out when he would be returning to St Petersburg.

Balakirev was, of course, the dominant personality in this friendship. Mussorgsky wrote to him, on 19/31 October 1859: '. . . I have recognised your superiority; in our arguments I have always been aware of a greater clarity in your views, and more firmness . . . I am very grateful to you, Mily, because you were successful in arousing me from my torpor.'[5]

Here is an acknowledgement of the infectious vitality with which Balakirev urged on his pupils out of the Russian lassitude which sometimes overtook them.

Borodin met Mussorgsky in 1859. He had not yet met Balakirev. Writing of those times, Borodin says that Mussorgsky was living in an atmosphere of musical innovations of which he himself did not have the smallest notion . . . Mussorgsky talked enthusiastically about Schumann's symphonies which Borodin did not know and played parts of the one in E flat major. When he had reached the development section he stopped and declared: 'Here come the musical mathematics.' All this was new and delightful to Borodin.[6]

In this way Balakirev drew men to him in the late 'fifties and 'sixties. He widened the horizon of all with whom he came in contact. His amazing gifts and powerful personality precluded all criticism. Borodin, however, was the last of the 'mighty handful' to join his circle, for late in 1859 he went abroad to continue his scientific studies. He did not meet Balakirev until late 1862 (November or December), at one of the Saturday 'At Homes' of the famous Petersburg doctor, S. P. Botkin.[7] After his death, Balakirev told Stassov that until then, Borodin thought himself a mere amateur, and did not consider the impulse that drove him towards composition to be important. 'I was the first to tell him', Balakirev wrote, 'that his real business was—composition. He eagerly started work on his E flat major symphony.'[8]

Every bar was overhauled and criticised by Balakirev. Borodin much later wrote that when Balakirev returned the score of his first symphony, there were comments scattered all over it suggesting the very things he (Borodin) had done at first, but altered because he (Balakirev) had advised it![9]

Even Borodin did not remain entirely unruffled, though his temperament was so equable. Of course Balakirev was not infallible, and he *was* dogmatic. Furthermore, he put Borodin to work immediately on a symphony, a curious method of starting off a new composition pupil. A rough draft of the first movement was completed in a month or two, but the symphony was not completed until 1867. Its first performance was in January 1869.

Mussorgsky started on a Symphony in D major early in 1861. The symphony was to be inscribed to the companionship of the weekly Wednesday meetings at Balakirev's house.

No trace of this symphony remains. On 11/23 March 1862[10] he wrote to Balakirev that he was at work on the *Andante*, and that although he had never actually avoided work, he had failed to achieve much because of his Russian laziness.

In late 1861 (26 November/8 December) the pianist Canille introduced the young seventeen-year-old naval cadet Rimsky-Korsakov to Balakirev.[11] He at once succumbed to Balakirev's magnetic personality. Balakirev was shown some piano pieces and the beginning of a symphony in E flat minor. He insisted that the youth should continue with his symphony.

Balakirev had no promising pupil at the time except Mussorgsky, about whose ability he was beginning to have doubts. Gussakovsky[12] seemed to be losing interest in music and was soon to marry and go abroad. Balakirev did not meet Borodin until the following year. He took a fancy to Rimsky-Korsakov, writing that he put his trust in him as an old aunt in a young lawyer nephew.[13]

The first movement of the E flat minor symphony was finished within a month—Balakirev certainly inspired his pupils to work.

In helping Rimsky-Korsakov to orchestrate it, Balakirev thought he showed a considerable bent in this direction. The Scherzo and Finale were soon completed, but the 'first Russian symphony' (as he called it, ignoring Rubinstein's 'Russianness'!) had to be interrupted. On 8/20 April 1862 Rimsky-Korsakov left the naval college as a 'guardemarine' (one stage lower than a midshipman) and joined the clipper *Almaz*.[14]

Balakirev did not want to lose him, for the *Almaz* was destined for a long cruise in foreign waters. However, Korsakov's elder brother (his father was dead) insisted that he remain in the service and the *Almaz* left Kronstadt for England in October.

Some of Balakirev's correspondence with Korsakov on the *Almaz* is preserved and is most illuminating.[15] It shows how Balakirev tries to keep the young 'guardemarine' interested in music, and how intimate were teacher and pupil. On 14/26 November, Balakirev wrote him a long essay on the art of orchestration (based on Berlioz' treaty). Korsakov answered that he was sorry not to have replied to 'auntie' earlier, requested Balakirev to send his next letter to Gravesend, and bade good-bye to 'dear auntie', adding, 'your beloved nephew kisses you on the lips'.

On 14/26 December, Korsakov sent Balakirev, for his Christmas tree, as he put it, a 'home-made *Andante*', based on a folk tune given to him by Balakirev. The slow movement was the one that he had had difficulty over in his symphony, as Balakirev at this time was very strict about keeping melodies from becoming too sentimental—though Balakirev's strongest point was never to be the composing or judging of slow melodies. Korsakov had seen the sights of London, including the Crystal Palace, the British Museum and Westminster Abbey.

A fortnight later Balakirev wrote that the Andante had not arrived. Next month Korsakov, writing from Greenwich, expressed dismay about this. Soon afterwards he was upset because he had not heard from his mother, or Balakirev, or Cui. He was *losing his urge to compose*. Balakirev quickly replied, trying to relieve his depression, and mentioning that Wagner had arrived in St Petersburg. He had heard some *Tannhäuser* music which was 'revolting'.

In an interesting letter of 3/15 April 1863 Korsakov appears to have had a dream in which, to his great distress, Balakirev refuses to speak to him. He adds: 'I don't believe in dreams . . .' Writing from Piatigorsk, Balakirev gave advice about the use of the harp, whose lower register, which he compared to a saucepan or frying pan, should be avoided.

The *Almaz* returned to Russia for a few months before another long voyage to America. The correspondence all but ceased, and Rimsky-Korsakov had at this time rejected the idea of becoming a musician. He returned to Kronstadt in the summer of 1865. All his dreams of artistic activity had flown away, he wrote. Nor did he regret them.[16] He did see Balakirev once or twice in the summer but, being transferred to Petersburg in September and coming under Balakirev's strong influence again, he returned to his musical interests with renewed vigour. He finished his symphony, wrote a trio for the Scherzo, and orchestrated it all closely supervised by Balakirev—probably learning a great deal about orchestration in doing so. His naval duties were not arduous, and he sometimes even slept at Balakirev's. In November 1865 his setting of Heine's 'Lehn deine Wang an meine Wang' was published, but not with his own accompaniment. Balakirev provided this himself.

The E flat minor symphony, Op. 1, was performed by Balakirev at a Free School Concert on 19/31 December 1865. It was well received, and was performed together with Mozart's *Requiem*. In fact, not only the inspiration Balakirev afforded him, and the urge to compose, but the pushing forward of his music, the publishing of a song and the performance of his symphony, show how great is the debt Korsakov owed to Balakirev in these early days.

In the summer of 1866 he wrote an Overture on Three Russian Themes based on the style of Balakirev's two overtures, two of the themes being taken from Balakirev's collection published in the same year. He was still very much under Balakirev's influence.

Borodin's first symphony was finished in 1867. It is clear that the first movement is much influenced by Balakirev, while the

Scherzo and Finale are more originally Borodin's own. It is these two movements which were really successful at the first performance, given by Balakirev at a Russian Music Society concert on 4/16 January 1869. Even the critic F. M. Tolstoy, who hated the 'new music', praised the Finale.[17] The success of Borodin's first symphony, with the public at least (some critics wrote unfavourable notices about it), was probably the spur which urged him on to compose his second, and this chance was given to him by Balakirev's performing the work.

Balakirev, although he performed the first version of Mussorgsky's choral work *The Destruction of Sennacherib* at a Free School Concert in March 1867, refused to perform his *Night on a Bare Mountain* (then called *Witches*), of which he disapproved. Mussorgsky never attempted another purely orchestral work as a result; but he refused to obey Balakirev's directions. In September 1867 he wrote to Balakirev[18] that whether he agreed to produce *Witches*, or not, he would not alter the plan or the working-out ... for both were carried out in a spirit of sincerity.

Korsakov, too, was beginning to stand on his own feet and to kick against Balakirev's predisposition for symphonic development, which Korsakov considered to be not always suitable or desirable.[19]

Both Rimsky-Korsakov and Mussorgsky were introduced to Ludmila Shestakova in 1866, when she emerged from a three-year retirement following the death of her little daughter Olia. (On the death of Olia, Balakirev had generously offered to take two promising piano pupils free in her memory.) She wrote, speaking of this time, of Mussorgsky's deep respect for Balakirev,[20] and of the feverish activity of Balakirev's group. The days were not long enough for them to play and talk music. And so, leaving her house (she was very hospitable), they would spend much time escorting one another home.

In speaking of the 1866–7 period, Rimsky-Korsakov related[21] that he used to visit Mussorgsky at his flat, which he shared with his brother and sister-in-law. Here they could talk freely, safe from Balakirev's and Cui's 'interference'. According to Korsakov,

Borodin, Mussorgsky and he were subordinate and obeyed, while Balakirev and Cui gave the orders.

Cui certainly had a high opinion of himself. He was speedily rising to the top rank in the army, and his bigoted views were often ascribed to Balakirev himself. He was music critic of the *St Petersburg Vedomost* (Gazette). He had just finished an opera, *William Ratcliffe*, which was praised by Balakirev's circle, but was of little merit. By the 'seventies, like Korsakov, he began to display academic tendencies—perhaps as a reaction to Balakirev's hatred of them—and he wrote an offensive notice on *Boris Godunov* in 1874.

But, until 1869 or so, all was harmony (outwardly, at any rate) in the group, and the 'feverish activity' of Mussorgsky, Rimsky-Korsakov and Borodin received its first impetus entirely from Balakirev. It was he who 'kept them at it' and, though his criticisms might sometimes annoy them, he was a constant inspiration to them all.

### NOTES ON CHAPTER 4

1. Except of course for the pro-Western Anton Rubinstein.
2. CC (Paris, July 1911), p. 7.
3. M(2)A, p. 25.
4. *M. P. Mussorgsky: Letters and documents* (*M. P. Mussorgsky: Pisma i dokumenty*), ed. by A. Rimsky-Korsakov, Moscow, 1932.
5. ibid., p. 53, quoted also in FA, p. 12.
6. When Clara Schumann visited St Petersburg early in 1864, there was great excitement among the group (K(3)B, pp. 209–211).
7. TA, No. vi, p. 57.
8. M(2)A, p. 29.
9. CA, p. 117—this refers to October 1871. Balakirev had borrowed the score of the first symphony to make a piano arrangement of it (which never materialized) and was unwilling to return it unless Borodin made these changes! Balakirev was still fussing about 'necessary alterations' in the early 'eighties.
10. CB, p. 44.
11. TA, No. vi, pp. 55–56.
12. A. S. Gussakovsky (1841–75) was a pupil of Balakirev from 1857–61. The first allegro of his Symphony in E flat major was performed at a University concert in January 1861. He never finished the symphony (L(1)D, p. 28).
13. AE, p. 24.
14. ibid., p. 25.

15. The Balakirev–Rimsky-Korsakov correspondence is taken from L(1)D, pp. 17–210.
16. AE, p. 29 et seq.
17. S. A. Dianin—*Borodin: Zhizneopisanie Materialy i Dokumenty*, Moscow 1960, p. 75.
18. CB, p. 80. This work is much influenced by Liszt's *Danse Macabre*, first performed in Russia in 1866.
19. ibid., p. 103.
20. See introduction.
21. CB, p. 66.

# CHAPTER 5

*1866–1867: Balakirev in Prague – the Austro-Prussian war – Glinka's operas performed on second visit – behaviour of Smetana – Stassov's article – Free School Concert in honour of Slav visitors – Pan-Slavonic views – appointed conductor of Russian Music Society – invites Berlioz to Russia – Balakirev's programmes – resignation of Lomakin from directorship of Free School.*

In 1866 Ludmila Shestakova asked Balakirev to go to Prague to arrange the production of Glinka's operas there. She wrote in her *Recollections* that she would never forget Balakirev's devotion to her brother's memory. 'Whenever I planned to make his music better known, Balakirev seized on my idea and with love, energy and patience carried it through to the end. In spite of the hard work involved and his poor health, he forgot everything and gave himself up wholly to the task'.[1]

He set off in June on what was to be the most adventurous journey of his life.[2] In later years he loved to recall his journeys to Prague, starting with the words: 'When Ludmila Ivanovna sent me to Prague . . .'[3] On his arrival in Prague discussions had only just begun when the Austro-Prussian War broke out. Balakirev's first letter to Ludmila Shestakova was written from *Vienna:* 'You, no doubt, are very surprised, my dearest Ludmila Ivanovna, to see the name Vienna at the head of this letter, aren't you? Hear and be astonished at my successes.'[4] Balakirev had been to Prague. 'I was received much more hospitably than I had expected. Talks started at once about putting on *A Life for the Tsar.*' But the Prussians were getting closer to Prague. He speaks of 500 wounded men arriving on one day, 1000 on the next (large numbers for these days!). By then it was too late to leave, as the Austrians had cancelled nearly all passenger trains except for one express a day.

I had to stay, like it or no, for another day. All the following day I was in a state of extreme excitement. Every hour they posted on street corners new telegrams from which, however, one could gather nothing except that the Austrians were fighting with stubborn determination against the Prussians.

Balakirev intended to return to Russia by way of Leipzig to try to arrange for the publication of Glinka's operas there. But having reached Bamberg and discovered from the officers of the Bavarian regiment which was quartered there that they were going to occupy Kissingen (which is on the route to Leipzig), and that some were going to Leipzig to try to drive the Prussians out of that city, he was obliged to return to Vienna.[5]

On 30 June/12 July he wrote to Ludmila Shestakova:[6] ' . . . there is nothing else for me to do but return to Russia as quickly as possible'. He continues:

Today a telegram has been published in Vienna about a battle between the Prussians and Bavarians at Schweinfurt near Kissingen. This road was the only one to Leipzig and the Bavarians advised me to return from Bamberg to Vienna. As regards Prague it is already in the hands of the Prussians, [rumours were certainly flying about!] and they will probably be in Vienna itself in four or five days. I have tried to write to Prague. At the post office they are accepting no letters or telegrams for Prague. Franz Josef is behaving as befits an Austrian hero—that is to say, he keeps retreating. Yesterday, they say, the all-wise Austrian state council met at the palace and decided, after profound deliberation, not to defend Vienna, and to withdraw to Pest,[7] where the Empress has already betaken herself. As you see, there is no possibility of remaining in these parts, and I must hurry while the road is still open from Cracow to Russia. To my good fortune, I have found a fellow traveller, a Galician Russian, bound for St Petersburg, and we have decided to leave tomorrow. We shall travel, via Pest, by rail as far as possible, then for the rest, we shall have to travel about 200 versts[8] on horseback to Cracow ... You won't believe how upset and irritated I am ... I have become nervous and jumpy and am only consoled by this one thought—that I'm not the only one who is sleeping badly. The local Kaiser[9] is also sleepless at nights in his Schönbrunn, and has already had attacks of fainting sickness. I can't wait to leave and shall only feel calmer when I have reached Russian territory.

He adds a postscript: 'The news has been received that the Prussians are 60 versts from Vienna.'

While he was in Vienna, Balakirev had found in the Public Library there a book of Czech folk-songs which delighted him.[10] It was entitled *Marriage among the Czechoslovak people*, by B. M. Kulda.[11] From this little book he took three tunes, and started work on a Czech Overture, based on them, when he arrived safely back in St Petersburg in July.

Six months later he was ready to depart for Prague again. The 'Seven Weeks War' was over. Austria had lost her hegemony in Germany to Prussia.

On 20 December 1866/1 January 1867 Balakirev wrote to Ludmila Shestakova from St Petersburg:[12] 'Yesterday I had such a fever that I thought that instead of going to Prague I should end up in Botkin's[13] clinic. But now I'm so much better that I can leave tomorrow, and I shall leave provided the ceiling doesn't fall in and kill me ...'

Balakirev arrived in Prague on 24 December/5 January. On the next day he wrote:[14] 'I hasten to inform you, dearest Ludmila Ivanovna, that I have arrived in Prague safely, that is with hands, feet and head—all in one piece. I got here yesterday evening'.

And on 26 December/7 January: 'They put on *A Life for the Tsar* in my absence—very badly.' He saw this version on the next day, and was able to judge what kind of cast and orchestra he would have to deal with. On 28 December/9 January: 'At last I have seen *A Life for the Tsar* here. What a horror it was! I haven't quite come to my senses yet. The overture was so-so. But the curtain rises and oh! horror, what costumes. The peasants were waving some kind of peaked caps and wore overcoats with white buttons, and they had beards, but not Russian ones, Jewish ones!'[15] Smetana, the principal conductor of the Prague opera, had been responsible for this production.

Balakirev's main collaborator in the production of the opera was Josef Kolář (1830–1910), the Czech scholar, writer and expert on Slavonic languages, who translated Glinka's operas into Czech.

On 11/23 January he was able to write to Ludmila Shestakova:

Today, at last, everything has been decided. I was with the directors for final discussions . . . Thank goodness, Smetana will not be training the chorus. He is being replaced by Tausig, a proper musician, who sympathizes with the music of Glinka, and so it is now easy for me to remove Smetana's influence . . . The artists are very anxious to sing Glinka's operas properly because they like them. They assure me that Smetana deliberately gave them the wrong tempi in performance in order to put them off, in which he sometimes succeeded . . . They say that Smetana and Prohazka are forming a large party in order to hiss *A Life for the Tsar* off the stage, but another party is being formed to sabotage them . . . The main leaders in all these local plots are the Poles, living here in large numbers, and they have already managed to form a whole anti-Russian coalition amongst the Czechs. On the other hand, the professors and students take a totally different attitude, and I am convinced that in spite of all their Jesuitical attempts I shall defeat them. Smetana and I are no longer on speaking terms. We only bow to one another. It is obvious that he knows that I know everything.[16]

Smetana's intrigues, however, gained ground with the directors. On 28 January/9 February,[17] he wrote that they had been behaving so badly towards him that Kolář told them that if

73

they went on behaving in such a way, Balakirev would take the music and walk out on them.

> They are being more polite as a result of this. I am very glad, but I am afraid the choruses are going very badly . . . However, the soloists make me happy. They are attentive, industrious and have artistic souls . . .
>
> These beastly directors, somehow contrived to lose the piano reduction of *Russlan*. Good. So I, to the astonishment of all, accompanied the whole opera (at a rehearsal) from memory, after which the piano edition turned up and was not lost again. In a word, I'm in a very good frame of mind. *Russlan* is near and Petersburg is nearer.

The first performance of *Russlan and Ludmila* was on 4/16 February, subsequent performances were on 5/17 and 7/19 February (the latter was Balakirev's 'benefit' performance).

Earlier on the day of the first performance, a Saturday, Balakirev wrote:[18]

> I am unable to write much to you, as today we give the first performance of *Russlan*. I shiver as if in a fever. I don't know what the result will be. There have only been three rehearsals, of which one (yesterday evening) was the dress rehearsal . . . I shall not forget Smetana, and as for the other directors, they are no better than he. I'm convinced that *Russlan* will be spoilt like *A Life for the Tsar* after I've gone . . . Yesterday Smetana noised it abroad that on my departure he would make cuts and change the cast! (in order no doubt to injure the opera) he found that my tempo in Gorislava's aria was incorrect, that Glinka himself was quite mistaken when he indicated *allegro* and in his (Smetana's) opinion it ought to be *adagio*.

On 6/18 February he wrote to Cui that he was now the 'complete director'. On the same day he informed Ludmila Shestakova:

> *Russlan* has at last been given and was received with an

74

enthusiasm the like of which has not been seen here before. The audience applauded unceasingly, threw bouquets and wreaths on to the stage just as they do in Petersburg (the Czechs normally behave in the theatre like the Germans, that is, like fish). I'll tell you in detail how it all went. I arrived in the theatre with my heart in my mouth . . . the fatal moment, seven o'clock, arrived, and I started on my way to the rostrum, thinking to myself, 'now my famous *Russlan*, make your effect upon the Czech public, and strike all these pro-Poles and pro-Germans on the snout'. As I went to the rostrum I could see that all would be well.[19]

The young composer Antonín Dvořák was playing the viola in the orchestra at this performance. He had a very high opinion of Balakirev both as a musician and composer, and used to recall in his later years how he had played on this occasion under Balakirev's baton.

Balakirev continues:

I was greeted by deafening applause and I had to bow to all parts of the theatre even before the overture. The overture went off—although not as well as in St Petersburg—at least, not badly. Further applause. The curtain went up, and I myself was staggered. Before my eyes, real Russian costumes and décor, not at all badly done . . . At yesterday's (the second) performance, a large company of Poles arrived intending to hiss the opera off the stage, but the public drowned them with applause so that I did not even hear them hissing. Tomorrow there will be a third performance of *Russlan* (my benefit). They say the Poles are going to hiss it more persistently. On Friday there will be *A Life for the Tsar*, and to annoy the Poles I am making all the actors kneel at the prayer 'God Save the Tsar'. None of the Dresden Russians have thought it necessary to come except Mrs Ivanova, in the first place because they are all aristocrats, and secondly because the Poles have given them a great fright by spreading the rumour that there will be a lot of unpleasantness for all Russians in Prague. Mrs Ivanova receives a daily letter from her mother, begging her to leave as quickly as possible. The *Dziennik Poznanski*, No. 35, printed that the staging of Russian operas in Prague is Muscovite propaganda for which the Russian Government have paid 30,000 rubles.

*A Life for the Tsar* was given only one performance, on 10/22 February. Balakirev was then asked to go home. The political atmosphere was too much for the directors. In the rumours of Russian bribes for the staging of the operas, the sum had increased to 50,000 rubles![20]

Stassov wrote an article, 'Glinka's opera *Russlan and Ludmila* in Prague', for the *St Petersburg Vedomost*.[21] Balakirev's successes were laid before the Petersburg public. They did not remain unrewarded.

Busy as he was in Prague, he had been working on his Overture on Czech Themes, which he finished quickly.[22] It was revised, rescored and published as the Symphonic poem *In Bohemia* in 1906. It is dedicated to Kolář. He was fond of the Czechs in spite of all that had happened and wrote to M. D. Calvocoressi, (who was arranging a performance of it in Paris) on 21 February/11 March, 1906: 'With all my heart I hope that this composition will be successful in Paris. It would give me great joy if the French could *like the Czech themes* which are of a Slav character and of a type to draw attention to the delightful Czech people, who resist with such energy the attempts of the Germans to absorb them.'[23]

The first performance, for which Balakirev had so quickly turned out the work, was at a Free School Concert on 12/24 May 1867, given in honour of the Slav visitors who had come to Russia for the All-Russian Ethnographical Exhibition in Moscow.[24] It was in a notice about this concert that Stassov first referred to Balakirev's group as the 'moguchaya kuchka', literally, 'mighty little group' or 'mighty handful'.[25] He was not to know then that it would stick to them, nor that it would be misleadingly altered to 'Les Cinq' or 'The Five' in French and English.

Balakirev's romantic Pan-Slavonic views are even more clearly stated in a letter of 5/17 May 1880 to Stassov, who by then had modified his ideas on the subject:

You say: Slavdom is crushed, hence it is worthless. You apparently know nothing of the history of the Czechs, whose country was incomparably more advanced than the Germano-Roman world by which it is surrounded—and, moreover, it was *quality* that was crushed by *quantity*. You don't give a brass farthing either for the frantic, unbelievable energy displayed by the Czechs, who held out against the crusades of the whole of Europe; or for the capacity this people had of producing and incarnating a government service such as that of King Yuri Podebradsky, which was without equal in Europe at that time. You want to know nothing, for example, about what a heroic nation the Serbs are, and what energy they displayed when they defended themselves against the Turks under George the Black and Milosha Obrenovich, and finally beat them back . . . And the Montenegrins? What have you to say about this little nation, who, having neither food nor a port (their port was ceded to Austria by command of Alexander I) nevertheless did not ever submit either to the Turks or the Germans? And the Poles? Can it be that you see nothing in them but humourous good-nature and passivity? . . . You . . . greatly admire success, and turn aside with contempt from misfortune . . . [The Slav race] was apparently endowed from the very beginning with a degree of mental and emotional development which the Germanic race was only able to achieve after a long process of change under the influence of Christian civilization . . . The spiritual and political life of the Slavs was forcibly interrupted. I should say that this loss was irreparable, were it not that I believe that humanity, albeit by long and difficult paths, will nevertheless arrive at the same state to which the civilization of the Slav peoples, in their day *leaders in the battle for thought and civic consciousness*, would have brought us.[26]

Balakirev's father had lost his job at Yaroslavl because of a change in the establishment; but he was given instead a post as assistant to the district treasurer at Klin near Moscow. Balakirev visited his father and sisters Maria and Varvara in June and July of 1867. From Klin he wrote to Zhemchuzhnikov on 19 June/1 July:

> Although my expedition to Prague yielded me (minus) 400 rubles (i.e. 400 rubles of debts), in compensation it yielded me other advantages (!): beings higher than we mortals, such as Count Bobrinsky, took me tenderly by the hand, le célebre Tolstoy (A.K.) came to me twice and invited me to call on him without fail at Pustynka . . . I stayed there for a full round of the clock and saw *much to edify me*, starting with him and his wife and finishing with her nieces. . . .[27]

Anton Rubinstein wanted, because of his many other commitments, to resign the conductorship of the Russian Music Society which he had founded in 1859. Some of the board of directors (one of whom was the influential Kologrivov) suggested that Balakirev be appointed to succeed him, and although there was some opposition, he was generally considered to be the most promising young Russian conductor. He was appointed in the summer of 1867.[28]

One of his first acts was to persuade the board to invite Berlioz to conduct six of the ten concerts in the 1867–68 season. To some extent, it would therefore seem, he was overshadowed in his first season by the Frenchman. But he saw the chance that was given him here *not* as an opportunity to increase his reputation as a conductor, but as the acquisition of a wider platform for the music of the more modern composers with whose work he wished to make the Russian public acquainted.

The first three concerts, on 19/31 October, 26 October/7 November and 2/14 November, were conducted by Balakirev himself. They included performances of the Introduction to Act I from *Russlan*; Wagner's *Faust* overture (the only work of Wagner of which Balakirev approved); Schumann's 1st Symphony; introduction, recitative and aria from the third act of Dargomyzhsky's *Rusalka*, sung by E. K. Skordula, who also performed Glinka's song 'The Lark', and Balakirev's 'Come to me' (No. 10 of his group of twenty songs); and, in the second concert, Rimsky-Korsakov's *Serbian Fantasy*, which had first been performed at the Free School Concert of 12/24 May.[29]

Berlioz conducted the 4th, 5th, 6th, 8th, 9th and 10th concerts in the series. The Petersburg public were certainly surfeited, in Balakirev's first season, with the music which he wanted them to hear. A wise man would have taken his directors' advice and given the public, in the following season, more of what *they* wanted to hear.

In November 1867 Lomakin resigned from the Directorship of the Free School of Music, and a council was appointed to direct the policy of the school. And Balakirev's second big opportunity came his way.

### NOTES ON CHAPTER 5

1. TB, p. 148.
2. Before his departure for Prague he moved flat from the Nevsky Prospekt to share with his friend E. K. Le-Dantu (L(1)D, p. 461).
3. TB, p. 149.
4. Timofeyev (TB, p. 152) gives the date of this letter as 19 July (31 July), thus making it come after the other letter, dated 30 June (12 July), in which Balakirev writes that he is returning to Russia without delay via Budapest and Cracow. Clearly the dates of these letters have been muddled, and the first letter should probably have read 'June 19'. There is only *one* difference in 'June 19' and 'July 19' in the Russian language, and Balakirev's writing may not have been clear. Balakirev's itinerary was obviously as follows: St Petersburg–Prague–Vienna–Bamberg–Vienna–Budapest–Cracow–St Petersburg.
5. TB, p. 153.
6. ibid., pp. 151–152.
7. The newer town of the twin towns Buda and Pest, now capital of Hungary.
8. One verst equals 3500 feet.
9. Franz Josef.
10. TA, No. vii, p. 60.
11. AA, p. 364, col. 2.
12. TB, p. 153.
13. See above, chapter 4.
14. TB, p. 154.
15. ibid., p. 156.
16. ibid., pp. 162–163.
17. ibid., pp. 180–181.
18. ibid., p. 183.
19. ibid., pp. 183–185.

20. K(3)B, p. 240.
21. No. 35, 1867, V. V. Stassov: *Selected Works in Three Volumes* (*Izbrannye Sochineniya v trekh tomakh*) Vol. III, pp. 202–206.
22. On 5/17 January 1867, orchestrated soon afterwards (TB, p. 160).
23. CC, p. 4.
24. TA, No. vii, p. 60; G(3)A, p. 33.
25. G(3)A, p. 17; AE, footnote, p. 33.
26. FA, pp. 23–23.
27. FC (iii), p. 100.
28. M(2)A, p. 48; TA, No. vii, p. 61.
29. K(3)B, pp. 242 and 244.

6. Balakirev photographed in Tiflis (1863)

7. 'The Mighty Handful' and Vladimir Stassov

(*1st line*) Balakirev, Stassov, Mussorgsky

(*2nd line*) Rimsky-Korsakov, Borodin, Cui

# CHAPTER 6

*1868–1869 (summer): Appointed Director of Free School – 'All music in his hands' – Free School and Russian Music Society – holiday in the Caucasus – Balakirev as conductor – Dargomyzhsky's* Stone Guest – The Fire-Bird – *intrigues to oust Balakirev from the Russian Music Society – Berlioz's disgust – first Russian performance of* Lohengrin – *R.M.S. Concerts – Balakirev and Tchaikovsky* (Fatum) *– forced resignation from R.M.S. – appraisal of the situation – 'mud-slinging' articles – death of his father.*

On 28 January/9 February 1868 the new council of the Free School appointed Balakirev as successor to Lomakin. In this way, most of the orchestral concerts were now under his control, since the Russian Music Society and the Free School of Music were the main bodies which existed at that time in St Petersburg to promote concerts. As Cui put it,[1] '. . . he had all music in his hands'. The position of the Free School of Music became much stronger, while it contributed a considerable share in the concerts of the Russian Music Society, the School choir taking part in the society's concerts as the following extract from a rough copy of the report of the Petersburg section of the R.M.S. and the conservatoire for the years 1868–69 shows:[2] 'The choirs were made up of amateurs, mostly from members of the Free Music School. The members of this institution, under the direction of M. A. Balakirev, took part unpaid, with the readiness of true lovers of the art of music, in six symphony concerts. Among other things they performed Mozart's *Requiem* and Beethoven's ninth symphony.' The financial position of the Free

School was to some extent eased. Balakirev asked the directors of the R.M.S. 'to allow him to move certain classes of the Free School into the hall of the Conservatoire, when the latter was not occupied by students. The directors, who were in full sympathy with the rapid development of the Free School, were glad to accede to M. A. Balakirev's wish, and when the classes were in the evening, gave permission for the hall to be lit free of charge.' Balakirev made a reduction on the price of tickets for members of the R.M.S. for a Free School concert given on 18/30 March 1868. Some of Balakirev's friends, too, dreamed about the possibility of gradually merging the Russian Music Society and the Free School of Music.

Just after his thirty-first birthday, then, Balakirev stood at the height of his career as a practical musician. All composition virtually ceased, except some work on *Tamara* during the summer at Kislovodsk in the Caucasus. Of his conducting ability, most reports are favourable, a few only with reservations. Rimsky-Korsakov's later lukewarmness may be attributed to Balakirev's behaviour towards him in the late 'seventies, when he publicly told Korsakov how to conduct at a Free School rehearsal.[3] Kashkin[4] thought he devoted too much attention to detail but neglected the architectural whole, but Lyapunov wrote that the principal features of his performances were:

> Simplicity, precise observance of all the composer's indications, not permitting any sort of exaggeration, undue emphasis or inappropriate hurrying up or slowing down . . . There was no false expression, pretentiousness or artificiality about him. His tempi were correct, exact and unexceptionable. But his performances were never dry or lifeless. The warmth of his nature was transmitted to his performances without detracting from their high artistic value.[5]

Borodin says of his conducting of Schumann's second symphony, in an article in the *St Petersburg Vedomost* (1868):

> We have never had anyone who has conducted Schumann's work with such animation, such lucidity and such subtle under-

standing as Mr Balakirev. In his conducting even the defects in Schumann's orchestrations are somehow smoothed out . . . But the main difficulty in performing Schumann's works is to put over correctly the infinite variety of delicate nuances which demand from the conductor an artistic flair of an unusually developed kind.[6]

Tchernov, who knew him in later years, wrote in his *Recollections*:

M. A. always conducted in a very calm manner, but with extreme skill and brilliance. He never had recourse to any undue emphasis or artificial expression . . . In former times Balakirev always conducted from memory. Only at the end of his life did his memory begin to fail him.[7]

By 1868 Dargomyzhsky had nearly finished the composition of his opera *The Stone Guest* (based on the story of Don Juan). Neither Balakirev nor Stassov had thought much of it in 1866. On 30 January/11 February 1866 Balakirev had written:[8] 'He [Dargomyzhsky] played us over his castrated *Don Juan*', and on 17/29 May Stassov wrote of it, 'how simply miraculous it is!' (*sic*). But they had changed their views by January 1868, by which time the opera had been radically altered. Balakirev, Stassov, Cui, Mussorgsky and Rimsky-Korsakov all began to frequent Dargomyzhsky's house to hear it. On 26 April/8 May, Stassov told Balakirev:[9] 'Dargomyzhsky charges me to invite you to his place on Wednesday evening (1st May): they'll be singing all that he's written so far of *Don Juan*.'[10]

The project of his opera, *The Fire-Bird*, was still simmering in Balakirev's mind. He had approached a new librettist, D. Averkiev, who was a Slavophile and an experienced playwright. Averkiev sent him the libretto of a first act for *The Fire-Bird* in 1868, and worked out a general plan. Balakirev, who was busy with his concert work, wrote to Averkiev on 30 April/12 May:[11] 'Forgive me for not writing before. I have been very busy . . . As regards the libretto, I was very surprised at finding so much of my own previous material . . . There is a lot that is unsuitable . . .'

Averkiev's first act had literary qualities that Balakirev's other libretti did not possess, but he was not satisfied. The whole thing was again put off.

This year he spent another summer holiday in the Caucasus at Vladikavkaz and Kislovodsk (where he gave recitals). He knew by this time that he had alienated the Imperial Patroness of the Russian Music Society, the Grand Duchess Helena Pavlovna. She was already trying to oust him from the conductorship of the R.M.S. as Balakirev wrote to Stassov on 14/26 September from Kislovodsk, and put in his place one Seifriz.[12] Evidently, the board of directors rose up in arms against this, and thanks to Kologrivov, D. A. Obolensky, U. F. Abaza and Nicholas Rubinstein, supported Balakirev. The party hostile to Balakirev insisted that the Grand Duchess write to Liszt, Wagner and Berlioz for a testimonial about Seifriz, and besides this, Berlioz was asked to give an unfavourable reference on Balakirev! Liszt and Wagner gave a reference on Seifriz—a conscientious and knowledgeable conductor—but Berlioz, of course, sent no answer to the board, and wrote on 21 August/2 September to Stassov telling him: about the letter he had received. 'I shan't do what they ask', Berlioz wrote. '*Quel diable de monde est-ce là!*' The party hostile to Balakirev included Zaremba, who was an important figure on the staff of the Conservatoire. He would have needed all the tact in the world to have overcome such a tricky situation.

In early October Balakirev returned to St Petersburg, and soon afterwards the first Russian performance of *Lohengrin* took place. Balakirev, Dargomyzhsky, Cui, Mussorgsky and Rimsky-Korsakov took a box and sneered; Balakirev wrote to Stassov on 3/15 November: 'After *Lohengrin* I felt cracked enough in the head to "contemplate the universe" ' (a phrase recently used in an article by Serov).[13] 'All night long, I dreamt of a goose.' [14]

Balakirev had no intention whatever of modifying his programme in accordance with the wishes of the members of the board of directors who were hostile to him. He did not intend to 'give way' to the academic and 'Germanized' opposition. The second concert of the 1868–69 season, for instance, shows little relief from his radical programme-building:[15] Schumann's second symphony, 'Eastern dances' from Act IV of *Russlan* orchestrated for the occasion by Balakirev, Mendelssohn's overture, *Calm Sea and Prosperous Voyage* and songs by Schumann, Rubinstein and Liszt. (It was in a notice on this concert that Borodin wrote so favourably about Balakirev's conducting of the Schumann symphony.)

Only a day or two after, one of Balakirev's main supporters on the board of directors resigned in protest about the way things were heading. On 9/21 November he wrote to Stassov:[16] 'That was a very dirty trick they played on us with Kologrivov's walking out.' Kologrivov refused to have anything further to do with the Russian Music Society's business.

At the concert on the 23 November/5 December, the third and fourth movements from Berlioz's *Romeo and Juliet* symphony were performed. In the first concert of 1869, Borodin's first symphony was played, and subsequent concerts included excerpts from Rimsky-Korsakov's *Maid of Pskov*, *Sadko* and *Antar*, Liszt's Two Episodes from *Faust* on 1/13 February 1869, and, on 17/30 March, the first performance of Tchaikovsky's *Fatum* fantasia. Balakirev first met Tchaikovsky early in 1868, when their correspondence started (Tchaikovsky lived in Moscow). On 18/31 March (1869) Balakirev writes[17] that Tchaikovsky's *Fatum* had been played at a Russian Music Society concert on the day before and had not received much applause. He says it is hastily written, not well thought out, creaks at the joints, and he compares it with the form of Liszt's *Les Préludes* which is the nearest work to *Fatum* in form that he can think of. But in that work one thing follows naturally on another. He also advises Tchaikovsky to compare it with Glinka's *Night in Madrid* for masterly fusing together of sections. He talks about the frightful verse by Batyushkov that Tchaikovsky chose as an epigraph.

Balakirev's position was fast becoming intolerable. The last concert in the series was given on the 26 April/8 May; on the very next day the Grand Duchess Helena Pavlovna informed him that his services were no longer required.[18] There is no doubt that Balakirev, with his tactless outspokenness and undeviating pursuance of his own path, was to some extent to blame for the impossible situation in which he found himself in the spring of 1869. The Petersburg public, quite naturally, wanted a staple diet of classical music in their main series of subscription concerts. What concert organiser, either then or now, would introduce so many modern works into a subscription series? The Russian Music Society gave only two concerts a month, from October to April, and the amount of music which for the Petersburg public was novel that Balakirev managed to cram into only two seasons as conductor is quite astonishing—praiseworthy in one sense, rather foolhardy in another. Serov, Famintsyn and F. Tolstoy 'savagely fell on' Balakirev, as Karatyghin puts it,[19] because of his 'radical programmes'.

But although his tactlessness, his 'rather disobliging' nature, as Cui wrote much later,[20] and his unwise programme planning were factors which led to his enforced resignation, the behaviour of the opposition to him on the board of directors chief among whom were Helena Pavlovna and Zaremba, was unpardonable. Particularly, their disgraceful endeavour to try to get an unfavourable opinion on his ability from Berlioz must earn the contempt that it deserves.

His resignation was followed by one of the most extraordinary series of mud-slinging articles that any capital city can ever have seen. Cui must have forgotten, in later years, how outspoken his own articles were at this time. Stassov wrote an article on 6/18 June entitled 'Musical Liars' against Famintsyn and F. Tolstoy. Tchaikovsky, too, wrote an article in the Moscow *Contemporary Chronicle* in which, after praising Balakirev's conducting, he wrote: 'Balakirev can say now what the father of Russian literature declared when he received the news of his expulsion from the Academy of Sciences: "It is possible to dismiss the Academy from Lomonosov, but it is impossible to dismiss Lomonosov from the Academy." '[21]

Balakirev determined to concentrate in the next season on his Free School Concerts, confident that the public would support him, and his new series of concerts were in direct rivalry to those of the Russian Music Society.

The Grand Duchess Helena Pavlovna financed a new magazine

in 1869, called *The Musical Season*, in which the main object seems to have been, in the first numbers, to explain what had been wrong with Balakirev's conducting, and generally to vilify him. No doubt this periodical was established to redress the balance, for Stassov and Cui in Petersburg, and the whole Moscow section of the Russian Music Society and the Moscow press were in Balakirev's favour.

Nevertheless some of the things which were said were quite inexcusable. Feelings ran high on both sides, and Balakirev was determined to fight Helena Pavlovna and the new conductor of the R.M.S., Napravnik, to the end. He even seemed to take joy in the battle.

On 3/15 June Balakirev's father died at Klin and he had to go to settle his affairs, spending some time in Moscow as a result.[22] He saw much of Tchaikovsky and Nicholas Rubinstein and must have been much cheered by their support in his adversity. Nevertheless, Tchaikovsky did find Balakirev's presence oppressive and rather disliked his dogmatically expressed one-sided opinions.

Balakirev's father had been ailing for some time. Balakirev had written from Prague in 1866 that it only remained for him to return to Russia and find his father dead[23] and his cup of woe would be full. He did *not* inform his sick father of his enforced resignation in his last letter to him on 30 April/12 May, in order not to upset him.[24] And he seemed to be remarkably resilient and cheerful in face of his misfortunes.

NOTES ON CHAPTER 6

1. See introduction.
2. FA, pp. 34–35.
3. AE, p. 66.
4. N. D. Kashkin (1839–1920) was a professor at the Moscow Conservatoire. He knew Balakirev well.
5. L(2)A, No. viii, p. 33.
6. ibid., p. 34.
7. M(2)A, p. 48.
8. K(3)B, p. 235.
9. ibid., p. 249.
10. Dargomyzhsky died early in 1869 before completing his opera. Cui finished

the final scene and Rimsky-Korsakov took charge of the scoring. It was performed early in 1872, but was received coldly.

11. G(2)A, pp. 378–379.
12. K(3)B, pp. 253–254.
13. ibid., p. 257, in *Novaya Vremya*, 1868, No. 231.
14. A reference to the swan in *Lohengrin*.
15. K(3)B, p. 257.
16. ibid., pp. 257–258.
17. L(2)B (St Petersburg, 1912), pp. 26–29.
18. FC (ii), p. 93; TA, No. vii, p. 61.
19. K(2)A, p. 65. F. Tolstoy wrote under the pseudonym 'Rostislav'.
20. See introduction.
21. K(3)B, p. 266—in the paper *Sovremenny Letopis*.
22. TA, No. vii, p. 62.
23. TB, p. 152.
24. FC (ii), p. 89.

# CHAPTER 7

When Balakirev had been on holiday in the Caucasus in the summer of 1868, he had again written down a number of themes which he had heard. It has always been supposed that the themes collected on this occasion included the one known in the Caucasus as 'Islamey', which was used by Balakirev in his piano fantasy of that name. But B. M. Dobrovolsky is of the opinion that the folk-tune 'Islamey' was written down by Balakirev on his visit to the Caucasus in 1863, as it is a Kabardian dance from the *North* Caucasus, and all Balakirev's other North Caucasian folk-songs date from that year.[1]

It was at Tchaikovsky's house in Moscow that Balakirev subsequently heard an American actor sing a Tartar melody from the Crimea. The actor's name was de Lazar, and apparently at that time he frequented Tchaikovsky's house.[2] On 9/21 August 1869 Balakirev started his piano fantasy *Islamey* using de Lazar's theme for the slow middle section. As he composed it he played it through with Tchaikovsky, to whom the bass part was allotted.

Nicholas Rubinstein promised to play it at a Free School Concert in the coming series—a series about which the Grand Duchess Helena Pavlovna was furious—and in this way he was able to demonstrate his support for Balakirev.

*Islamey* was finished on 13/25 September in St Petersburg, at 9.30 in the evening, according to a note on the score. Perhaps the unusual speed with which he completed it was achieved because of his desire to have the work played as soon as possible by Nicholas Rubinstein at one of his concerts, to demonstrate to the Petersburg public where the Moscow authorities' sympathies lay in this quite exceptionally acrimonious battle.

As soon as he had finished it he sent it off to Rubinstein. Tchaikovsky wrote to him on 2/14 October: 'Your Armenian—Georgian—Jericho fantasy' (Balakirev used to call Moscow his 'Jericho' at this time) 'has been received, and Rubinstein is already playing it through every day at the conservatoire.'[3]

Rubinstein, in an undated letter, wrote to Balakirev: 'I am working, poor wretched fellow that I am, at your piece, which fills me with terrible delight, and for which I thank you; I shall certainly play it at my concert in Moscow; but it is so difficult that few will cope with it; I want to be one of those few.'[4]

Rubinstein, to whom it is dedicated, performed it at a Free School Concert on 30 November/12 December. Three days later (3/15 December), Borodin wrote to his wife:

> The hall was full and there were great ovations both for Rubinstein and for Balakirev, whose piece, by the way, was clearly not to the public's taste. The majority were perplexed by this eastern fantasy and understood none of it. This piece of music, anyway, is actually rather long and confused; the technical side is too obvious; even Balakirev's admirers admit this. It's a pity, but there is nothing to be done.[5]

Although many people to the present day agree with Borodin's verdict, yet it was through *Islamey* that Balakirev's name became known throughout Europe in the nineteenth century—Rubinstein played it in Paris and other Western European cities, and Liszt played it frequently. Even today, it is probably—perhaps unfortunately—Balakirev's best-known work. In spite of its defects, it exercises a 'terrible delight', a horrible fascination.

While in Moscow, Balakirev had been introduced by Tchaikovsky to the publisher P. Jurgenson, to whom he made the mistake of selling his most popular piece in perpetuity for all countries. His financial situation was bad, and he needed hard cash immediately. *Islamey* was published in 1870 in its first edition (with speed indications and so on in *Russian*; subsequent editions had them in Italian).

Balakirev's programmes in his 1869–70 series show a mixture of older and newer music, but still the newer music predominates. In Stassov's handwriting, written in red pencil, is the following note at the foot of a letter he received from Balakirev on 28 October/9 November asking him to come to a rehearsal of a Free School Concert the next day:[6] 'Programme of the 2nd concert of the Free School'. And the programme of the concert (on 2/14 November) was enclosed with the letter:

Overture, *Iphigenia in Aulis* .................... Gluck
Overture, *Midsummer Night's Dream* ........ Mendelssohn
Two excerpts from the monodrama *Lélio* ........ Berlioz
Violoncello Concerto ..................... Schumann
Group of songs sung by A. A. Khvostova.
Musical Picture for orchestra *Ivan the Terrible*
A. Rubinstein
(1st performance)

Although he did not like Anton Rubinstein's music, Balakirev consistently performed it, and in this he shows a broadmindedness not often attributed to him.

On the day after this concert, Borodin wrote:[7] 'Although the hall was not quite full, at least there was no sign at all of brass hats, of directors, of headmistresses and girls from boarding-schools, of pages, of bare-shoulders and court ladies.'[8]

On 16/28 November, Balakirev's programme[9] included Litolff's third piano concerto, with Leshetitsky as soloist, movements from Liszt's oratorio, *Legend of St Elizabeth*, another performance of *Sadko* and Schumann's first symphony. These programmes are very good examples of the music Balakirev gave his public.

Borodin testifies to another move in the fight. Anxious to draw away the pupils of the Free School, Helena Pavlovna had opened free choral classes in the conservatoire:[10]

'The pupils of the Free School are certainly going there to *drink* tea, but continue to *sing*[11] at the School just the same.'

Of Balakirev's financial position, and general demeanour at this time, Borodin wrote:

All this is very hard for poor Mily. His services are given to the school free, like the school itself, and one must live somehow; and he also has both his sisters on his hands. But in spite of all I have never seen Mily in such excellent spirits as now; it is not only that he does not lose heart, but he bustles about his work with more passionate energy than ever before. He's grown more robust in physique. There's a true artist for you![12]

And referring to the numbers of the *Musical Season* and other periodicals which had been devoted to slandering Balakirev Borodin says of the public's support of Balakirev's concerts and his personal reception:[13] 'But, like their anger, Mily's reception at each concert grows ever warmer and warmer.'

Unfortunately public support was not enough. Balakirev also needed financial support for the concerts. Besides the receipts from the sale of tickets, there were two other sources of financial aid for the Free School Concerts: an annual State subsidy of 500 rubles, and members' payments and donations.[14] Balakirev tried very hard to increase the numbers and amount of these donations.

In addition to all his other activities, Balakirev was also urging Tchaikovsky on with his *Romeo and Juliet* overture. A letter dated 4/16 October is headed 'Perlin'—in allusion to the way Petersburg was becoming 'Germanized', no doubt. In it he replies to a letter of Tchaikovsky:[15] 'It seems to me that your inactivity is a result of lack of concentration, in spite of your "cosy workshop".' Ironical words indeed in the light of later developments! Balakirev gives a line on his method of composing: 'Just at the moment, thinking about you and the overture, an idea has come to me involuntarily.' Balakirev jots down a few bars of an opening 'fierce *Allegro*', with a clash of swords. He continues:

> If I were composing the overture, I should become enthusiastic over this germ, I should brood over it or, to put it better, I should turn it over in my mind, until there was a possibility of something vital springing from these roots . . . The last letter I received from you made me so unusually light-hearted that I went out straight away into the Nevsky Prospekt for a walk, skipping along and even composing something for my *Tamara* . . .

He goes on to speak acrimoniously of the Russian Music Society, for which he is not to be blamed. But his sarcastic treatment of Haydn rather reveals his one-sidedness:

> The Music Society will give in their first concert[16] a symphony of Haydn. I haven't heard for a long time now such paradisic strains as:

> Later will come a symphony of Gade, Svendsen and company. It has come to my ears from fantastic sources (you know where) that at the time of N. Rubinstein's stay in Petersburg,[17] a general battle with the tall Minerva[18] will take place . . .

On 12/24 November, speaking of the first concert of the Russian Music Society (conducted by Seifriz—Napravnik conducted all the others) Balakirev wrote:[19] 'In order that the Patroness [the Grand Duchess] should not sit in an empty hall, she sent round 400 free tickets [for Seifriz's concert] and paid out 3000 francs.' He asks Tchaikovsky to send him all that he has written so far for *Romeo and Juliet*, and promises 'not to say anything—either good or bad—till it is finished'.

Tchaikovsky sent him the four chief themes (the first of which he later changed in accordance with Balakirev's advice). Balakirev's reply is illuminating. The heading 'Perlin, den $\frac{13 \text{ ten}}{1}$ December, 1869' adds the date in German (with the Russian calendar date coming below the other), a further playful reference to Teutonised St Petersburg.[20] The letter is very long and testifies to the infinite trouble he took over *Romeo and Juliet* despite his own difficulties.

As it is almost ready and will soon be performed, I shall tell you frankly what I think of the main themes. The first theme does not please me at all. I can't say whether it may improve in the development, but in the crude state in which you have sent it to me, it has neither beauty nor strength and does not sufficiently suggest Father Laurence's character. Here there ought to be something in the style of Liszt's chorales ('Der Nächtliche Zug', 'Hunnenschlacht' and 'St Elizabeth') in the character of the Catholic church . . . but your theme is of quite a different sort, rather like a theme from a quartet by Haydn, that genius of vulgar music which induces an inordinate thirst for beer. There is nothing of the church, nor of Catholicism in it; rather, it reminds me of Gogol's 'Comrade Kunz' who wanted to cut off his nose to avoid spending money on snuff. However, it may be that in its development your theme may turn out to be of quite a different character, in which case I shall eat my words.

He approved of the other themes, writing of the main love-theme in D flat: 'The second D flat major theme is simply fascinating. I often play it and should like to hug you for it. In it is the tenderness and longing of love, and much more that ought to go straight to the heart of the immoral Albrecht.' But his praise is not unqualified for, as he put it, Romeo and Juliet were Europeans, not Persians. He gives as an example the second theme of Schumann's overture *The Bride of Messina*. 'But this theme has its own weak side, too—towards the end it is somewhat sentimental . . .' Balakirev's analysis of Tchaikovsky's theme is most interesting—it shows how careful he was to avoid sentimentality in a slow melody.

About his concerts, he writes:

> The concerts are not making a profit and meanwhile it is neces-sary to spend the whole time at the school. I am devising an audacious plan—I don't know whether it will work—to do Mozart's *Requiem* (not as one of the subscription series), and for this there will be Italian singers as the soloists. Please don't speak of this to anybody! I am afraid lest the news should leak out to the Music Society, and they will leave no stone unturned to do the dirty on me. Their behaviour is foul and disgusting. They now criticise Napravnik[21] and attribute their 'fiasco'[22] to his programmes. I expect Rubinstein[23] has told you all about my concerts. I must tell you that his behaviour to me is be-coming more and more saintly, not only as an artist, but as a man—it was he who first called my Jericho fantasy 'Persian Powder', since it paralysed the brains of all the musical bugs . . .

The subscription concerts had numbered five altogether, four in 1869, and one in March 1870; the total deficit for the season had been 426 rubles. The tide was beginning to turn against Balakirev. Napravnik was an excellent conductor who was gradu-ally receiving the whole-hearted support of the directors of the Russian Music Society, which received a much more substantial state subsidy[24] than the Free School. Meanwhile, Balakirev's finan-cial position, as well as that of the Free School, was becoming more and more uncertain.

In order to recoup his finances, Balakirev planned a pianoforte recital to take place at the annual fair at his home town of Nizhny-Novgorod.[25] This was going to be his salvation. On this he pinned all his hopes.

The concert failed—Nizhny had forgotten him. The total profit was 11 rubles (about a guinea). It was only after the failure of this concert that he became really down-hearted. He wrote to Stassov: 'Although I remained cheerful the whole time, in spite of the likes of Helen and her beastly menials, yet the subsequent failure of my public concert and the extremity of my financial position as a result of this has cracked me up, and my spirits are very low in consequence.' [26]

He afterwards called this concert a 'second Sedan'.

Borodin describes the situation in a letter of 24 November/ 6 December:

He did not expect this [the failure of his concert]. Besides being a blow to his self-esteem, it was a frightful blow to his pocket. This year will then be extremely important to Mily: in order to extricate himself from the financial difficulties by which he is tied hand and foot, there is only one remedy: lessons, lessons, endless lessons without respite. To couple the subscription concerts of the school with lessons, in Mily's own words, is an impossible task, because last year, to keep the concerts going he had to rush about hither and thither, looking for support from all sorts of connections, which were vital to him in the struggle with Helena and company. This, together with orchestral and choral rehearsals, took up all Mily's time, all his strength and energy. [27]

Balakirev confided in the gentle and tactful Zhemchuzhnikov to whom he turned at this difficult time. On 23 December 1870/ 4 January 1871 he wrote to Zhemchuzhnikov: 'You are the only person who can rescue me. It is absolutely necessary that I have 150 r., which I must pay not later than 24th December, i.e. tomorrow, and the money on which I counted I shall not receive before January. Do not refuse me this request . . .' [28]

At this time Balakirev arranged musical evenings at Zhemchuzhnikov's house, and introduced him to Canille and Borodin.

On 22 January/3 February 1871, Balakirev wrote to Tchaikovsky: [29]

I am sorry that I have not answered your letter sooner . . . My concerts are not taking place, as I am teaching incessantly so that I am only now able to find time for the school, and up to January I found it impossible to promote the classes and rehearsals. So, your overture [30] is going to be performed. I am very happy about the early part, but the end doesn't please me

**8.** Letter of Balakirev to Zhemchuzhnikov probably written in 1871

*Translation*

Dear Vladimir Michailovich!
As a postscript to my letter I must tell you further that Canille will be with you on Tuesday, and three of us will be coming: Borodin, Canille and I. Consequently we'll be playing music for 4 hands. Don't forget their other names: *Alexander Porfirevich* Borodin, *Fedor Andreyevich* Canille.

Yours, M. Balakirev

12th March
Did you receive my 1st letter? Invite *fewer*, it will be more pleasant.

9. Balakirev in the early eighteen-nineties

at all; it's impossible to write about it in detail. It would be much better if you came here, so that I could tell you what I think of it. In the middle section you have done something new, and you have done it well—the alternating chords over a pedal-point, a little *à la* Russlan. But the end is very routine stuff . . . why those sudden thumped chords in the very last bars? This is contrary to the meaning of the drama . . .

Balakirev, who ended *1000 years* (*Russia*) and was to end *Tamara* softly, could not understand a desire to play up to an audience at the end of a work. He adds, 'Nadyezhda Nikolayevna' (Rimsky-Korsakov's future wife) 'has scored out these bars with her own fair hands . . . Give my regards to Nicholas Rubinstein and Kashkin.'

And on 19/31 May:[31] 'I'm sorry that you, or rather—Rubinstein, have hurried the publication of the overture. Although the new introduction is much better, yet I was very anxious for you to make certain further alterations in the overture . . .'

So Balakirev fussed over Tchaikovsky's composition.

His demeanour in 1871 was causing grave alarm amongst his friends. His failure seems to have made him more irritable with his own friends. He started taking advice from a young sooth-sayer with 'big black eyes', with whom he was reputed to be in love.[32] He enquired of her, apparently, how his battle with the Russian Music Society would fare. She revealed their intentions to him.

At this time Balakirev convinced himself of the aimlessness of existence and came near to suicide. On 9/21 March, the anniversary of the death of his mother, he remained at home alone and gave himself up to reflections about his life and on this day, according to his own words, his conversion to religion took place.[33] Evidently he let Zhemchuzhnikov know about his experience in the period 10–12 April. Balakirev tried to conceal his conversion to religion from his musical friends, fearing their ridicule. On 12/24 April he wrote to Zhemchuzhnikov 'Please do not say a word to anybody about my *conversion to religion*. I am telling only those who must be told. . . .'[34]

Borodin heard a rumour that Balakirev had gone mad. '. . . this news about Mily becomes very probable'[35] he wrote to Rimsky-Korsakov in August, 'when one recalls his former inflammation of the brain, his perpetual headaches, his nervous irritability, his circumstances, and finally the whole of his recent behaviour'.

Borodin had written to his wife in June saying he had become unpopular with everybody because of his behaviour—he made offensive remarks about *Boris Godunov*, was indifferent to *The Maid of Pskov*, was angry at Stassov's ridiculing of his recent conversion to religion; Cui was annoyed that he had lost interest in his musical circle.

But Balakirev roused himself from his depression and wrote to Tchaikovsky on 29 September/11 October:[36] 'This season I shall give five concerts . . . The Music Society wants to perform your overture *Romeo* and I don't want to bid against them for it.' And this, when the work was dedicated to Balakirev! He had almost given way.

On 3/15 November he wrote to Tchaikovsky: 'I am sending you the programme of all five concerts . . .'[37] This was his last letter to Tchaikovsky for a decade.

On 18/30 December 1871, Balakirev conducted the following programme at the Free School: *Carnaval Romain* Overture of Berlioz; Rimsky-Korsakov's *Antar*; a chorus by Tchaikovsky; and the piano concerto in D minor by Litolff. It almost looked as though things were back to normal.

At the fourth concert of the series (on 3/15 April 1872), Balakirev performed the Polonaise from Act III of *Boris Godunov*. In spite of Balakirev's previous tactless remarks about *Boris*, when Mussorgsky heard of Balakirev's decision, he wrote on 22 March/ 3 April that he was delighted that Balakirev considered the polonaise worthy of being performed at one of his concerts, saying that he had never before heard a performance of a purely orchestral work of his own.[38] (Balakirev had refused to perform *Night on a Bare Mountain*.) Balakirev suggested a few alterations, some of which were apparently carried out, but he had nothing to do with the rest of *Boris*.

The concert was not well attended. Ten years were to elapse before Balakirev again raised his baton.

## NOTES ON CHAPTER 7

1. FC, p. 433, '*Zapisi Kavkazskoi narodnoi muzyki*' (commentary by B. M. Dobrovolsky).
2. TA, No. vii, p. 63.
3. L(2)B, p. 35.
4. TA, No. vii, p. 64.
5. *Letters of A. P. Borodin (Pisma A. P. Borodina)*, Part I, Moscow, 1927–28, pp. 174–175, and K(4)A, pp. 227–228.
6. K(3)B, p. 272.
7. *Letters of Borodin*, Part I, p. 162.
8. M(2)A, p. 51.
9. K(3)B, p. 267.
10. M(2)A, p. 53.
11. Borodin plays on the Russian words for to drink, 'pit', and to sing, 'pet'.
12. *Letters of Borodin*, Part I, p. 159, and FA, p. 35.
13. ibid.
14. L(1)D, p. 373.
15. L(2)B, pp. 36–40.
16. In fact, it occurred in the *seventh* concert (ibid., p. 38).
17. In two months' time, to play *Islamey*.
18. The Grand Duchess Helena Pavlovna.
19. L(2)B, p. 43.
20. ibid., pp. 48–51.
21. The conductor of the opera, and newly appointed conductor of the Russian Music Society.
22. The lack of support for the Society's concerts.
23. Nicholas Rubinstein.
24. TA, No. vii, p. 65.
25. M(2)A, p. 53.
26. FA, p. 37 (footnote).
27. M(2)A, p. 54.
28. FC (iii), p. 102.
29. L(2)B, p. 64.
30. *Romeo and Juliet*.
31. L(2)B, p. 66.
32. CA, p. 127.
33. FC (iii), p. 112
34. ibid., p. 105.
35. *Letters of Borodin*, p. 286, and FA, p. 17.
36. L(2)B, p. 68.
37. ibid., p. 71.
38. CB, pp. 121–122.

# CHAPTER 8

*1872–1877: Retirement and re-appearance: Financial failure of Free School Concerts – post on Warsaw railway – explains position to Stassov – withdrawal from public life – bigoted orthodox christianity – offer from Moscow – Kashkin sees 'cruelly stricken man' – correspondence with Ludmila Shestakova – Rimsky-Korsakov's début as conductor – Korsakov takes over directorship of Free School – Balakirev reproves him for programmes – Stassov and Mussorgsky horrified – The Fire-Bird – emerges from retirement and starts work on* Tamara *– Borodin's delight – Glinka's operas prepared for publication – attitude towards Rimsky-Korsakov – Filippov.*

In the 1871–72 series of Free School Concerts Balakirev had roused himself to make a supreme effort. But the fifth and final concert in the series had to be cancelled because of lack of funds.[1] For Balakirev, this further failure was the last straw. His financial position was so desperate that he had to make some money, somehow, immediately. Through the influence of his friend, Le-Dantu, he took a job with the Central Railway Company, Warsaw line, as an official in the goods department. This had the great advantage of a *fixed* salary, though it was only 80 rubles, something over £8, a month.[2] Having publicly admitted his failure by taking this step, he sank into a deep depression and lost interest in music.

On 6/18 July 1872 Balakirev entered the following pathetic words in his note-book: 'Today my work in the office of the Warsaw railway began. May the Lord have mercy!!!'

Two months later he wrote a pathetic letter to Zhemchuzhnikov: 'My circumstances have not improved, in fact quite the reverse. They are *demanding* my rent, and it must be paid by 1st October at the latest. I don't know what will happen. Besides my rent I must have 40 or 50 rubles to get myself clothes in which I can go out to give lessons, which I have had to postpone until 1st October because I am without respectable clothes.'[3] In addition to his clerical work, Balakirev taught on every week-day evening.

In a letter to Stassov[4] (15/27 March 1873) he explained his feelings:

> If I had to abandon the school and concerts, I hope you will not say I have done it out of caprice. It was not easy for me to make this decision, but *I have no desire to go back on it*. Even if the possibility of giving concerts as formerly were to arise, I should not return, since without me there is still someone to draw up a good programme and conduct—I mean Korsinka,[5] who I assume is quite fitted to do this.[6]

And he explained it to Lyapunov later in this way: that if his career as a railway official had not been accidentally cut short, he might have received promotion and his salary would have become large enough to have allowed him to stop teaching and concentrate on composition.[7]

Balakirev withdrew entirely from public life. Rimsky-Korsakov wrote: 'In the period 1872/73 Balakirev remained invisible to all, retired from his musical activities and withdrew from the society of his former friends.' And Borodin wrote: 'By the way, about Balakirev. He is always running off to church . . .'[8]

Balakirev sought refuge from his troubles in a rather bigoted form of orthodox christianity. In every room of his flat there were ikons with lamps in front of them. He stopped wearing furs, smoking and eating meat. He liked fish, provided that the manner of demise had been by knocking on the head—an extraordinary facet of strict orthodoxy. He crossed himself constantly. And he completely ignored his former friends and would have nothing to do with music.[9] Stassov's ridiculing of his new religious passions may have contributed to his withdrawal. But the mental crisis through which he went was undoubtedly very serious.

When he heard of Balakirev's difficulties and retirement, Nicholas Rubinstein, much perturbed, wrote offering him a professorship at the Moscow conservatoire with a guaranteed salary of 3000 rubles a year. According to Kashkin he deeply appreciated the offer, but refused on the grounds that he lacked the necessary technical knowledge. 'Balakirev said that . . . he had never studied musical technique systematically, and that he had assimilated all that he knew by instinct and practice.'[10]

Balakirev thoroughly disliked the cut-and-dried methods—fugues, strict counterpoint, adherence to harmonic rules and so on—favoured by conservatoires at that time. As he himself implied he felt that instinct and practical experience were more valuable than any of these, and the financial benefit did not attract him, though it would have attracted a less honourable man, even one whose pecuniary position was less shaky than Balakirev's. Indeed, in 1871 Rimsky-Korsakov accepted a professorship at the St Petersburg conservatoire with no text-book knowledge whatever, though it must be said that Balakirev was in favour of his accepting the post at that time to get a footing inside the hostile conservatoire. In reckoning up the advantages of accepting the post, Rimsky-Korsakov wrote in a letter to his mother on 15/27 July, that his first consideration was—pecuniary.[11]

Korsakov did, of course, later make up his initial musical deficiencies. But Balakirev did not consider himself deficient.

Kashkin, visiting St Petersburg shortly afterwards,[12] was told by Stassov that although Balakirev would have nothing to do with his former Petersburg friends, being a Muscovite, he might be admitted to his flat. Kashkin found a horrible change in him. He seemed to exhale an atmosphere of deep depression. His manner appeared to be the same as before, but he was painfully constrained—he seemed to be afraid of touching on personal topics or of being questioned. Balakirev had the appearance of a cruelly stricken man.

Ludmila Shestakova became very worried about the safety of his compositions and sketches. On 6/18 December 1873 she wrote asking him a great favour, that he would give them all to her for safe custody:

> I'll seal them up in your presence and preserve them until you want them again.
>     . . . The List of your music which I remember:
>     1. Concerto for pianoforte in E flat major.
>     2. *Tamara*, instrumental composition.
>     3. Fragments and materials from the unfinished opera *The Fire-Bird* and the libretto for it, if it is preserved.
>     4. Arrangement for several voices of *The Cherubim*.
>     5. Pianoforte piece *Novelette*.[13]

Stassov had written to Balakirev on 28 March/9 April 1872, trying to persuade him to continue with *The Fire-Bird*. 'You would create a marvel. A few days ago Mussorgsky played the Persian excerpt to all our musical group (as much as he could remember). You really cannot imagine how incomparable this is.'[14]

But Balakirev was not to be persuaded.

He did, however, grant Ludmila Shestakova her request, and sent her the following manuscripts (according to the following list he made from them) on 18/30 December 1873 (this list does not, of course, include already published music):

Completed compositions in score:
1. Czech Overture.
2. Music to *Lear*.
3. Eastern dances from *Russlan* arranged for one orchestra.[15]
4. Georgian song [orchestrated version—the version with pianoforte accompaniment had already been published—E.G.].

Unfinished:
1. Concerto (E flat).
2. Symphony (C major).
3. Scherzo of Chopin—orchestration.

4. Sketches of *Tamara*.
5. Various fragments: quartet, piano scherzo, etc.

and he adds: 'All the main things are here. Some, which I am not sending, are missing, as everything in my chest is in rather a mess, but some of them may come to light. However, of these the more important may prove to be only two overtures: the Spanish and Russian. Anything else I find, I shan't delay sending to you . . .' The manuscript breaks off here.[16]

On 20 December/1 January Ludmila Shestakova again wrote: 'Another thing comes to my mind. For health and other reasons you have recently withdrawn from public life, and you are not establishing any *permanent* musical institution, so I suppose that you will not object if I remove my *brother's piano*, which you have, to the conservatoire.' On 5/17 January 1874, Balakirev made this laconic comment in his note-book: 'Today, at about ten o'clock, they took from me M. I. Glinka's piano.'[17]

It seems that Ludmila Shestakova did not at all trust Balakirev with anything in his possession, including his own manuscripts. As early as June 1861 he had written to Stassov that he was contemplating burning his manuscripts (Gogol felt the same urge), and probably Stassov had told Ludmila Shestakova of this and asked her to do what she did—she was the only person who still had any influence with Balakirev.

On 18 February/2 March, Rimsky-Korsakov made his début as a conductor at the conservatoire. Balakirev roused himself to write a kindly letter of encouragement and good wishes just before the event.[18]

Soon after this Korsakov was persuaded to take over the directorship of the Free School, which Balakirev resigned. But the first concert was not given until March 1875.[19] How different from Balakirev's programmes! The programme consisted of music by Haydn (Balakirev's bête noire), Palestrina, Allegri, excerpts from *Israel in Egypt* and the *St Matthew Passion*. Balakirev wrote a letter of protest about the programme—he must have felt that he had passed on the most progressive platform in Russia, in all good faith, to a 'traitor' to his cause. Stassov was horrified, and Mussorgsky wrote in the following terms of Rimsky-Korsakov's and Cui's recent academic and eclectic tendencies: 'Released from Balakirev's iron grip, they felt in need of rest; where did they look for that rest? In tradition, of course . . . They have laid down the glorious banner of war in a cosy corner, hiding it carefully and locking it with seven keys behind seven doors . . .'[20]

But Borodin wrote to L. I. Karmalina on 15/27 April that many people were up in arms because Korsakov had become absorbed in the study of musical antiquity. But Borodin understood—he himself had started with the classics and then come on to Glinka, Liszt and Berlioz, but with Korsakov the opposite was the case, and the classics still had for him a novel freshness.

Nevertheless, the 'mighty handful', bereft of Balakirev's leadership, seemed to be disintegrating. Who can blame Tchaikovsky for his letter to Madame von Meck in 1877?[21] Balakirev's only published original works at this time were *1000 years* (1869, a revision of the Second Overture on Three Russian Themes); twenty songs; a couple of Mazurkas and a polka for piano, and *Islamey*. Cui he rightly considered a gifted amateur. Borodin, whose second symphony and *Prince Igor* had not yet appeared, was 'a professor of chemistry'. Mussorgsky he considered to have too profound a belief in his own genius.

But Rimsky-Korsakov escaped his censure. That newly self-styled academician wrote soon afterwards to Kruglikov, saying of his four former comrades in the 'mighty handful', that their technique was deficient, and that for this reason he did not envy them a bit, though they were more talented than himself.[22]

Balakirev's idea of using his job on the railway as a means of subsistence failed. Le-Dantu left, and Balakirev left with him.[23] He had to subsist on music lessons, and he also became inspector of music at two St Petersburg schools—the Maryinsky Institute and the College of St Helen.[24]

He was dissatisfied with the orchestration of his *King Lear* music, but he gave permission for the overture to be performed in March 1874. He did not attend the rehearsal or the concert.

But Ludmila Shestakova was ceaselessly urging him to continue with *Tamara* and his opera *The Fire-Bird*. Balakirev did not fulfil her requests that he should write out the episodes of *The Fire-Bird* which he remembered. It is possible that certain episodes were used in *Tamara* and other works. Lyapunov explains the failure of the opera in this way:

> The plan of the opera did not satisfy him. As in *Russlan* there was too little action and a complete absence of any dramatic cohesion. His fiery temperament demanded life and passion in an operatic subject. Only a dramatic fable could have won him over completely, but the story of *The Fire-Bird* only provided material for fantastic pictures for which he improvised on the piano some surprisingly talented episodes which unfortunately he never wrote down.[25]

There is extant, however, one Georgian folk-tune which he wrote down in the summer of 1863, and which was intended for *The Fire-Bird.* This tune Rimsky-Korsakov used as the first theme of the second part of *Sheherazade*, with slight alterations.

Stassov wrote to Rimsky-Korsakov on 17/29 July 1876: 'Balakirev is angry with you. Why didn't you send him a word in reply to his offer to give to you his material for *The Fire-Bird?'*[26] A few months later Balakirev again wrote to Korsakov on 4/16 March 1877: 'Searching about in my music, I have found the libretto of the first act of *The Fire-Bird.* Would it be of use to you?'[27]

Apparently Balakirev persisted, as both the libretti of the first act, by Krylov and Averkiev, were found amongst Rimsky-Korsakov's papers after his death. (It is, of course, well known that Korsakov's pupil Stravinsky's first great work was a ballet based on this tale.)

Balakirev was gradually emerging from his shell. Stassov wrote to Borodin on 30 March/11 April 1876: 'I don't know if Ludmila Ivanovna has told you the splendid news: Balakirev has promised her, IN VERY POSITIVE TERMS, to write down on paper all his *Tamara* . . .'[28] On 1/13 June, Borodin wrote to L. I. Karmalina: 'As a result of the continued warm and energetic persistence of Ludmila Ivanovna, Balakirev has again started writing his unfinished *Tamara*. God grant!'[29] And Borodin again wrote on 19/31 January 1877:

> Balakirev, dear, gifted Balakirev has risen from the dead and is alive for music . . . Balakirev is again almost the same man as the old Mily Alexeyevich, champions the keys of D flat major and B minor and fusses about the smallest musical details, to which he would not listen a short time ago. He again bombards Korsakov with letters about the running of the Free School, takes a lively share in the devising of its programmes, is working at his own *Tamara*, and has finished a piano duet version of Berlioz's *Harold* commissioned by a Paris publisher —in short, he is alive again. But he still does not show himself anywhere—at concerts, theatres, nor amongst his acquaintances (except for Ludmila Ivanovna and the Stassovs). How the change has come about, nobody knows.[30]

It had taken Balakirev four years to throw off his depression. The refuge he found in religion must have helped in this; also he was undoubtedly unable to live for long away from the music he loved, which was his own life blood. A less strong-willed man than he might not have recovered. Perhaps it was, however, a more detached man who emerged from the crisis, and this is understandable. It was embroiling himself too much, getting involved in too many things, that had resulted in his breakdown and, if only subconsciously, he had to armour himself against any future recurrence by a certain detachment. But he was still as anxious as ever to help, as generous as before in assisting his friends, as willing to give up his time to others, though he had become a little disenchanted with this world.

He took up *Tamara* where he had left off, and the interruption does not seem to have affected the work at all. Also, as well as arranging Berlioz's *Harold in Italy* for piano duet, he started work on preparing the score of Glinka's *Russlan and Ludmila* for publication. Balakirev had promised Ludmila Shestakova some years before that he would edit the works of her brother, and one of the ways in which she may have tempted him back into musical life was by pleading with him to start the preparation of *Russlan*.

For with just such an unselfish act might she have drawn him from his dejection. The works of Glinka were never mentioned without kindling a fire in him.

However that may be, in November 1876 he invited Rimsky-Korsakov and a young pupil of his, Anatol Lyadov, to collaborate in his preparation of *Russlan*, and later of *A Life for the Tsar*.[31] Balakirev also resumed his attitude of mentor towards Rimsky-Korsakov, who gave way to begin with because of his submissive nature, as he put it.[32] He upbraided Korsakov for entering a chamber music competition, and insisted that he introduce a chorus of begging pilgrims in Act IV of a revised version of his opera, *Maid of Pskov*—so that they might sing a folk-song from the collection of one Tertius Ivanovich Filippov (a folk-song enthusiast with whom Balakirev had recently become very friendly—he had the same Slavophile and religious tendencies as Balakirev).[33]

Balakirev also sent Korsakov private pupils in elementary theory, one of whom was a Mrs Glazunova.[34] But his interference in Korsakov's work along with what can only be described as 'bullying', began to irritate Korsakov more and more, and the relationship between the two men became strained.

### NOTES ON CHAPTER 8

1. TA, No. vii, p. 65.
2. ibid.
3. FC (iii), p. 106.
4. Stassov tried to cheer up Balakirev in a charming letter written at the end of 1872: 'In a few minutes it will be 12 midnight and the *New Year* will begin. I thought, Mily, that I'd write you a few words during these minutes, so as to pass over from one year into the next in your company and to remind you once more that there is somebody who loves and appreciates you as much as ever . . . ' (V. V. Stassov: *Pisma k Deyatelyam Russkoi Kultury*, Moscow, 1962, p. 99). On 2/14 January 1873, Stassov's birthday, Balakirev visited him. It was to be the last time for a year or two.
5. Rimsky-Korsakov.
6. FA, pp. 47–48.
7. L(2)A, No. viii, p. 41.
8. M(2)A, p. 58.
9. ibid., pp. 58–59.

10. N. D. Kashkin: *M. A. Balakirev and his relations with Moscow;* (*M. A. Balakirev i evo otnosheniya k Moskve*), in *Muzyka*, 1913, No. 152, p. 677 et seq. When Tchaikovsky resigned from the Moscow Conservatoire in 1878, Balakirev was offered his post, but refused for the same reasons (*M. A. Balakirev: perepiska s N. G. Rubinsteinom i s M. P. Belyaevym*, Moscow, 1956, p. 7, commentary by V. A. Kiselev).
11. AE, p. 42.
12. See note 9.
13. FA, p. 48.
14. G(2)A, p. 377.
15. K(3)B, p. 257: he performed these at an R.M.S. concert in 1868.
16. FA, p. 49.
17. ibid., taken from the Institute of Russian Literature, f. 162.
18. AE, p. 53.
19. ibid., pp. 54–56.
20. M(2)A, p. 58. Letter of Mussorgsky to Stassov (19/31 October 1875) published in the *Russian Muscial Gazette* (*Russkaya Muzykalnaya Gazeta*), 1911, No. 24–25.
21. See introduction.
22. AE, p. 71.
23. TA, No. vii, p. 66.
24. L(2)A, No. viii, p. 43.
25. L(2)A, No. vii, p. 59.
26. Letter of Stassov to Rimsky-Korsakov—*Russkaya Mysl*, 1910, No. vii, p. 89; quoted in G(2)A, p. 381.
27. G(2)A, pp. 381–382.
28. S. A. Dianin—*Borodin: Zhizneopisanie Materialy i Dokumenty*, Moscow, 1960, p. 203.
29. TA, No. vii, p. 66.
30. ibid., and L(2)A, pp. 43–44.
31. TA, No. vii, p. 67.
32. AE, pp. 61–62.
33. TA, No. vii, p. 67.
34. See next chapter (p. 113).

# CHAPTER 9

*1878–1884: Publication of Glinka's operas – Korsakov's concerts at Free School – first performance of* Polovstian Dances *– attitude to Mussorgsky – views on Korsakov's arrangements of* Boris – *Stassov – new offer from Moscow – resumes directorship of Free School – Glazunov – Belyaev – publication of Overture on Three Russian Themes – completion of* Tamara *– Liszt's thanks for dedication – letter from Bourgault-Ducoudray – urges Tchaikovsky to write* Manfred *symphony – advice about its composition – through Filippov's influence, appointed Director of Music at the Imperial Chapel – new duties – Balakirev's celibacy.*

T he newly edited score of *Russlan and Ludmila* was published on 10/22 November 1878. Timofeyev writes: 'This event was celebrated at the house of L. I. Shestakova, where a gathering again took place, as in former times, of the whole circle, including V. V. Stassov – "Bach", as his friends called him.'[1] The score of *A Life for the Tsar* was finished at the end of 1880 and published in 1881.

Balakirev's correspondence with the publisher Jurgenson, broken off for five years or so, was resumed in 1877 with discussion of preparation of other works of Glinka including at that time Balakirev's arrangements of *Jota Aragonesa* and *Night in Madrid* for piano.[2]

Rimsky-Korsakov was still Director of the Free School, and at Balakirev's instigation, conducted four concerts in January and February of 1879. The concerts are important, since they included the first performance of the *Polovtsian Dances* from

*Prince Igor* (hurriedly orchestrated for the occasion); some ex-cerpts from Korsakov's own *May Night* and the scene in Pimen's cell from *Boris* also received their first performance. It looked as if the Free School was again becoming as important as it used to be in providing a platform for the most advanced works in Russia, and that the 'mighty handful' were regaining their position of pre-eminence. But Balakirev's interference was prov-ing a great trial to Rimsky-Korsakov, and he was again assum-ing his school-master's attitude to Mussorgsky. Balakirev wrote to Stassov on 28 July/9 August, that he was pleased to find Mussorgsky less complacent and proud than formerly; the latter listened carefully and uttered no word of protest when Balakirev told him that he must work at harmony lessons with Rimsky-Korsakov.[3] Mussorgsky may have been humble on this occasion, but not so Balakirev himself, who was still convinced that he knew the remedies for all ills. It took rather a blind man to speak as Balakirev did to the composer of *Boris* and *Pictures from an Exhibition*. Indeed, by this time Mussorgsky had composed nearly all his great works, and had hewn his way towards the goal of 'reality' and 'truth' in music. But his ideas about music had grown quite different to those of Balakirev, who was incapable of appreciating Mussorgsky's achievements, in the same way that Hugo Wolf was incapable of seeing Balakirev's own achieve-ments when in bigoted disparagement, he remarked: 'What a glutton for notes that man is!'[4]

Balakirev, probably at the same meeting, persuaded Mussorg-sky to remodel *Night on a Bare Mountain*, which he did in 1880, though not on the lines suggested by Balakirev.

About his relationship with Mussorgsky in the last years he wrote to M. D. Calvocoressi on 22 July/4 August 1906: 'In the last period of his career, his views on music were in certain respects contrary to mine, but because of his bad health I thought it inappropriate to enter into discussions with him on this score.'[5]

Both Balakirev and Stassov were most anxious about Mus-sorgsky's condition, for he had become an alcoholic. He died early in 1881, the first of the 'mighty handful' to die. The other members of the group, including Balakirev, held the veil in front of a memorial plaque erected to him in 1885.

Balakirev's views on Rimsky-Korsakov's later arrangements of *Boris* were expressed in a letter to Calvocoressi on 25 July/ 7 August 1906:[6]

> ... Rimsky-Korsakov has re-orchestrated this score and has corrected harmonies in it; but in addition to this he has intro-duced many modifications to his own taste, disfiguring Mussorgsky's music and spoiling the opera by altering the order of the scenes. As a matter of fact, I hear from Stassov that he has recognised his error and is preparing a new edition of *Boris Godunov* in which the correction of the harmony and the orchestration remain, but in which all Mussorgsky's intentions will be scrupulously respected ...'[7]

These were the views of the editor-in-chief of Glinka's works.

Meanwhile, since June 1876 Balakirev had been working at *Tamara*. The bulk of the work was finished three years later, and most of it was written during *these three years*. Between 1867 and 1872 very little had been actually written, and between 1879 and 1882 (when it was finally completed) very little remained to be done. Stassov wrote to Borodin on 17/29 June 1879: 'A few days ago Balakirev played us the whole of *Tamara*, with large new passages inserted and a wonderfully poetic introduction de-picting a deserted place and the quiet sound of a river. This is incomparable! Now only the final touches are needed, and the orchestration.'[8]

Although Balakirev's relationship with Stassov was still cordial, the letter of 5/17 May 1880 (quoted in Chapter 5), reveals a disagreement in 'Pan-Slavonic' views—Stassov rather cynical, Balakirev the complete Slavophile. Similarly, Stassov's religious scepticism remained unchanged throughout his life. Balakirev's religious mania irritated him. Their friendship could never be quite as cordial as it had been in the 'sixties, though it still continued warm for the next few years. To some extent, Stassov was replaced by T. I. Filippov, whose Slavophile and religious views exactly corresponded with Balakirev's own.

In 1881 a very important opportunity came Balakirev's way. Had he been willing to reverse some of his former views, and also if he had been less scrupulous and less a man of principle, he would have accepted. For the offer must have been tempting in many ways. Nicholas Rubinstein died in Paris, and Balakirev, at the age of forty-four, was offered by the Moscow section of the Russian Music Society the post of Director and Principal Conductor of the Moscow Conservatoire. It would have given him further great opportunities of spreading abroad the music he loved, besides affording him much influence on Russian musical life. Perhaps because he had failed with the Petersburg section of the Russian Music Society—his experience with 'directors' had hardly been happy—and also because of his hatred of the very word 'conservatoire', he declined, and although the offer was pressed he excused himself on the grounds that the duties would be too involved and arduous for him. His suggestion that Rimsky-Korsakov be appointed in his stead was not followed up, since he was not considered to be a good enough conductor.[9] Balakirev had had enough of dealings with Music Societies and Institutions and, perhaps wisely, realised he was not suited to this kind of work.[10]

There was one exception to his abhorrence of institutions, however—his beloved Free School of Music, which he himself had founded. In September 1881 Rimsky-Korsakov resigned the directorship for a variety of reasons, and not long after, Balakirev, at first hesitant, again took over the directorship.[11] Stassov wrote from Paris on 5/17 October to congratulate him: 'It was only when I arrived in Paris that I found in the post there a letter from Ludmila [Shestakova]. She just wrote a few words in all, but this was immediately on receipt of your letter to her. What did your letter say?—that you are again taking over the Free School and will again direct it. Imagine my joy, my delight, my raptures!!!'[12] At the first concert he conducted, on 15/27 February 1882, Berlioz's *Te Deum* was performed. This had always been one of his favourite compositions. A month later, on 17/29 March, he performed Sasha Glazunov's first symphony. Glazunov, the son of the lady whom Balakirev had sent to Rimsky-Korsakov for lessons, was only sixteen years old, but his first symphony, though very much influenced by Balakirev and showing Russian national traits which were later to disappear from his music, is the work of a very talented youth indeed.[13] Present at this concert was a certain Mitrofan Petrovich Belyaev, a millionaire timber merchant whose liking for this symphony led him to go to Moscow in August to hear Rimsky-Korsakov conducting it at a concert held as part of the All-Russian Art and Industrial Exhibition. Belyaev introduced himself to Korsakov and asked to be allowed to attend the rehearsals.[14] So started a new 'circle' with important repercussions not only on Russian music but on Balakirev's position with the younger Russian composers if not as leader, at any rate as 'elder statesman'.

In 1881 Balakirev started on his revision of earlier works which occupied him in much of his spare time during the 'eighties and later. The Overture on Three Russian Themes was published by Jurgenson in a revised form in the following year.[15] The revisions are mostly in orchestration and in many cases, though certainly they improve the score, do not justify the time and labour they involved. They produced slightly better results, but cannot make up for the lack of any great new work in that time—except for *Tamara*. His correspondence with the folk-song collector and husband of a pupil of his, A. Pypin, shows that he was toying with the idea of an opera on a Polish subject—the legend of King Kazimir III and the Hebrew woman Esther, but nothing came of this.[16]

In 1881, too, Stassov had been assisting Balakirev with the proof-reading of the latter's edition of *Russlan*. Upset at the continued non-appearance of Balakirev's own *Tamara*, which seemed to him to have made no progress for the last two years, he wrote to Balakirev on 18/30 July:

> I can't tell you how strange it is to me that you have substituted the role of proof-reader for the role of composer!!! What is the reason for this change which passes all comprehension? Surely even without you there are plenty of proof-readers, but in the field of composition no one can replace you! In the winter

you can never compose because of lessons, in the summer it is—proof-reading; when will there be time, then? But the strangest thing of all for me is this: that you have lost the urge to get on with your lovely *Tamara*, and that you can bring yourself to put in its place one thing after another so many times and for such a long period. I don't understand it at all.[17]

But at last *Tamara* was nearly finished, a year later. In a letter to Stassov of 15/27 July 1882, Balakirev wrote in a typically laconic manner, referring to Ludmila Shestakova's constant perseverance: 'Forgive her for this: that if *Tamara* is written, then she is to blame.' [18]

The final orchestration was finished on 14/26 September, and the first performance took place at a Free School Concert on 7/19 March 1883, conducted by the composer.[19] It was received with enthusiasm by the public and was performed again in the following year.

This masterly and imaginative work is almost perfect in concept and design; its form is admirably suited to the story, a romantic tale of a cruel but amorous Georgian princess who lived in a lonely tower on a rocky crag. Over every demi-semiquaver Balakirev has taken infinite trouble. It is almost true to say that most of Rimsky-Korsakov's later works of any merit in the more 'oriental' vein spring from *Tamara*. They reflect, in the coolness of outside observation and therefore in a manner more appreciated by Western audiences, the passionate deeply felt inside feelings of Balakirev's exotic princess. Most of the other lesser Russians who composed in this vein were also influenced by *Tamara*, particularly Lyadov and Ippolitov-Ivanov.

*Tamara* was published by Jurgenson in 1884 and inscribed with the following dedication: 'Dedicated to Franz Liszt with the most profound respect: Mily Balakirev.' Liszt wrote to Balakirev:

I am very honoured, dear colleague.[20] My sympathy and admiration for your works is known. When my young disciples want to please me, they play me your compositions and those of your valiant friends. I send my heartfelt greetings to the masters among this intrepid Russian musical phalanx, endowed with rare vital energy: they do not suffer from anaemic ideas—a terrible disease which has spread in many countries. Their merits will be recognised more and more and their names will become renowned. I accept with gratitude the honour of the dedication of your symphonic poem *Thamar* which I hope to hear next summer in its orchestral version. When the edition for 4 hands is brought out, you will greatly oblige me by sending me a copy. From mid-January to Easter I shall be in Budapest. Allow me to express, dear colleague, my feelings of great esteem and cordial devotion. F. Liszt.[21]

*Tamara*, though it never achieved popularity, was performed quite frequently abroad, particularly in France. In 1894 Balakirev received the following letter from Professor Bourgault-Ducoudray:[22]

Sunday 16 December, 1894.            Villa Molitor.

Dear Sir and friend, I have been to the Lamoureux concert at which *Thamar* received a remarkable performance. I think that you would have been very satisfied if you could have heard this interpretation of your beautiful work. It was warmly received by the public, but not warmly enough to my way of thinking. You have revealed new paths. I do not only admire the richness of your developments and the novelty of your rich orchestration, but while listening to *Thamar* I seem to be breathing the heady perfumes of *exotic* flowers. We are here transported into a completely new world and the penetrating poetry with which your composition is impregnated is of quite a different type to that which we know in the west. With all my sincere congratulations for this well-deserved success. Your devoted admirer, Bourgault-Ducoudray.[23]

This is the kind of impression which *Tamara* made on discerning Frenchmen, and it must have been a revelation to Debussy and other French impressionists; France was just beginning to emerge from her Saint-Saëns–Massenet epoch, and works such as *Tamara* and Rimsky-Korsakov's post-Tamara compositions played a considerable part in it.

Another guide to Balakirev's methods of composition may be found in his correspondence with Tchaikovsky, which had petered out in 1872, but which was resumed in 1881 by Tchaikovsky. (A new edition of *Romeo and Juliet* was being prepared—in the first edition the dedication to Balakirev had been omitted by mistake.)

Stassov, probably during the winter of 1868–69 (when Berlioz visited Russia), had sketched out a programme for a symphony with a motto-theme on the subject of Byron's 'Manfred', which he gave to Balakirev. The idea had not appealed to Balakirev, who had written (during his holiday in the Caucasus in 1868) to Berlioz to try and persuade him to write such a programme-symphony (on lines similar to his *Symphonie Fantastique* and *Harold en Italie*). In this letter to Berlioz (10/22 September) he had copied out Stassov's programme (without mentioning that Stassov had originated the scheme).[24] But Berlioz was a sick man and nothing came of this.

Balakirev wrote to Tchaikovsky on 28 September/10 October 1882 (having just received a copy of the new edition of *Romeo*) that he would like to give him 'the programme of a symphony which you would carry out splendidly'. In another letter he wrote down Stassov's 'Manfred' programme, inserting his own comments (as he had done for Berlioz fourteen years before). But Tchaikovsky's reply was not enthusiastic, although he had at first expressed interest.

It was not until Balakirev had seen Tchaikovsky, who visited St Petersburg in October 1884 for the first performance of *Eugene Onegin*, that he really warmed to the idea. The day before his departure, Balakirev sent him Stassov's original programme, adding his own suggestions for keys (B flat minor, D flat major and D major predominating!). Underneath, Balakirev wrote:

Manfred's own theme ought to be introduced in all the movements. In the scherzo this theme could appear in the form of a trio.

## HELPFUL MATERIALS

For the 1st and last movements.

| | |
|---|---|
| Francesca da Rimini . . . | Tchaikovsky |
| Hamlet . . . . . | Liszt |
| Finale of *Harold* . . . . | Berlioz |
| Prelude in E minor . . . | Chopin |
| Prelude in Eb minor . . . | Chopin |
| Prelude in C sharp minor No. 25 . | Chopin |

(separate from the others)

For the Larghetto

Adagio from the *Symphonie fantastique*    Berlioz

For the Scherzo

| | |
|---|---|
| La Reine Mab . . . . | Berlioz |
| Scherzo (B minor) from the 3rd symphony . . . . | Tchaikovsky |

For the Requiem in the last movement it would be well to introduce the organ.[25]

Naturally these works were only to be taken as prototypes, not copied. Tchaikovsky finished his *Manfred* symphony—in *B* minor—within a year, and soon afterwards wrote to Balakirev (to whom the work is dedicated):

Among my closest friends some defend *Manfred* passionately, while others are not satisfied and say that I am not myself in it, that my inner nature lies hidden. I myself am of the opinion that it is my best symphonic composition . . . My dearest friend, I am having four copies of *Manfred* sent to you tomorrow. One for you—the others I ask you to give to Nk. Andr. Rimsky-Korsakov, Lyadov and Glazunov . . . au revoir, best of my friends, and again thank you from the bottom of my heart. P. Tchaikovsky.[26]

But Tchaikovsky's feelings about *Manfred* were rather changeable. In a letter to Taneyev (13/25 June 1885) he wrote of his hesitation to compose *Manfred* and of his promise to write it 'incautiously given to Balakirev'. On the other hand, on 22 December 1885/3 January 1886 he told Jurgenson that he valued it very highly (artistically, for in the same letter he offered it to Jurgenson free of charge). By 1888 his opinion of it had fallen to such an extent that he could write of it as 'abominable' to the Grand Duke Constantine (letter of 21 September/3 October 1888).[27] But this may have been because the Grand Duke disliked *Manfred*—Tchaikovsky was not above changing his epistolary views to suit the opinion of their recipient.

In 1883 a new post was offered to Balakirev. Two years before he had been commissioned to edit a new harmonisation of the Orthodox Church Liturgy. On the accession of the Tsar Alexander III, Bakhmetev, who had been Intendant of the Imperial Chapel since 1861, retired. He was replaced by Count Sheremetyev, who was not a musician, so that the post of Director of Music had to be revived. Balakirev's friend, T. I. Filippov, was a very influential man with the church and in government circles (he was a senator) and on 3/15 February 1883, after a certain amount of pulling strings, Balakirev was appointed to the Directorship, with Rimsky-Korsakov as his assistant.[28] It was a post entirely suited to his new religious outlook on life, but the administrative and choral duties took up a great deal of time.

He was determined to make a success of the new job and threw himself with vigour into his new duties. The whole chapel moved to Moscow for three weeks for the coronation of Alexander III. In the winter the Imperial Chapel was, of course, based in St Petersburg, but the Tsar's Peterhof palace was the centre of summer services.

Balakirev at last was able to give up all private piano lessons. He carried out numerous reforms in the material conditions of the younger pupils and choirboys. The scope of technical and practical classes was much extended. Classes for instrumentalists and choir-masters he entrusted to Rimsky-Korsakov. Balakirev was paternally disposed towards the boys, whom he sometimes helped with money if they were in need, and he devoted some of his fees for private recitals and for odd compositions to this purpose. One or two of his choral arrangements of traditional church chants appeared in print. (He was also responsible for the censorship of church music in Russia.)

Balakirev recognised that only the musical side of the chapel was his province (although he was very anxious to set in motion a project for the reconstruction of the chapel buildings which was continually shelved by the authorities). Rimsky-Korsakov disliked some aspects of the atmosphere, but it may be inferred that Balakirev kept himself clear of any scandalmongering which may have occurred. He was dictator in the musical realm; he could be as (benevolently) autocratic as he liked. For this reason, however, his relations with Rimsky-Korsakov soon became even more strained. But Rimsky-Korsakov never considered the chapel as more than an extra 2300 rubles a year. Balakirev, as with any job he had ever taken on, directed much of his energy towards it. After his appointment to the Imperial Chapel, Balakirev wrote to Zhemchuzhnikov (who was in Switzerland suffering from tuberculosis) in order to try to repay to him some of the money he had borrowed in the early 'seventies: 'My present salary is 212 r. 34 k. a month (plus a yearly rent allowance of 800 rubles), and out of this I could easily pay off my debts to you at the rate of 50 r. a month . . .' Balakirev was worried about his friend's health and thought he might need the money in Switzerland. Zhemchuzhnikov refused Balakirev's offer; he died a few months later.[29]

Balakirev's embracement of an extreme form of orthodox religion and the fact that music was his first love probably precluded the need of intimate feminine companionship. That he was rumoured to be in love with the female soothsayer whom he consulted in the early 'seventies,[30] and the gossip about his early love affair in Kazan seem to rule out the possibility of repressed homosexual tendencies. Olenin relates that he gave jolly parties for members of the female sex exclusively. (When one of his young male friends happened to call unexpectedly during such a party, Balakirev politely but pointedly informed him that he was always delighted to see his musical friends on *Tuesdays*;[31] the young man hastily made his excuses and withdrew.)

Up to the time that Balakirev became Director of Music at the

Imperial Chapel, he had been much too poor to be able to marry;[32] it is unlikely that he even considered it, especially during his mental illness in the 'seventies. Again, the life which Balakirev led at the Imperial Chapel was more suited to a bachelor than to a married man (though Korsakov was, of course, married). Everything tended to favour a monastic existence.

To a man of Balakirev's rather narrow outlook and autocratic temperament, however, a happy married life might have proved to have a broadening and softening influence which could have brought him to the full flower of manhood. As it was, age perhaps only tended to increase the less endearing aspects of his character; on the other hand it in no way detracted from his more lovable traits.

## NOTES ON CHAPTER 9

1. TA, No. vii, p. 67.
2. L(1)C, p. 24 et seq.
3. CB, pp. 195–196.
4. Collected Criticisms of Hugo Wolf (1886).
5. CC, p. 8.
6. By this time Balakirev and Korsakov were completely estranged.
7. CC, p. 8.
8. S. A. Dianin: *Borodin: Zhizneopisanie Materialy i Dokumenty*, Moscow, 1960, p. 216.
9. N. D. Kashkin: '*Articles on Russian Music and Musicians*' ('*Stati o russkoi muzyke i muzykantakh*'), Moscow, 1953, pp. 30–32.
10. Balakirev may also have refused because he could not bear the thought of living away from St Petersburg. A. A. Olenin (in *My Reminiscences of Balakirev*) writes of his dislike of Moscow, which he found provincial: 'He constantly and uncompromisingly poked fun at the manners of Muscovites. . . . He went there very seldom . . . "You must realize", M. A. would begin "that the Muscovites are very obliging people. I was once passing through on business and was staying at the hotel Dyuss. I had hardly unpacked in my room when I suddenly heard a noise in the corridor. What was it? It turned out that they were dragging along to my room a splendid instrument—a piano. I tried to convince them that I had no intention of ordering such a thing. They replied that the piano was being put in my room on the instructions of X" (M.A. mentioned a very celebrated Moscow name). "I was extremely astonished and touched at such excessive kindness. That evening there was a knock on my door—and who should come in but the culprit who had sent the piano. So I rushed towards him to express my thanks, and saw

that he had under his arm an enormous portfolio—the score and piano part of his latest composition. He sat himself down and compelled me to listen for at least three or four hours. The citizens of Moscow are astonishingly kind!" concluded M.A.' (FC (x), pp. 348–349, trans. E.G.)

11. TA, No. vii, pp. 67–68. Filippov asked Borodin to arrange for Liszt to send Balakirev a letter of congratulations on his 'return to society' (*Borodin* by Serge Dianin, tr. by Robert Lord, London, 1963, p. 126). Filippov's letter is quoted on p. 255 of Dianin's second Russian book on Borodin (see note 8).

12. V. V. Stassov: *Pisma k Deyatelyam Russkoi Kultury*, Moscow, 1962, p. 116.

13. M(2)A, p. 59.

14. AE, p. 75.

15. L(1)C, p. 4. The revised version of this Overture was performed at the Moscow concert mentioned above. Stassov wrote that after the Overture the audience called out again and again 'Balakirev, Balakirev', and would not stop applauding.

16. L(1)B, p. 397.

17. V. V. Stassov: Op. cit., p. 115.

18. FB, p. 161.

19. TA, No. vii, p. 71; L(2)A, No. viii, p. 45.

20. The original letter is in French. The word here is 'confrère'.

21. TA, No. vii, p. 70.

22. Louis Albert Bourgault-Ducoudray was born at Nantes in 1840 and died at Auteuil, near Paris, in 1910. He became Professor of the History of Music at the Paris Conservatoire, and collected Greek and Breton folk music.

23. TA, No. vii, p. 71 (in French).

24. For a full account of the history of Tchaikovsky's *Manfred* symphony, see Gerald Abraham's preface to the Eulenburg score (London, 1958).

25. L(2)B, pp. 81–83.

26. ibid, pp. 95–96.

27. Preface to the Eulenburg score of the *Manfred* symphony, pp. vii–viii, by Gerald Abraham.

28. L(2)A, No. viii, p. 46; TA, No. vii, pp. 68 and 71 et seq. M(2)A, pp. 60–61; AE, p. 76.

29. FC (iii), p. 109. Total annual salary: 5290 rubles, including allowances for board (2250 r.) and lodging (800 r.)

30. see page 97.

31. Balakirev was 'At Home' on Tuesday evenings to all his young musical protégés (see next chapter).

32. Also, he had to support his sister Maria after his father's death, and his sister Anna Gusseva came to live with him after her husband's death in 1877. (To Balakirev's great grief, Maria committed suicide in 1879.) His youngest sister Varvara married M. N. Shmelev, who died of tuberculosis in 1896.

# CHAPTER 10

*1885–1893: Party in honour of Tchaikovsky – Olenin and his sister – dislike of Belyaev – Olenin's lessons – hopes in Lyapunov – work on Lyapunov's compositions – Au Jardin and two Mazurkas – relationship with Jurgenson – publication of Russia and Overture on a Spanish March theme – Tuesday evenings – views on Liszt, Wagner, Glinka, Korsakov, Tchaikovsky – 'Valerian Gorshkov' – Olenin's anecdote – boycott of Anton Rubinstein's jubilee – death of Borodin – concerts for Glinka memorial at Smolensk – first visit to Chopin's birthplace.*

A t the beginning of 1885 Balakirev's position, as Director of the Free School and Director of Music at the Imperial Chapel, was still very strong. New faces were fast appearing at the weekly 'Tuesday evenings' to which Balakirev invited his young musical protégés. Early in 1884 the twenty-four-year-old composer Sergei Lyapunov had come to St Petersburg after finishing his course at the Moscow conservatoire.[1] He was one of the most important friends and pupils to remain constant to Balakirev until his death. Olenin and Tchernov were also among his new pupils and admirers.

Balakirev gave a party in honour of Tchaikovsky, who was going abroad. He insisted that his new pupil Olenin bring his sister Maria Olenina who was a young singer very interested in the new Russian music; she was the centre of attraction at the party, at which were gathered all the greatest musical forces in Russia. Amongst those present at the party were Belyaev, Tchaikovsky, Rimsky-Korsakov, Glazunov, Lyadov,

Shcherbachev and all the Stassovs. Maria Olenina sang to this distinguished company, accompanied by Balakirev and Olenin, Stassov exclaiming, 'Splendid, sir! Marvellous, sir!' to her father, the while.[2]

Belyaev's presence at this party was significant. This extraordinary man, himself a viola player, was very fond of chamber music. Not long before, he had had the score, parts and piano duet arrangement of Glazunov's first symphony printed at his own expense in Leipzig, and gradually started to issue other works in the same way. He soon found himself to be a music publisher.

But he was as headstrong and masterful as Balakirev himself. Belyaev refused to buy up the business of Stellovsky, which was on the market, and included Balakirev's own early works and most of Glinka's and Dargomyzhsky's music. He also refused to buy the rights of the newly revised *1000 years*, now entitled Symphonic Poem *Russia*, though it had been awarded one of his anonymous prizes. (He outbid Jurgenson for the publishing rights of Balakirev's group of forty folk-song arrangements in 1884.) Furthermore, he refused to support the Free School, but instead started a series of 'Russian Symphony Concerts' in 1886. Balakirev saw the platform of new music being taken out of his own hands. Until these new concerts were instituted, for instance, all Glazunov's earlier works were performed at the Free School. But after 1886, many of them were given first performances at Belyaev's concerts, and were of course published by him.

He also loathed the touch of philanthropy in Belyaev's approach. And the most talented young composers of the day started going to Belyaev's Friday evenings rather than to Balakirev's Tuesdays—among these were Lyadov, Blumenfeld, Ippolitov-Ivanov, Arensky and Glazunov. Rimsky-Korsakov was his adviser. Who can blame these young men for making use of the advantages Belyaev had to offer—publication of their works, generous payment for the rights, performances of their compositions at suitably subsidised concerts . . . But, inevitably, as Belyaev and Balakirev had quarrelled, they saw less and less of Balakirev, whose position was definitely undermined as a result. Olenin put it this way:

There's a man (Belyaev) whom Mily Alexeyevich could not endure. He would not recognise in him any service to Russian art; he considered his patronage the outcome of empty vanity and conceit, and declared that he was corrupting Russian musicians. Everything, positively everything, in this man disgusted M.A. He regarded his concerts as of no importance whatever . . . He loathed the Friday gatherings at Belyaev's . . . But his greatest offence in Balakirev's eyes was that he enticed to his house, as it were, Rimsky-Korsakov, Lyadov, Glazunov and others, not by lofty ideas but by 'money', by his fees, which seriously lowered the quality of the music of these composers.

Of Rimsky-Korsakov, Balakirev (rather typically!) went so far as to say: '. . . he sold his talent for 30 pieces of silver to Satan who, disastrously for Russian music, revealed himself in the form of M. P. Belyaev'.[3]

Olenin records of Balakirev's teaching at this time:

I once took him a rather long pianoforte composition—it ran to about 25 pages. M. A. made me play it. After two or three pages he stopped me, and flung his arms around me. The work pleased him so much that he sat down at the pianoforte and began to play it, praising a passage here, another there. 'Now I see that you'll be a composer', he reiterated, 'You're in an excellent way. But this thing needs to be gone through in detail and finally polished up. Make me a special visit and we'll see about it!' You can understand how delighted I was; we were both of us moved . . . I took it to M. A. several times, I don't remember how many. He started off by deciding that something must be cut out. I grudged the cutting of certain episodes, and grumbled. Then we got to the keys. 'No', he said, 'We'll have F minor here instead of E minor; you come to it naturally and easily'. No sooner was the alteration made than he found, as he always did, that the old key would be better. And the changes he required in the distribution of the parts, and even in the arrangement of the chords! Everything had to be rewritten again and again. I rebelled, and did the work reluctantly . . . In the end the whole piece was transcribed anew—and how much labour that cost me![4]

Balakirev's most promising pupil was Lyapunov, in whom he may have felt he had the ideal pupil, one who agreed with his own views of true art, who strove not only to use it as well as his master, but to surpass him in a similar idiom. In Lyapunov, Balakirev placed his hopes. He wrote from Peterhof (where he spent the summer with the Imperial Chapel) on 1/13 July 1886: 'I am very bored without your symphony, and I ask you to send to me out here at Peterhof as much of the exposition as is ready, and I shall look it over by the autumn.'[5]

Balakirev had not only started Lyapunov on a symphony (in the accustomed way) but interfered in its composition as he had been wont to do with Borodin, Rimsky-Korsakov and Mussorgsky. In May 1887 he wrote to Lyapunov: 'Your symphony progresses and before leaving town I have done a little work on it and brought it up as far as the F sharp pedal . . .'[6]

And on 7/19 August 1891 Balakirev told his pupil, 'I set to work copying out the score of your Scherzo from the symphony, in some places orchestrating it differently.'

Referring to Lyapunov's first pianoforte concerto in E flat minor, Balakirev wrote on 14/26 June 1890, 'Your concerto has been copied out. It was necessary to alter one or two passages where the harmonies did not agree at the end . . .'[7]

Balakirev had virtually stopped composing himself. Early in 1884 he wrote a study-idyll for piano in the style of Henselt, *Au jardin*, which was published by Jurgenson in 1885; and two mazurkas, Nos. 3 and 4, which were published in 1886. Of these pieces he wrote to Kruglikov on 12/24 March 1884: 'Recently I have been working particularly hard on chapel affairs, so that I have only been able to compose small stuff, like *Au jardin* and one or two nice little mazurkas which are nearly ready for publication.'[8]

Balakirev's relationship with his publisher P. Jurgenson was deteriorating. He took a great interest in music publishing and attached much importance to externals. The appearance of the published text, the design of the title-page, the position of the publishers' stamp, the quality of the print and dye, the skill of the engravers, placing of lines and proof-reading—all these matters keenly interested Balakirev and are discussed at length in some of his correspondence with Jurgenson.[9] The title pages of *Islamey* and *Tamara* are particularly beautiful.

Balakirev felt very strongly about a composer's rights in relation to his publisher—and this before these rights became an object of wide public discussion. Mutual relations between composer and publisher were complicated by the existence of a special law in Russia about the rights of composers. According to this law the publisher, on buying a musical work, became the unrestricted owner of it, not only during the composer's life, but for fifty years after his death. Because of the absence of an agreement by Russia to join an International Convention, the composer (or publisher) could publish a given work abroad, but did not have the right to import it commercially into the Russian Empire. Infringement of this decree was punishable with imprisonment. Unless the composer had stipulated his conditions in a special clause, if a publisher who owned the rights of a given work for some reason *failed* to publish it, or published it in a distorted form, then the composer was deprived of the possibility of publishing and disseminating it in his native country—where it would probably be most in demand. The only alternative was to break the law deliberately by publishing the work abroad and bringing it into Russia illegally. This method was widely practised by various firms of music publishers, who reprinted Russian editions and sold them in Russia through their agents. But it could not, of course, be practised by Russian *composers*.

Therefore, when he sold his work to a publisher, not only the composer himself but also his heirs lost their rights to it. It was only after a period of fifty years after his death that his works became the property of the public or of his heirs.

In such a situation the arbitrariness of the publisher could not be checked. Examples of this can be found with the music of Glinka and Dargomyzhsky. Stellovsky was chiefly to blame for the fact that many of Glinka's works were so long in appearing.

In 1884 Balakirev finished revising and rescoring his *1000 years* with the title, symphonic poem *Russia*, (or to be more exact *Russ*, the old name for Russia). When he tried to republish the score, he found himself in conflict with V. Khavanov, who had bought A. Johansen's business and, therefore, owned the rights of *1000 years*. Khavanov caused a great deal of unpleasantness.[10] Negotiations lasted for two years. Attempts were made to transfer the rights to P. Jurgenson, but he insisted that *Russia* should be made over to him outright and in all countries. Balakirev refused, and when Jurgenson asked why, replied (20 November/December 1886):

> You ask me why I do not want to grant you exclusive rights to publish my works abroad. I do not grant such rights to any one, since I have no desire to be entirely dependent on publishers, for they may be of all sorts. The incident with Khavanov is instructive. Tomorrow, as in the case of F. T. Stellovsky, some gentleman may turn up to whom you will find it profitable to sell your firm and your business, and then I shall find myself in the position of a fly entangled by a spider. And I fear nothing so much as to be subjected to shameless and persistent exploitation.[11]

Jurgenson had written on 2/14 November 1886: '. . . there is little foundation for your view that I am seeking to make good certain losses at your expense. The truth is that I have never so much as hinted to you that (with the exception of *Islamey*) all your music published by me up to the present has brought me only a large deficit.'[12]

Balakirev's main stipulation was that his publisher should be granted the right to any given work only 'within the boundaries of the Russian Empire' (or, 'not for all countries'). The inclusion of this clause in the contract would give him the legal right not only to publish his work abroad, but to bring it into Russia, should the publisher, who owned the rights to it 'within the boundaries of the Russian Empire', either not publish the work at all, or fail to publish it in the agreed time, or publish it in a mutilated form.

To begin with, Jurgenson did not seem to grasp the hidden meaning of this stipulation, or did not regard it as significant. But he was very jealous of his publisher's rights, especially as his own business expanded and others (such as that of Belyaev) grew. He also wrote that there was no reason for him to bear losses resulting from the publication of Balakirev's works if he did not have the right to publish them freely and sell them everywhere. Subsequently Balakirev did grant Jurgenson (for an additional payment) the rights to these works in their entirety, but *only* after he had completed publication in the agreed time and in a proper form.

From the time that Jurgenson had written about the 'large deficit', Balakirev almost entirely stopped publishing his works with Jurgenson. He gave Jurgenson, free of charge, an arrangement by Liszt (different from the one published by Bernard in 1842) of Vyelgorsky's song 'I loved him' for piano solo in compensation for the losses Jurgenson had incurred on his account, and did not write to him again about his own works. If he made an exception for a second series of songs he wrote in 1895–96, it was only because he had much earlier promised them to Jurgenson. An attempt to publish an arrangement for piano of Glinka's song 'Do not speak' led once more to an exchange of letters about the fee and, later, about the area of distribution of certain editions and the reasons for this arrangement. He also tried to have Lyapunov's first piano concerto, symphony and Solemn Overture published, but was only successful with the Solemn Overture.

After the quarrel with Jurgenson in 1886–87, Balakirev's position became rather difficult. The publisher Bessel bought the rights to publish a revised and rescored version of the Overture on a Spanish March Theme in 1886, and in 1887 also bought the rights of the Symphonic Poem *Russia* which he published in 1889. But Bessel had no desire to become Balakirev's sole publisher; nor had Gutheil, who eventually bought most of the works Balakirev had originally sold to Stellovsky. The only other man who could have been of use to Balakirev in the publishing field was Belyaev, but that was out of the question.

Balakirev, then, besides being very fully occupied with the Imperial Chapel, found himself without a publisher. He still had his unfinished C major symphony and E flat piano concerto on his hands, but can have felt no urge to continue work on them in these circumstances. And so until his retirement from the Imperial Chapel, the impulse to compose became much less strong in him.

Of Balakirev's Tuesday evenings, Olenin says:

They began about 8 o'clock, at which hour Balakirev expected us. I was nearly always the first to arrive. Mily Alexeyevich invariably gave us a cordial welcome. It was his custom to bestow a triple embrace on his intimate friends. He always wore a black lustring jacket and trousers of the same material, and a small iron cross hung on his waistcoat. The guests arrived by degrees and we seated ourselves round an oval table.

Usually conversation began with the musical topics of the day. Mily Alexeyevich always shone by his wit, which was rather of the popular order. At the same time he was a thorough master of the Russian language and embellished his conversation with shrewd and happy epithets...[13] The discussion was extended to music in general and then, almost as a matter of course, playing began. What we should play was never suggested beforehand. The roles were distributed as follows: all the solos, his own and those of other composers, were taken by Mily Alexeyevich; S. M. Lyapunov performed his own things; when it was a question of compositions for eight hands (arrangements of orchestral works), others had to be called upon. I remember that Constantine Tchernov and I were chosen, but I usually set my partners such a pace that they dropped me from the ensembles ... Of the composers performed, Liszt had priority, then came Chopin and Schumann, that is, the most pianistic composers. Mily Alexeyevich always played them himself, and it was the most enjoyable part of the evening's programme.

We spent a few evenings in the study of pianoforte passages alone. Mily Alexeyevich showed us some that were very fine, but pianistically weak; others that were excellent from the point of view of pianism only; others, again, that were superb pianistically and, as regards content, ideal in every respect (Chopin, Liszt); or were brilliant but unbelievably insipid (Thalberg, Kalkbrenner); or, lastly, were shockingly trivial (Meyer, Herz and others)—all played from memory.

So many views have been expressed about Balakirev himself that it is most interesting to know of his views about other composers. Olenin recollects:

Liszt occupied the throne at our gatherings. And how Mily Alexeyevich played him! In performing his compositions he seemed to be specially inspired.

Mily Alexeyevich had an intense, all-absorbing hatred for Wagner. Everything in him was intolerable—the music itself, with its specific peculiarities, and Wagner's very personality. He once expressed himself thus: 'For me Wagner's music is as rascally as the Dreyfus affair.'

He worshipped Glinka. Every bar of Glinka's, every reminiscence of him, was sacred . . . From Glinka's music he obtained indications of the path which Russian music was to follow.

He considered Rimsky-Korsakov unapproached in the first songs, *Sadko*, *Antar*, the Serbian Fantasia, *The Maid of Pskov*, and found something to praise in *The Snow Maiden*; but from *Christmas Eve* onwards he turned his back on the creative work of Rimsky-Korsakov; he did not adopt a severe attitude towards it—he simply did not want to know anything about it.

He acknowledged Tchaikovsky's immense talent, but this very admission engendered a feeling of exasperation—he expected big things of Tchaikovsky, and in his view they were never forthcoming . . .

It is rather ironical that Tchaikovsky thought exactly the same about Balakirev! 'He said that, with the exception of such masterpieces as *The Tempest*, *Romeo and Juliet* and *Manfred*, there was nothing of Tchaikovsky's that he had not spoilt in some way with his own hand.'[14]

In 1887 on the twenty-fifth anniversary of the founding of the Free School Balakirev conducted a jubilee concert which started with his Overture on a Spanish March Theme and finished with his *Tamara*.[15] Soon afterwards he received a state pension of 1500 rubles a year for his Services to the Free School.

Balakirev's piano-idyll *Au jardin* had been published in 1885 and dedicated to Henselt, whom he admired; on the occasion of the fiftieth anniversary (in 1888) of Henselt's début as a pianist Balakirev wrote an article for the periodical *New Times* under the pseudonym of 'Valerian Gorshkov'. He featured under this name in a novel written by his boyhood friend, P. D. Boborykin (with whom he had shared a flat in Kazan).[16]

An anecdote of this time, typical of his lack of tact and of his brand of impishness, is told by Olenin. (Balakirev's views of the 'German' school in St Petersburg, including Anton Rubinstein, were, of course, well known. He thought that their music, as he said of Serov's, was merely an accompaniment, leading up to a point and never reaching it, lacking in genuine melody):

One day Balakirev's servant Adrian brought him the visiting card of an officer in a Guards' regiment, who bore a famous name. Mily Alexeyevich was surprised.

'This is not for me,' he said to Adrian. 'Tell him the midwife lives on the next floor up.' The officer, however, insisted and Mily Alexeyevich received him. A very elegant guardsman entered, with a stylish shagreen port-folio under his arm. He had come on the recommendation of so-and-so (another very high-sounding name) for advice, and he apologised to Balakirev for troubling him. The latter was perplexed:

'But,' he said, 'I'm quite incompetent in military matters.'

'It's purely a matter of music,' replied the guardsman, smiling bewitchingly. 'You see, I've composed an opera.' Mily Alexeyevich was on his guard: 'An opera? Then you must have studied. But where?'

'Oh, yes,' the officer went on, 'I've done a lot of study abroad.'

'That's interesting, very interesting,' replied Mily Alexeyevich. 'Nevertheless, I can't be of any use to you; I'm of very little consequence in theatrical circles.'

The visitor interrupted him again: 'It's not a matter of staging. I've come to ask your advice about whom I could commission to write an accompaniment for my opera.'

Mily Alexeyevich looked him in the eye and said without the flicker of a smile: 'I think you should apply to Rubinstein and nobody else—he's a specialist in that line.'[17]

Olenin's elder son was Balakirev's godson. According to Olenin:

Balakirev always took a great interest in him ... When my son wanted to go into the navy as a profession, M.A. was horrified. He thought that all sailors were drunkards and idlers. He wrote to me: 'Dissuade Alesh from this step in every possible way, and if your talk has no effect, ruin yourself and buy the piano score of Rubinstein's *Ocean* symphony and play it over to your son, and that will surely bring him to reason'.[18]

But Balakirev's behaviour towards Rubinstein in 1889 was unpardonable. In that year he was celebrating his jubilee in St Petersburg. Balakirev refused to attend the festivities, and went so far as to write a letter to the organisers, protesting that Rubinstein's influence on Russian music had done nothing but harm.[19] This created a sensation, and can hardly have added to his popularity.

Borodin died in 1887. On the second anniversary of his death (15/27 February 1889) Stassov, Glazunov, Lyadov, the Rimsky-Korsakovs and Belyaev met in his old house in his memory.[20] Balakirev was not one of their number. His relationship with Rimsky-Korsakov became really frigid when, in 1890, although he headed a delegation of congratulation to him from the Imperial Chapel on the occasion of the twenty-fifth anniversary of his début as a composer,[21] Balakirev refused to attend the official luncheon. Korsakov was deeply offended.

Apparently the reason for Balakirev's refusal was some argument about the publication by Belyaev of Lyapunov's Symphony —Balakirev did not think that Rimsky-Korsakov had done enough to arrange this and took it to heart, especially as he himself had just gone to a great deal of trouble to secure a state pension of 1500 rubles a year for Korsakov on the occasion of his jubilee (though it is possible that the latter did not know that Balakirev had been responsible for this).[22]

The Belgian Countess Merci d'Argenteau took a great interest in the music of the 'mighty handful' and arranged for its performance in Belgium. Cui wrote a pianoforte suite which he called *Merci d'Argenteau.* The Countess visited St Petersburg on a number of occasions. She fell ill on her last journey (in 1890) and died in Cui's flat. Olenin writes: 'After her death it turned out that she had bequeathed to Cui an enormous sum of money. As we were looking through Cui's suite at M.A.'s we mentioned this. He remarked, "You know, in the second edition of this suite César must change its title: for the suite is surely no longer "Merci d'Argenteau", but "Merci pour l'argent".'[23]

Six years earlier Balakirev had conducted concerts in Moscow and elsewhere to raise funds for a memorial to Glinka at Smolensk (in which government he had been born). The monument was unveiled on 20 May/1 June 1885.[24] Balakirev conducted two concerts for the occasion—his services were, of course, given free.

Another example of the disinterested trouble Balakirev took over those he admired is to be found in the early 'nineties. In 1891 he spent part of his holiday on a visit to Poland to see Chopin's birthplace at Zelazowa Wola, travelling by way of Warsaw. On 7/19 October Balakirev returned to Warsaw and gave an interview to a Polish journalist, who wrote a column in the *Warsaw Courier* under the title 'In homage to the memory of Chopin'.[25] The following is an extract from the interview:

> 'And so, in fact, you undertook a long and arduous journey only to . . .'

'Yes, just in order to see with my own eyes the place where one of the greatest musicians of all countries and peoples was born . . .'

'Am I right in thinking that the aim of such a journey was some special research for a biography of Chopin?'

'Oh, I am not a writer! Consider my journey to Zelazowa Wola, about which there doesn't seem to me to be anything out of the ordinary, merely as the expression of a sincere, profound, ardent admiration for your Chopin—the expression *for your Chopin* is a bad one, because he belongs to all mankind!'

As Mr Balakirev said this his eyes shone with sincerity, and his voice sounded so warm and natural that there was no question of pose or affectation, and our conversation was from the start quite unlike a dry official 'interview' . . .

'We travelled by the Viennese railway', Mr Balakirev continued, 'to the station Ruda Gusowska . . . at last we arrived at Zelazowa Wola—and, don't deceive yourself, very few people know how memorable this place is, even in the district.'

'It is a fairly small estate, isn't it?'

'Yes, a small estate . . . There is a small dwelling house with about six rooms, and opposite it another even smaller house, something like a lodge . . . The owner of Zelazowa Wola is at present a certain Pawlowski . . .'

'Mr Pawlowski was probably quite surprised by your visit?'

'And he had good reason to be. I think that my immediate predecessor, who came as a guest from a great distance to Wola, was Mr Napoleon Orda,[26] eleven years ago.'

'Do you know Orda's drawing?'

'Yes, but Orda drew the house in which Pawlowski now lives—that is, the manor house. But Chopin could only have been born in the lodge opposite the main building. In 1809 the manor house was inhabited by Count Skarbek, so that Orda's drawing can hardly be a picture of the birth-place of the composer of the Nocturnes. I examined the little lodge in detail. At one time,' Mr Balakirev went on, 'before there was a railway, this locality was cut off from the world (as if it had been nailed up with boards), so that the character and customs of the people, and above all their folk-songs and melodies, must have been preserved. There is no doubt that from his earliest years Chopin listened to and absorbed them. There were woods, there are undulating hills and valleys, there was evidently a fair-sized orchard, so that his first impressions of nature could have implanted a sense of the beautiful in the child's soul.

'Unfortunately I arrived at a time when all the work in the fields was over and on a week-day, so that I was not able to hear a single folk-song. You ask what impression my visit to Zelazowa Wola made on me?—A depressing one. I spoke with indignation yesterday and the day before at two Russian gatherings about the unbelievable neglect of a place worthy of reverend memory . . . we played Chopin and nothing but Chopin at these two meetings . . . I think that the idea of preserving Chopin's house from final ruin was taken to heart . . . What will come of this, I don't know. In any case it would be an excellent plan to raise the matter in the Polish press.'

'Have you any proposal to make?'

'Well, at least there might be established in the lodge, which ought to be kept up, something in the nature of a Chopin museum. I don't think that the present owner of Zelazowa Wola will have any objection to this, if one takes into account that the collection of relics, the notice-board on the wall of the house and other similar adornments which would affect the number of visitors and tourists.²⁷ Finally, one way or the other, it is simply society's duty to concern itself with everything connected with a genius such as Chopin . . .'

A delegation from the committee of the Warsaw Music Society went to buy the lodge soon after, but were unable to do so because of the excessively high price named by the owner. Z. Noskowski, a professor at the Warsaw Conservatoire and

Director of the Warsaw Music Society, wrote to Balakirev and told him of this.[28] After a fire at the end of 1891 in Zelazowa Wola, Balakirev advised Noskowski to see that the little house was restored, and suggested that he organise a museum there. The necessary funds were to be raised by public concerts and the collection of subscriptions in Warsaw, St Petersburg, Moscow, and in the rest of Europe. But after considerable effort, Balakirev only succeeded in helping the Warsaw Music Society to obtain a *private* permit to collect funds for a museum and to build a memorial to Chopin. No advertising in the press or posters were allowed on a private permit, and since the money obtained from concerts in this way was insufficient, Balakirev made efforts to secure a public permit. This, however, was not finally obtained until 1894.

## NOTES ON CHAPTER 10

1. TA, No. vii, p. 74; L(1)B, p. 390.
2. A. A. Olenin: *My Reminiscences of M. A. Balakirev*, FC(x), p. 321.
3. ibid., p. 346 (trans. S. W. Pring).⎫ Pring's translation was published in the
4. ibid., p. 329 (trans. S. W. Pring).⎭ *Musical Quarterly*, January 1930.
5. L(1)B, p. 392.
6. ibid.
7. ibid., pp. 392–393.
8. K(4)A, p. 240.
9. L(1)C. I have made extensive use of the introduction to this volume.
10. ibid., pp. 74–80. Letter to Jurgenson of 1/13 May 1884.
11. ibid., pp. 104–105.
12. ibid., p. 102.
13. His mastery of the Russian language is also abundantly revealed in his correspondence.
14. A. A. Olenin: *My Reminiscences of M. A. Balakirev*, FC(x), p. 325 et seq. (trans. S. W. Pring).
15. L(1)D, pp. 202–203.
16. TA, No. vii. pp. 72–73; K(3)A, p. 193.
17. FC(x) p. 350 (trans. S. W. Pring).
18. FC(x), p. 350 (trans. E.G.).
19. TA, No. vii, p. 75.
20. AE, p. 84.
21. His début had been at a Free School Concert on 19/31 December 1865, when Balakirev had conducted his first symphony.
22. L(1)D, p. 182.

# CHAPTER 11

*1894–1910: Second visit to Poland – Chopin celebrations – last public appearance as pianist – piano playing – retirement from Imperial Chapel – relationship with former friends – Stassov – complete works of Glinka prepared for publication – songs, 1895–96 – C major symphony – last appearance as conductor – R. Newmarch's description – second group of folk-songs – meets J. H. Zimmermann – later piano music – invitation to France – views on 'modern' French composers – Olenin's sister's concert – songs, 1902–03 – Lear music, In Bohemia, Glinka cantata – cancellation of 'last concert' – second symphony and E flat piano concerto – deteriorating health – death and funeral – Ludmila Shestakova's assessment.*

In April 1894, concerts sponsored by the Warsaw Music Society were widely advertised after the grant of a 'public' permit to raise funds, and by the autumn the necessary sum for the construction of a memorial to Chopin had been raised.

Balakirev once again journeyed to Warsaw, to take part in the celebrations. He wrote to his pupil U. P. Pypina, on 27 September/9 October:

> And so I'm in Warsaw again, and I go, as I used to, to the Church of the Holy Cross, in which stands an exquisite bust of Chopin and where his heart is buried . . . Here I have been kept busy obtaining various permits in connection with the forthcoming celebration, since, as Noskowski assures me, they are allowed to do nothing.

Yesterday I was at a meeting of the council of the Music

139

Society here, and the programme for the celebration was finally decided: on Sunday 2nd[1] will be the unveiling of the memorial in Zelazowa Wola, when Noskowski's Cantata[2] and the Polonaise in A major will be performed by choir and orchestra.

On Wednesday 5th[3] the concert in which I am participating will take place. The following is the programme:

1. Noskowski's Cantata
2. 4th Ballade
3. Romances (sung)
4. (a) Mazurka (A minor)
   (b) Nocturne (G major)
   (c) Polonaise (C minor)
5. Romances (sung)
6. Sonata in B flat minor
   (a) Intrada ed allegro
   (b) Scherzo
   (c) Marche funèbre
   (d) Finale
7. Polonaise in A major for chorus and orchestra[4]

What a curiously mixed programme! One wonders what Chopin would have thought of a grand choral and orchestral version of the A major Polonaise.

On the other hand, Balakirev's performances of the piano items must have been well worth hearing. Olenin's opinion of his playing is interesting:

He was a pianist of the front rank, and in recalling his playing I can compare it most nearly to Anton Rubinstein's, in its extraordinary self-possession, its noble singing tone, its freedom from affectations of any kind. Mily Alexeyevich hated an exaggerated *ff*, and had an even greater detestation of exaggerated *pp*s . . . M. A. held that the timbre of the instrument is so beautiful and characteristic that there is no necessity to add an artificial tinge to it. His pianoforte always sounded like a pianoforte. It is curious, however, that in his compositions he sometimes indicated '*quasi flauti*' or '*quasi corno*', and yet in his playing he never specially underlined them. His technique was amazing. He played such things at Liszt's *Études*, *Dies Irae*, *Scherzo und Marsch*, etc., as if they were jokes. But the chief feature was his extraordinary penetration of the spirit of the work he was performing.[5]

And Mrs Rosa Newmarch, who visited him at St Petersburg in 1901, wrote of his playing:

Balakirev is not a tremendous technician like Paderewski, for example. His technique is irreproachable, but it is not only of his virtuosity that one thinks when hearing him for the first time.[6] Also, he does not carry you away by his passionate spirit. Such an enthusiastic temperament could not be called cold, but he does not possess the power of emotion nor the profound poetry which made up the masterly qualities of Rubinstein's playing. What strikes us more in Balakirev's art is his sympathetic and intellectual nature. He observes, he analyses, he instructs, putting it all over in an atmosphere of lucidity . . . Nevertheless one must not imagine Balakirev as a dry pedagogue. If he is a professor, it is an enlightened professor, a sympathetic and inspired interpreter who knows how to reconstruct for us the period and personality of a composer instead of substituting his own.[7]

In fact, this description of his playing shows that Balakirev's ideas on interpretation were not tinged with the romantic thought of the late nineteenth century. The music Rosa Newmarch heard him play was Beethoven's *Appassionata* Sonata, Chopin's B flat minor Sonata and Schumann's G minor Sonata. His playing was much closer to that of, say, Svyatoslav Richter (who also excels in profoundly poetic interpretations of Liszt's works) than with de Pachmann's extravagant but extraordinarily fascinating outpourings.

According to S. N. Lalayeva Balakirev's playing of Chopin's sonatas, ballads, scherzi, preludes, studies, mazurkas and nocturnes was particularly dramatic and expressive. His extensive repertoire also included most of the piano works of Schumann, arrangements of excerpts from Berlioz's orchestral compositions, the *Pastoral* and *Appassionata* sonatas of Beethoven, a large number of Liszt's works, and of course Russian compositions.[8]

His Warsaw concert on 5/17 October 1894, was the last time he appeared in public as a pianist.

Earlier in 1894, Rimsky-Korsakov resigned his post as Balakirev's assistant at the Imperial Chapel. Later in the same year, Balakirev took the opportunity afforded by the death of Tsar Alexander III to resign his directorship. His last act was to direct the chapel choir at the funeral of Alexander III.[9] After his resignation, Balakirev went on living in St Petersburg, in the same flat in which he had lived since 1882, 7 Kolomensky Street, flat 7.[10] He spent the summer months at Gatchina, a small resort not more than thirty miles south-east of St Petersburg.

By this time Balakirev's relations with most of his former friends except Cui—whom he saw occasionally—and, of course, Ludmila Shestakova, had been broken off. His relationship with Stassov, who disagreed with his religious and slavophile views and who did not share his hatred of Belyaev, had become much less intimate. On 4/16 January 1894, having forgotten to congratulate him on his 70th birthday at the proper time (2/14 January) and having found out what was happening in connection with this celebration, Balakirev wrote a dry official note of congratulation. He continues:

> Entertaining as always a great respect for the trend of your musical criticism during the 'sixties which, together with the articles of César Antonovich[11] at that time, were a very great help to me at the beginning of my musical activity, I hasten to send you my sincere though somewhat belated congratulations, and to express my joy that your past work is at last beginning to be appreciated as it deserves. With heartfelt gratitude for the past, M. Balakirev.[12]

On 2/15 January 1903 Stassov, calling on Balakirev and finding that he was out, wrote the following charming little note, with the words 'Mily' and 'V. S.' (his initials at the end) in *Slav* characters: 'Abandoning on the way all petty, transient things, a 79-year-old-man came to thank his old friend "Mily"for this— that [the friendship] is *not over* and that it is rich and beautiful for *ever*. "V. S." '[13]

His friendship with Ludmila Shestakova remained as warm as it always had been. Until her death in 1905, he frequently visited her early in the morning and invariably congratulated her on her name day and on her birthday—and he always called on her on his own birthday also, as the old lady was herself unable to go out any more.[14]

In the 'eighties and 'nineties Balakirev frequently participated in musical evenings at the house of his great friends the Pypins. Both S. N. Laleyeva and V. V. Yastrebtsev write enthusiastically of his performances at the Pypins, where a circle of friends (called the 'Weimar circle' after an evening devoted to Liszt's music in memory of that composer's death in 1886) provided a sympathetic audience. In March 1895 at a musical evening before Balakirev's departure for the Crimea (for health reasons) to stay with Le-Dantu, who by this time was engaged in vine growing, V. E. Payevsky delivered an address of appreciation to him on behalf of the 'Weimar Circle'. It was apparently a very cold spring in the Crimea, and instead of a prolonged stay there Balakirev spent barely three weeks in the South. No sooner was he back than he was anxious to arrange another musical evening at the Pypins!

The importance of these gatherings to Balakirev is made very clear in the following excerpt from S. N. Lalayeva's *Reminiscences*:[15]

In February 1896, Mily Alexeyevich wrote to Yulia Petrovna (Pypina) that he wanted to play at her house on 12 February and asked her to invite the whole circle . . . At 8 o'clock we were all there, and Balakirev arrived, beaming and full of life. Turning to our dear hostess, he said 'Today is an important day for me: it was 40 years ago that I made my first public appearance at a University concert, and played the *allegro* from my concerto with an orchestra under the direction of

Karl Schubert on 12 February, 1856. This evening I should like to celebrate with *you* . . .'

Balakirev's warm-hearted enthusiasm and kindness still attracted young protégés in the latter part of his life. The young Yastrebtsev wrote in his diary in the 'nineties: 'this wonderful man, this Balakirev,' and later, 'There is no one like Balakirev, this absolute marvel, the soul of kindness and goodness.'[16]

Balakirev was, after his retirement from the Imperial Chapel, at last able to devote most of his energies to composition—not all of them, for he was still involved in the mammoth task, with Lyapunov, of editing the complete works of Glinka for publication (as well as continuing to be engaged from time to time in unselfish activities concerning the works of other composers). In an obituary article written for *Russkaya Mysl*, Vladimir Karenin (the pseudonym of Stassov's daughter) writes of his continued championship of composers whom he knew in his young days, such as Laskovsky, Gussakovsky (who had died abroad in 1875), Henselt, Vyelgorsky and Lvov.

> In no less touching a manner [she continues], M. A. concerned himself with animals, and not a few anecdotes about this circulated amongst his friends. At times his flat—especially at a time when a society did not exist for the protection of animals —became nothing less than a dog home. He took under his protection all homeless or neglected dogs, although they sometimes gave him a lot of trouble . . .[17]

Apparently if anyone complained at having his garments torn by one of them, Balakirev would say, 'Well, you can always go to the law about it!'

Balakirev's first composition after his retirement was a group of ten songs, published by Jurgenson. These songs have not the spontaneity or real passion of the early and greatest songs. They mostly reveal a strain of weak lyricism, far removed from his early style and also from the best of his later works. They were finished in 1895 and published in 1896. In the early 'nineties he had again started work on his unfinished symphony in C major.

10. A musical evening at Balakirev's flat

11. Balakirev in the late eighteen-nineties

The history of the genesis of this symphony could not be sus-
pected from the content of the work. As Gerald Abraham has
pointed out,[18] there is no stylistic clash between the thirty-year-
old and the sixty-year-old Balakirev. He took it up where he had
left off, and without the information of the thirty-year gap in its
composition, aurally one would be none the wiser. *As far as this
symphony was concerned* it was the same man who picked up his
pen in the 'nineties as had laid it down in the 'sixties—but a much
older one.

The first two movements were finished in 1893, the third in
1896 and the finale in December 1897. On 27 March/8 April
1898 Balakirev invited Cui, Rimsky-Korsakov, the Stassovs,
Glazunov, Lyadov, Olenin and Yastrebtsev to a musical evening
at which he and Lyapunov played a piano duet version of the
new symphony. All but Cui were able to go. The symphony was
greeted by almost complete silence. Eventually most of the others
found something to say about it, but Rimsky-Korsakov said
not a word. Stassov wrote to Lyapunov on 3/15 April: 'I confess
to you quite frankly that I could see practically nothing at all in
Balakirev's new symphony, and most unfortunately I could find
only feebleness and rust. What has happened to the former
Mily??!!"[19] (Stassov later changed his mind about the symphony.)

Balakirev conducted the first public performance at a Free
School concert on 11/23 April. The audience received the work
enthusiastically. As well as being the first performance of his first
symphony, it was his last appearance as a conductor, an appearance which the public fully appreciated, showering him with
wreaths, tributes, a mould of Liszt's hand and the like.[20]

Rimsky-Korsakov behaved himself very badly at the concert.
In Olenin's words:

He was sitting in the 3rd or 4th row with Glazunov (not far
from me). While the symphony was being performed he
every now and then shrugged his shoulders and exchanged
smiles with the latter. At the supper given by M. A. after the
concert, to which all his close friends were invited, A. A.
Petrov lost no time in apprising M. A. of this and alas! I was

obliged to confirm it. Rimsky-Korsakov's conduct was so obviously hostile that it was observed by his wife's sister A. N. Molas, a first-rate artist in every sense, and also by her husband, and she expressed her great indignation about it in conversation with me. At supper I told M. A. of this in order to sugar the pill which Petrov had made him swallow. M. A. was extremely hurt and on the next day went to her (he had hardly come in contact with her at all for some years) in order to thank her; he let me know of this triumphantly three days later.[21]

After their estrangement in 1890, Balakirev and Rimsky-Korsakov had become partially reconciled in 1894, but as a result of Korsakov's behaviour at this concert the rupture became total.

Balakirev might not have had to retire from his own Free School rostrum so early had he not had a weak heart. Timofeyev writes: 'His friend S. P. Botkin predicted that he would die of a diseased heart. This did not happen literally, but as he had a bad heart which was slowly developing, his end was inevitable . . .'[22]

In spite of his continual worrying about his health, he lived more than a decade longer. But, after his withdrawal from public life, his popularity soon waned; the Petersburg public forgot him. Naturally, he resented this neglect; and he spoke bitterly of the Russian public and Russian critics. However, a few composers and critics outside Russia appreciated his music, particularly Debussy, Ravel, whose mosaic styles owe something to him, and also Dukas, Calvocoressi, Sir Henry Wood and Rosa Newmarch; Mrs Newmarch's description of him (in 1901) is quite revealing:

Balakirev is not tall. I do not know about his ancestry, but he does not appear to be the tall fair type from Western Russia. I find in him, rather, something of the oriental. He has a thin head, a dark complexion, and a rather weary but at the same time nervous air; his eyes are full of fire, and of sympathy —the true eyes of a seer and a bard . . .[23]

In 1897 Balakirev had been appointed a member of the Commission of the Imperial Russian Geographical Society for the publication of Russian folk-songs in editions for performance. He wrote accompaniments for thirty songs collected earlier in the Arkhangel and Olonets districts, and in 1898 he arranged them for piano duet. These exquisite and delightful arrangements, original, except of course for the tunes themselves, are as characteristic as anything Balakirev wrote. Each song has had infinite care lavished upon it, and the result is that the song seems to be in entirely natural surroundings, whereas the embellishments, tasteful and restrained, are as much in Balakirev's own style as, for instance, his symphony in C.

In 1899 Balakirev met his 'ideal' music publisher in the person of J. H. Zimmermann (of Leipzig). This was the last and additional spur to composition, and until his death eleven years later his industry in this field is considerable. Zimmermann published the symphony, and Balakirev's first piano publication with him was a newly written-down version of the early Fantasia on themes from *A Life for the Tsar* by Glinka. In July 1899, Balakirev wrote to his pupil M. Gurskalina:

All this time I have been working on themes from *A Life for the Tsar*, induced to do this by dear Ludmila Ivanovna. I had the greater part of this fantasia already completed in 1855, and I had the impertinence to play the transcription of the trio 'Do not torment yourself, my dear' to Glinka himself. Glinka was extremely sympathetic in his attitude, even praised the transcription and made me play it often, when other people were present, too; and when we parted, just before his final departure, he wrote the theme of the trio for me on his portrait as a memento. I am extremely pleased that this fantasia has now been put in proper order and is completed and ready for publication.[24]

All Balakirev's piano music not already mentioned was composed in the last twelve years of his life.

The magnificent Sonata in B flat minor is the greatest work of this period. The B flat minor Scherzo (No. 2) is also very fine.

For a slow-moving, delicate piece the Berceuse in D flat major is unsurpassed; and the Mazurka in B flat major (No. 5, also used in the Sonata) is most effective, and perhaps reaches as great heights as the best of Chopin's mazurkas. Some of Balakirev's other mazurkas, however, contain more of a salon element than Chopin usually allows himself, while the infinite variety of poetry and mood in Chopin's mazurkas cannot in any way be rivalled by the mere seven composed by Balakirev. Nevertheless the sonata and these three pieces, almost perfect in every way, and a few others equally good, entitle Balakirev to a place in the piano repertoire, if only a minor one, which he has unfortunately not yet gained.

In 1902–03 there is evidence of admiration of Balakirev's music in France: he was invited to conduct concerts of Berlioz's works in Paris on the occasion of the centenary of Berlioz's birth (December 1903). But he refused, saying that the long journey would be too much for him—and he might not have been able to obtain his Orthodox Church food in Paris, he feared!

But his interest in Berlioz remained as great as ever, and his advice was sought in connection with Weingartner's and Charles Malherbe's complete edition of Berlioz's works,[25] particularly as regards the *Te Deum*, which he had performed as much as any other man. Berlioz, for Balakirev, was the one and only great French composer. In a letter of 9/22 June 1906, he wrote to Calvocoressi:

I permit myself to give you the friendly advice to renounce absolutely your project of making propaganda for completely unknown French composers of whom you write that they have taken the art of writing for the piano *further than Liszt*. Although the piano may be an instrument of uniform timbre, one senses very clearly in Liszt's piano music *instrumental timbres sometimes of the flute, sometimes of the oboe and others . . .* [my italics, E.G.] I can't imagine that, after Liszt, it can be possible to take the art of the piano any further: unless, that is, this instrument itself can be *notably perfected*, and afford

some future genius, no less endowed than Liszt, the opportunity of taking further 'pianistic instrumentation'. But of such
geniuses, one in a century is born! . . .[26]

So the bigoted and difficult Balakirev laid down his opinions—
he was autocratic to the end. But this letter does solve the difficulty of understanding, as Olenin said, his *uniform* piano-playing
on the one hand, and his frequent marking in his own compositions of *quasi flauti* and so on on the other.

Olenin tells of Balakirev's continued interest in his sister,
M. A. Olenina d'Alheim, who made her Moscow début in
November 1901 with great success. Cui, then a director of the
Russian Music Society, invited her to appear in St Petersburg
where, however, the critics adopted a negative attitude towards
her. This did not intimidate her, however, and in January 1902 a
concert of her own was announced. 'M. A. . . . was not a little
troubled. When her Petersburg concert was advertised he was
almost panic-stricken, being afraid of a complete failure.' Twenty
minutes before the concert was due to begin, Balakirev and Olenin
arrived at an almost empty hall.

He was dreadfully worried, and said with a groan, 'I know it
will be a failure, and not only Maria Alexeyevna but true art
as well will suffer.' 'She shouldn't, she shouldn't have risked
it', he repeated over and over again in varying tones. The
first bell rang, and suddenly the audience poured in; within
half an hour the hall was filled to over-flowing, and there was
not a vacant seat. You should have seen M. A.'s. delight and
excitement, though even then he abused the public in no
uncertain terms for their habit of being late: 'They oughtn't
to let them in', he grumbled. But this was evidently said to
himself, out of the abundance of his feeling. After the first three
or four numbers there was unanimous applause which became
a continuous ovation at the end of the concert. M. A.'s face
was simply radiant with happiness . . . The success was complete, colossal. The concert, with all the encores, lasted till
about midnight. When he came out, M. A., to my surprise,
engaged a cab to drive him to the Liteinyseyevich Prospekt,

and not to where he lived, the Kolomenskaya. It turned out that he was bent on going to my sister's to congratulate her. In this we have the whole Balakirev, the leader of the militant 'mighty handful'.[27]

Balakirev wrote ten more songs in the period 1903–04. 'A whisper, a timid breath', No. 7, is the most original and daring harmonically of the group, and is dedicated to Olenin's sister. Two others from the series are based very much on Russian folk-song (but are original melodies), 'Prologue' (which he orchestrated), and 'Song'; 'Starless midnight coldly breathed', No. 3, is an epic and heroic vision, a dream picture of an Orthodox Easter day in Catholic Prague, with the Orthodox hymn 'Christ is risen' solemnly sung in the cathedral in the final section, while the bells ring; in the last song, 'Sleep', the exquisite piano accompaniment dominates a voice part which is possibly too uninteresting in other respects to compensate for its lack of a strong melody.

It may have been a letter from Stassov which spurred Balakirev on to revise his *King Lear* music for publication; he started the revision in 1902. On 22 June/5 July 1901, Stassov had written: 'I should very much like to know what has become of *Lear*. This work is of particular interest to me! In the first place, it was splendidly original, and secondly, I was to a certain extent associated with it. This was . . . nearly 40 years ago . . .' (Stassov was collecting material for an article—'Art of the XIX Century'— to be published in the journal *Niva*, and he intended to mention the *Lear* music and its composer.)[28]

The *King Lear* music was published in 1904 with additions, and alterations in the orchestration, and with the 'Procession' also arranged for a single as well as a double orchestra. The new version was dedicated to Stassov on his eightieth birthday, 2/15 January.

The overture was performed on 11/24 March at a Russian Symphony Concert conducted by F. M. Blumenfeld, and it received another performance in Copenhagen on 22 November/4 December. In a letter of 13/26 February 1905 Balakirev's friend

S. K. Bulich informed him of the praise of the Danish critics, except for one who found it 'too restrained to live up to its subject'.[29]

An overture of the 'sixties still remained to be revised—the Czech overture. The revision was finished in 1905 and published in the following year as the symphonic poem *In Bohemia*. It is not performed nowadays, perhaps because of its title, just as the *Lear* music is neglected. (It might have been more appropriately called 'A Russian in Bohemia'.) It stands on the same exalted plane as the *Lear* music, *Russia*, *Tamara* and the C major symphony. It is beautiful, rhythmically alive, superbly orchestrated; and it ends with a splendidly effective flourish!

Ludmila Shestakova lived to see the publication of the almost complete works of her brother. Balakirev composed in 1904 a Cantata for soprano, chorus and orchestra to commemorate the centenary of Glinka's birth, in which there are quotations from Glinka's music. But political and other circumstances delayed the unveiling of the Glinka memorial in St Petersburg until 3/16 February 1906, when Balakirev's work was performed. He was much applauded on this his last public appearance. The 1905 revolution and Ludmila Shestakova's death had meanwhile taken place. But the cantata had already been performed in Paris by the Society of Conservatoire Concerts. Balakirev wrote to Calvocoressi a week after the Petersburg performance:

> My cantata was performed with great success under the direction of the conductor of the opera, Napravnik,[30] as I was unable to officiate myself because of the poor state of my health. The solo was very well sung by Mlle. Friede of the opera. In Paris, thanks to you, my cantata was performed before we did it, if I'm not mistaken on two occasions. I don't know how to thank you enough . . .[31]

Stravinsky's description of Balakirev in *Conversations with Igor Stravinsky* is of great interest:

> I saw him once, standing with his pupil, Lyapunov, at a concert in the St Petersburg Conservatory. [Probably at the Petersburg

151

performance of the Cantata—E. G.] He was a large man,[32] bald, with a Kalmuck head and the shrewd, sharp-eyed look of Lenin. He was not greatly admired musically at this time —it was 1904 or 1905—and, politically, because of his orthodoxy, the liberals considered him a hypocrite. His reputation as a pianist was firmly established by numerous pupils, however, all of them, like Balakirev himself, ardent Lisztians; whereas Rimsky-Korsakov kept a portrait of Wagner over his desk, Balakirev had one of Liszt. I pitied Balakirev because he suffered from cruel fits of depression.[33]

Balakirev's cantata was performed four times in all in Russia in his lifetime. Its last performance, on 18 February/3 March 1907, was at a concert to commemorate jointly fifty years from Glinka's death and seventy years from Balakirev's birth. It was given in the Petersburg Conservatoire under the direction of M. Vladimirov.[34]

Balakirev's own fiftieth anniversary of his Petersburg début (on 12/25 February 1906), had been quite overshadowed by the Glinka celebrations on 3/16 February, and in fact he did not receive the congratulations which were *invariable* in Russia on such occasions. The concert in February 1907 was possibly held in partial atonement for this omission.

In his last years, Balakirev could not help feeling bitter about the heartbreaking indifference generally shown towards him and his music. A concert of his music, 'his *last* concert', as Findeisen puts it in a French periodical, 'which had been fixed for 18 February 1909 (Balakirev was to have directed his overture *King Lear*) could not take place, the sale of tickets having been practically nil!' Findeisen finishes his article: 'Is this not a proof of more than the incorrigible ingratitude of the public?'[35]

Between 1900 and 1908 Balakirev composed a second symphony in D minor, of which the Scherzo alla cosacca (conceived as early as 1864 and at first intended for the C major symphony) and part of the finale (a polonaise) are particularly good and display fully the *classical* side of Balakirev's romantic art. The symphony was first performed, Lyapunov conducting, at a Free School Concert on 10/23 April 1909. (The overture and incidental music to *King Lear* were also performed at this concert.)

The last works that Balakirev was engaged upon were two songs, 'Dawn' and 'The Rock' with words by his Slavophile friend Khomyakov and his favourite poet Lermontov, respectively; a suite in D minor of three movements ('Préambule', 'Quasi Valse' and 'Tarantella') of not very original quality; and his E flat piano concerto begun in 1861–62. It was Zimmermann who had urged him to finish this concerto, as he wrote to Calvocoressi on 13/26 March 1906: 'It is curious that Viñes,[36] from whom I received a letter only today, dreams, like Zimmermann, of seeing me compose a work for piano and orchestra . . . Zimmermann asks me with such insistence that I cannot refuse . . .'[37] (Balakirev was also planning a fantasy on Greek folk-themes at this time, but it never materialised.)

The concerto was left unfinished, and Lyapunov completed the finale after Balakirev's death.

He interrupted the composition of the concerto in 1909 in order to orchestrate a 'suite' of four of Chopin's piano pieces— the Study in D minor, Mazurka in B flat, Nocturne in G minor and Scherzo in D minor. He also re-orchestrated his boyhood favourite, the piano concerto in E minor, and both these works were performed at the Chopin centenary celebrations in February 1910. Balakirev wrote to Calvocoressi on 15/28 February: '. . . I've been told that the commemoration of this day has been triumphantly organised by Lyapunov . . . My illness prevented my being present at the concert, but I am happy to have attended the rehearsal, all the same . . .'[38]

Balakirev's health had been steadily deteriorating during the past year. Lyapunov made a last effort to get him to write down what he remembered of *The Fire-Bird*. He had written on 29 June/12 July 1909: 'How would it be if you got together, perhaps in the form of an orchestral suite, the material from The *Fire-Bird*?' Lyapunov's efforts were fruitless, although, according to A. S. Lyapunova, the second theme of the 'Tarantella' from the suite in D minor was a theme from *The Fire-Bird*.[39]

As early as 7/20 February 1908, Balakirev wrote to Calvo-coressi: 'You ask news of my health. It gets worse, but my doctor is convinced that I'll live until the summer; and if he's not mistaken, the heat should help me regain some of my strength, and then I might hope to live till the autumn. It will be as God wills . . .'[40]

But he was still alive in April 1910 and wrote on 7/20 to Calvocoressi: 'In one of your last letters you raise the question of the orchestration of some of my songs. I have orchestrated three of them: 1) Georgian Song; 2) Dream; 3) Prologue. I shan't be able to orchestrate others, for, because of my age and my illness, such a task would be beyond my strength . . .'[41]

Balakirev had only another month to live. He died of a cold which resulted in pleurisy on 16/29 May[42] 1910, at 6.30 in the morning.[43] And so, after all, he did not in fact die *directly* as a result of his bad heart, which was probably fortunate, as otherwise a prolonged and painful end might have ensued.

Timofeyev writes of the burial:

Balakirev's funeral was a very solemn affair. Representatives of all the musical institutions in the capital filed past his coffin . . . Friends and admirers bore the coffin to the grave. He was buried in the cemetary of the Alexander-Nevsky monastery, near the graves of Glinka, Ludmila Shestakova and his friends Borodin, Mussorgsky and Stassov.[44]

It has been difficult, in the past, to get a true picture of Balakirev's character. Being a disputatious man (like Dr Johnson), he was never so happy as when he was fighting a battle—for the 'new Russian music', for Glinka's operas versus Smetana and the pro-Polish party in Prague; against the neglect of Chopin's birth-place, against the Russian Music Society (until, that is, the tide began to turn against him) and against Conservatoire-Teutonicism.

Rimsky-Korsakov, Tchaikovsky and Cui, for instance, have treated him unfairly, though they all agree about his enormous talent and extraordinary gifts; whereas S. Lyapunov, Calvocoressi and others, in order to redress the balance, have been at too great pains to refute the adverse comments. The following description, written during his lifetime, perhaps sums up his character, as well as is possible in the case of such a variegated and diversified person, in a few words:

> As a man he is an unusual personality. He suffers from nerves, his character is despotic. Sometimes he acts on the spur of the moment—these are all his shortcomings. But I cannot properly express the good, or to put it better, the outstanding side of his nature: he is disinterested, honest, kind, compassionate, and were he not to possess those few deficiencies which I mentioned above, he could without exaggeration be called a perfect man.[45]

Ludmila Shestakova knew Balakirev for fifty years (from 1855 until her death in 1905), and her description of Balakirev cannot be considered as other than sympathetic and free from any kind of prejudice.

## NOTES ON CHAPTER 11

1. 2/14 October 1894.
2. Written for the occasion.
3. 5/17 October 1894.
4. K(1)A, p. 430.
5. A. A. Olenin, *My Reminiscences of M. A. Balakirev*, FC (x), p. 326 (trans. S. W. Pring).
6. *À propos* Balakirev's technical prowess, Yastrebtsev wrote in his diary of Balakirev's 'wonderful' performance of *Islamey* in 1891 (FC (xii), p. 397).
7. NA (in French), 1902–03.
8. FC (xi), p. 370.
9. TA, No. vii, p. 74.
10. ibid., p. 75. His total pension was 4,500 rubles a year.
11. Cui.
12. FA, p. 53.
13. ibid.
14. TA, No. vii, p. 73.
15. FC (xi), p. 374.
16. FC (xii), pp. 387 and 389.
17. K(2)A, p. 202.
18. AF (*On Russian Music*), p. 179 et seq.
19. L(1)D, p. 210.
20. L(2)A, No. viii, p. 52. This was Balakirev's last Free School concert, but he conducted a Glinka memorial concert in Berlin in 1899.

21. FC (x), p. 347 (trans. E. G.).

22. TA, No. vii, p. 75. Balakirev's heart disease was angina pectoris.

23. See note 7.

24. SA, Vol. III, pt. 1, p. 316.

25. CA, pp. 143–144.

26. CC, pp. 6–7.

27. FC (x), p. 356 (trans. S. W. Pring).

28. V. V. Stassov, *Pisma k Deyatelyam Russkoi Kultury* (Moscow, 1962), p. 147.

29. FC (vii), p. 266. Its restraint is probably its greatest virtue.

30. Napravnik had been Balakirev's successor as conductor of the Russian Music Society.

31. Letter to M. D. Calvocoressi, 10/23 February 1906 (CC, p. 3).

32. Compare with Mrs Newmarch's description on p. 146. Stravinsky is a very small man, so that his idea of height is probably comparative.

33. Igor Stravinsky and Robert Craft, *Conversations with Igor Stravinsky*, London 1959, p. 45.

34. RA, pp. 349–350.

35. Obituary on Balakirev (in French), in *Société Internationale de Musique, revue musicale mensuelle*, July 1910, p. 418.

36. Ricardo Viñes (1875–1943), a well-known pianist, had given the first performance in the West of Balakirev's piano sonata (in Paris).

37. CC, p. 5.

38. ibid., p. 15.

39. L(1)B, p. 404.

40. CC, p. 13.

41. ibid., p. 15.

42. Not 10 May, as Muzalevsky states (M(2)A, p. 67). Timofeyev, Lyapunov, Karenin and Karatyghin all give the date as 16 May (old style).

43. K(2)A, p. 68.

44. TA, No. vii, p. 77.

45. ibid., pp. 73–74.

# Analysis and Criticism

# CHAPTER 12

## Orchestral Compositions (1): Overtures and Stage Music

## OVERTURE ON A SPANISH MARCH THEME

The original autograph score of Balakirev's Overture on a Spanish March Theme bears the inscription: 'Begun in St Petersburg on 29 January 1857, finished in Kuralov on 17 August 1857.' It was revised and rescored in 1886, and the first edition of this second version was published by Bessel in 1887. Under the words, 'Overture on a Spanish March folk-tune, given [to me] by M. I. Glinka', is written in ink, 'to the drama, *The Expulsion of the Moors from Spain*'. It looks as though Balakirev has thought of it as an overture to some play. But he has crossed out from 'to the drama . . .' onwards (in pencil), and a contemporary copy of the score does not bear this inscription under the title. Nevertheless it is clear that Balakirev had some definite dramatic subject in mind when he composed the overture, and the later version is prefaced in the following manner:

The composer bore in mind the history of the tragic fate of the Moors, who were chased and finally expelled from Spain by the Inquisition. Accordingly the first theme is Eastern in character; the orchestra in places represents an organ, the chanting of the monks, the more fiery blessings of *auto da fé*, before the ringing of the bells and the triumphal rejoicings of the people.[1]

159

As in his later overtures on Russian themes, so in this, his first orchestral work of note, Balakirev makes use of three varying themes, and the interplay between them is well developed for a man of twenty.

The first theme, the one which is 'Eastern' in character, depicting the Moors, is immediately exposed by a piccolo over a double pedal (tonic and dominant) on the first and second violins (ex. 1). The pedal and the piccolo give just the right effect for a

Ex. 1

Moorish-Muslim theme, and the deliberate augmented second from C sharp down to B flat is Balakirev's first venture into a realm which was to hold such fascination for him. The theme is worked up to a *forte* before what appears to be a bridge passage theme enters (ex. 2) while semiquavers continue, softly. This later turns

Ex. 2

out to be the theme of the chanting monks, and here alternates with the first theme.

Rushing semiquaver contrary motion scales usher in the Spanish march theme on the trumpets and horns, accompanied by the percussion (ex. 3). Each half of the theme is played twice. The original D minor has changed to B flat major in this passage (ex. 3)[2] which modulates to D major before a return to B flat (*poco più animato*) to the accompaniment of a flourishing chromatic scale descending heavily in crotchets. All the thematic material occurs in the exposition.

After some development ex. 1 asserts itself for a time (this may depict the 'chasing',[3] of the Moors from Spain). The march theme cuts it short with a *fortissimo* alternation of the chords of

12. Balakirev in 1910

**13.** Autograph of the first page of the Overture on Three Russian Themes

Ex. 3

F major and A flat major ninth, followed by two variants of the
bridge passage theme (ex. 2); the accompaniment in the second
of these versions is reminiscent of an organ. A few bars later the
Moors speak, *quasi allegretto*, but the tones of the organ allow
them no reprieve, *andantino*, and in a final and savage build-up
(*animato*) the march theme asserts its supreme authority, to the
chanting of the monks and the despair of the Moors (*poco più
animato*).

In this recapitulation the march theme is seen to be of more
importance than its fellows, which either act as counterpoints to
it, or as alternating passages to phrases of that theme. At the
finish of the overture two crashing chords alternate—the same
two as were introduced so unusually in the development, only
here, as the final key is D major, they are chords of D itself and
F major ninth.

This remarkable overture does not deserve the neglect into
which it has fallen. The working out may be on the diffuse side,
the developments rather naïve, and the counterpoints mechanical,
but no more so than many other nineteenth-century works of
much less merit which are in the regular concert repertory of

symphony orchestras. It is the work of a young man who shows much promise in the field of symphonic development.

## OVERTURE ON THE THEMES OF
## THREE RUSSIAN SONGS

According to a note on the score, Balakirev began his Overture on the Themes of three Russian Songs on 19 September/ 1 October 1857 in St Petersburg, and completed it at Ludmila Shestakova's country cottage at Zamanilovka on 26 June/8 July 1858.[4] The score was revised, and published by Jurgenson in 1882. It is the first purely orchestral work of Balakirev based on Russian folk-songs; its immediate prototype is Glinka's *Kamarinskaya*: Fantasia on two Russian Folk-songs. Balakirev merely adds a third, slow folk-song as an introduction and epilogue, but otherwise his scheme is not much more developed than Glinka's.

The three folk-songs are, A: 'The silver birch'; B: 'In the field stands a little birch tree'; and, C: 'There was at the feast'. This early overture had remarkable repercussions in Russian music. Tchaikovsky used theme B in his fourth symphony, destroying its essentially three-bar structure by inserting a 'pom-pom' in an unnecessary fourth bar. Stravinsky used theme C in *Petrushka*. Both these composers favoured variants of the themes employing a simple repetition of each figure, rather than Balakirev's varied repetitions.

After an energetic introduction in B major, based on theme B, eighteen bars in length, theme A, *andante*, is introduced on the flute and clarinet (ex. 4) with an inverted dominant pedal on

Ex. 4

the first violins, *divisi*. It is repeated twice, the first time with full lush accompaniment on the strings; the second repetition (on the woodwind and plucked strings, ex. 5) is particularly colourful.

Ex. 5

Without any bridge passage the *allegro moderato* follows on immediately. Theme B, in B minor, is announced by the clarinet (ex. 6). This virile theme, which so dominates the finale of Tchaikovsky's fourth symphony, also attains an ascendancy here over its mellower and more cheerful neighbour. Balakirev affords it a surprising variety of treatment. A modulation to D major prepares the way for theme C on the oboe (ex. 7), which transfers

Ex. 6

Ex. 7

itself to the cellos, basses and bass trombone, *fortissimo*, before a change of key signature to B flat major, obviously a sign that development and further modulation are not to be long postponed.

Theme B is the main subject for this part of the drama, appearing effectively in syncopated and flattened form. A mixture of themes B and C, after a return to two sharps, is quite effective (ex. 8).

Ex. 8

A rushing semiquaver passage leads to the recapitulation, *fff*, first of theme B, in simple form with simple repeats, the two halves of which are then rather cleverly telescoped (ex. 9).

Ex. 9

Theme C follows in B major, and a few bars of theme A (*andante* as before) bring to the quiet close of which Balakirev was so fond this simple and rather uncoordinated overture, which nevertheless reveals a considerable degree of contrapuntal ingenuity.

## OVERTURE AND INCIDENTAL MUSIC
## TO *KING LEAR*

Stassov asked Balakirev whether he was sticking to his intention to write music for *King Lear* in a letter of 19/31 July 1858. The play was being staged at the Alexandrinsky Theatre in St Petersburg. But Balakirev did not compose the music in time for these performances. In his letter, Stassov includes 'another' English theme—no doubt he had given to Balakirev at some earlier stage the 'English theme' which is used in the Prelude to Act IV, as this latter theme is not included in any of the extant correspondence.[5] Balakirev did not use the (second) English theme sent to him in the letter, but Stassov's suggestion for a 'Fool's song' is taken up: 'And here is the "Fool's song" for Shakespeare's play *As you like it.* This is the very music which was used for it in the English Theatre in Shakespeare's own day'[6] (ex. 10).

Ex. 10

Balakirev used the following version of the theme in the Prelude to Act III (ex. 11). Stassov's theme consists entirely of

Ex. 11

repetitions of figures (a) and (b), and Balakirev uses imitative stretto entries of figure (b) to heighten the obviously intended effect of the original.

Balakirev does not acknowledge the provenance of this theme, though the other one is called 'English theme' in the score (Prelude to Act IV, and Act IV Sc. 7—ex. 12).

Ex. 12

Balakirev composed the Prelude to Act V *first*—it was almost finished by July 1858.[7] The overture was completed and orchestrated by 18/30 September 1859 and first performed at a University Concert on 15/27 November; but the Procession (at the entry of King Lear and his court in Act I) was not finished until February 1861. Balakirev wrote to Stassov on 14/26 February:

> 12.30 in the evening: I have just finished the Procession. It only remains to orchestrate it . . . My head feels so very weak,

my feet are as cold as ice, a kind of nervous shivering has taken hold of me. Yesterday I was concentrating so hard (composing the Procession) that, for a moment, I imagined I should go out of my mind.[8]

And again, in a letter to Stassov two days later: 'Come round to me this evening . . . Mussorgsky will be here. I want to play over the Procession with him. I consider it to be the best of the Entr'actes, though not better than the overture . . .' Cui agreed with him in this. He goes on: '*Please come round*, I urge you most strongly . . .'

Yet Balakirev would not allow his music to be published. He was dissatisfied with it, particularly with the orchestration, which he apparently considered 'childish', and its final revision was delayed until 1902 (and was published two years later). Balakirev's friends disagreed with him. Ludmila Shestakova wrote on 27 December 1873/8 January 1874: 'I have a *big* favour to ask of you, my Mily; allow your *King Lear* to be performed again once only at a symphony concert, only once let me hear it before I die!' Again she wrote at the beginning of 1874: 'Cui and Korsakov have looked through the entire orchestration of *Lear*, there is *absolutely nothing childish in it*. Not only could it be performed and published, but it ought to be . . . *No* alterations *whatever* are necessary before its performance . . .'[9]

Balakirev gave way to the request, and the overture[10] was performed on 2/14 March 1874 at a concert of the Russian Music Society, with Napravnik conducting. He did not attend the performance. It had, however, after its first performance in 1859 been given fairly regularly in the following five or six years. The overture, and Preludes to Acts II, III, IV and V had been performed at a literary-musical Shakespeare recital-concert held in the hall of the Russian Society of Merchants on 23 April/5 May 1864, at which Balakirev conducted the orchestral items.[11] But he had not allowed any of his *Lear* music to be played after he took over the conductorship of the Russian Music Society, for the reasons given above. His fussy criticism of others, between 1867 and 1872, was matched by his self-criticism, a quality with which Balakirev became over endowed, so as to move even the gentle Ludmila Shestakova to mild reproach.

The overture starts with a short introduction, based on the music of the Procession, a brilliant Polonaise. The dual keys of B flat major and its dominant, and F major and *its* dominant are used in answering fanfares. This overlapping of keys gives a somewhat foolish air to the pomposity of the procession exactly in keeping with the character of Lear, as it appears to be, at the beginning of the play. Lear's theme occurs on the trumpets in the major key, accompanied by other brass, then softly and mysteriously on the woodwind and, after a short passage on the horns and timpani in a mixture of 3/2 and 6/4 depicting 'Kent's prediction', it is displayed in its entirety in B flat minor (ex. 13, A) at the beginning of the *allegro moderato*, with Goneril and Regan's cruel and evil theme (B) in the bass. The severe restraint which

Ex. 13

Ex. 14

Balakirev employs is classical in the truest sense, while the melody seems to portray Lear's character, and the fate which must inevitably befall him, with insight and clarity. At the end of Lear's theme, another motif adds to the picture of the burning agony of Lear's tormented soul (ex. 14). (Original crotchets were altered later to quavers.)

Goneril and Regan's theme, with added definition of rhythm leads to the second subject, in D major (ex. 15) which paints Cordelia in suitable colours. It speaks as clearly as the gentleman attendant in Act III, Sc. 3:

> You have seen
> Sunshine and rain at once; her smiles and tears
> Were like, a better way: those happy smilets
> That play'd on her ripe lip seem'd not to know
> What guests were in her eyes, which parted thence
> As pearls from diamonds dropp'd; in brief,
> Sorrow would be a rarity most belov'd,
> If all could so become it.

Ex. 15

Goneril and Regan's theme is soon blasted forth by the full orchestra, as if Lear's malediction in Act II, Sc. 4, has been called upon Goneril:

> You nimble lightnings, dart your blinding flames
> Into her scornful eyes, infect her beauty,
> You fen-suck'd fogs, drawn by the powerful sun,
> To fall and blast her pride.

This theme, besides acting as a bass to Lear's own theme, has furnished a bridge passage and, here, a codetta leading to the development section, which is the storm. It is restrained and telling; the thunder off-stage is produced by the cellos, basses and bassoons (ex. 16). The similarity to the semiquaver descending

Ex. 16

passage in the Fool's theme (ex. 10, see p. 165) should not be overlooked—the Fool plays a prominent part in the storm:

> He that has a little tiny wit,—
> With hey, ho, the wind and the rain,—
> Must make content with his fortune fit,
> For the rain it raineth every day.

Lear's theme is developed in its two separate parts, figures (a) and (b), to the almost continuous accompaniment of repeated semiquavers on the strings. Figure (b) is particularly effective, staccato, tossed about, *piano*, between strings and wind. The storm continues, with the addition of Lear's quaver theme (ex. 14, p. 167), imitatively treated, into the recapitulation, where Lear's theme is augmented to notes of twice the value. The repeated semiquavers become demi-semiquavers as Lear becomes abjectly pathetic in his madness. The theme of the cruel sisters interrupts and leads to the second subject, now in D flat major, *più tranquillo*. But Cordelia's death breaks Lear's heart as both figure (a) in augmentation, and figure (b), in notes of the original value, occur simultaneously in an infinite sadness, beautifully captured in only two parts written with great spareness (ex. 17). So Lear dies, and

Ex. 17

his spirit hovers in the mysterious passage which now has more significance than might have been foreseen at the beginning (*tempo del commincio*)—Kent's prediction has not, alas! proved false. The music dies away on a solo violin (ex. 18), accompanied by chords on the wind.

Ex. 18

In the overture, Balakirev has combined a strict sonata form, including an introduction and epilogue, with a concise rendering of the synopsis of the play. The skill involved in such a feat was considerable. Balakirev, aged twenty-two, shows almost as much grasp of the idea as the mature Beethoven in *Egmont*.[12] But his wayward, exploring talent did not develop much further on these lines, much to the chagrin of the more orthodox-minded musicians of his day.

The Procession occurs after Gloucester has said: 'The king is coming', at the beginning of Act I, Sc. 1. Shakespeare's stage direction is: 'Sennet. Enter one bearing a coronet, King Lear, Cornwall, Albany, Goneril, Regan, Cordelia and Attendants.' As Gloucester, Kent and Edmund are already on the stage, only Edgar and the Fool (of the principal characters) are not present on this magnificent occasion.

The word 'Sennet' could be defined as 'a trumpet or woodwind announcement of a stage entrance (in state)'. The brilliant Polonaise used by Balakirev is written for a double orchestra, the second orchestra being behind the scenes, and consisting of two piccolos, full quadruple woodwind, four horns, two trumpets, two tenor and bass trombones, tuba, triangle, side drum, tambourine and big drum. The main orchestra is not in any way depleted to allow for this—it consists of the normal full symphony orchestra, with three flutes and clarinets, a cor anglais, a full brass section including four horns, and a harp.

The mixture of keys in the opening fanfares is cleverly divided between the two orchestras. The main tonality is B flat; the stage orchestra's fanfare (trumpets and horns) is based on A with its dominant, the main orchestra's on F and its dominant, while the double basses and timpani outline their opening basis of B flat and F. A faintly comic and pompous version of figure (a) of Lear's theme provides the main subject of the Polonaise, allotted to the brass of the stage band (ex. 19).

Ex. 19

Allegretto maestoso ♩ = 84

The trio (ex. 20), is quite charming—Borodinesque, one would say, had it not been written in 1861. It is more subtle, too, than it at first appears. Compare it with figure (a) of the English theme (ex. 12, p. 165). Except that the third bar is decorated, in the trio, and the last note is different, the two are identical! The orchestration has a Mozartian translucence. Even when a *crescendo* leads to the entry of the theme on the stage band, accompanied by *fortissimo* semiquavers on the strings, the result is simple and uninvolved, but intellectually strong and sure.

Ex. 20

The return of the Polonaise itself adds its touch of subtle ridicule in a slightly idiotic canonic imitation of Lear's theme; the E natural (augmented 4th) increases the air of the ridiculous particularly in this passage (ex. 21)—an air of petty swagger. The

Ex. 21

pace increases and the Polonaise ends with a splendid flourish. Lear wanted the cares of state taken off his shoulders, but he also wanted to preserve all the deference and ceremony due to him as king.

Who else would have thought of bringing Lear on to the stage with a Polonaise? And yet, what could be more suitable than just such a splendid dance, pompous and unwieldy, slow moving but of great rhythmical impetus, hiding its idiotic traits behind a façade of ceremonial splendour. This is a masterpiece of characterisation. (There is a second version for single orchestra, less effective but more reasonable in respect of numerical demands.)

The Prelude to Act II consists of Goneril and Regan's music, with Lear's quaver theme (ex. 14, p. 167), probably representing his 'malediction'. There is an interesting mixture of E minor and E major six bars from the end, followed by contrary scales of E major and finishing on bare octave Es—it is all curiously harsh.

When Kent is put in the stocks at the end of Sc. 2, and is left alone on the stage, he says:

> Approach, thou beacon to this under globe,
> That by thy comfortable beams I may
> Peruse this letter! Nothing almost sees miracles
> But misery: I know 'tis from Cordelia . . .
> Fortune, good night: smile; once more turn thy wheel![13]

As Kent falls asleep, nineteen bars of the Cordelia music are played; and Fortune's wheel is represented by the harp.

The Prelude to Act III (Balakirev directs that Sc. 1 should be omitted) is a picture of 'Lear and the Fool on the heath. The Storm.' Figure (b) of Lear's theme is used (*andante*), alternating with the Fool's theme, *allegretto scherzando* (ex. 11, see p. 165). The storm music is very similar to that used in the development section of the overture.

The Prelude to Act IV actually depicts the scene at the beginning of Sc. 7; Shakespeare's direction: 'Lear on a bed asleep, soft music playing'; Balakirev's direction: 'Lear awakening in Cordelia's camp to the sound of the English folk-tune'. The theme (ex. 12, p. 165) is treated simply; it occurs first on the unaccompanied cor anglais. Lear's awakening is magical (ex. 22), at once demonstrating his pitiable condition and also, in its calmness, his cured madness. Both,

> Where have I been? Where am I? Fair daylight?
> I am mightily abus'd. I should e'en die with pity,
> To see another thus. I know not what to say:

and the Doctor's words to Cordelia,

> Be comforted, good madam; the great rage, you see,
> is cur'd in him . . .

are wonderfully painted.

172

Ex. 22

Variations on the English theme are finely wrought. Cordelia's theme, *l'istesso tempo*, ends this lovely episode. She seems to say

> O, look upon me, Sir,
> And hold your hands in benediction o'er me.

Twenty-six bars of the English theme occur in Sc. 7 itself when the Doctor says, 'Louder the music there!', directed to be played by musicians on the stage. This exquisite miniature, no less beautiful than the Prelude to Act IV, is written for flute, cor anglais, two clarinets, two bassoons and harp.

The Prelude to Act V (the battle, Lear's death by Cordelia's corpse, apotheosis), starts with calls to arms on the horns answered by martial runs on the strings and wind with accompanying chords based on the harmony of this chord:

Ex. 23

Only now has the E natural, employed so quaintly in the Procession music, achieved its truly tragic significance. So it seems—but of course, Balakirev composed this entr'acte first. He thought of the final tragedy first, and the initial drollery only three years later.

Lear enters with Cordelia in his arms (Cordelia theme, *allegretto quasi andantino*). She is dead. Lear bewails her death, and his last words are echoed in a tragic version of his theme (ex. 24):

> Oh, oh, oh, oh!
> Do you see this! Look on her, look, her lips,
> Look there, look there!

Ex. 24

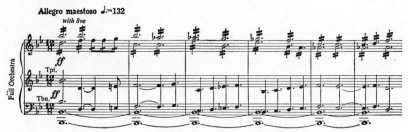

During the course of Act V the battle music is used on the entry of Lear, Cordelia and their forces in Sc. 2. The blinded Gloucester and Edgar speak *quasi recitativo* to a string and wind accompaniment:

> Here, father, take the shadow of this bush
> For your good host; pray that the right may thrive.

Both orchestras are used for the introduction of the third scene, when the battle music and fanfares on the brass announce the entry, in conquest, with drums and colours, of Edmund; Lear and Cordelia enter as prisoners. And so, but for a few other fanfares, ends Balakirev's music.

The extraordinary clarity with which Balakirev sees Shakespeare's drama is one of the most fascinating things about his music, which seems to add to our understanding of the play without adding anything superfluous to Shakespeare. In some ways the music is more restrained than the play. The tragedy is latent in the music, overwhelming in the play. But, to a musician, the music reveals the classical side of the play, its clear-cut form and its irresistible onward movement; and *King Lear* is surely one of Shakespeare's most simply constructed plays, with only one sub-plot, that of Gloucester, Edgar and Edmund, which is also entirely necessary to the action of the main plot. Shakespeare's remarkable stroke of creative genius, in Act III, Sc. 4, where Edgar, the Fool and Lear appear in the storm on the heath together is not matched in the music: the Fool, who acts the fool because that is his job, Edgar who is disguised and acts as a madman to escape capture by his father, and Lear who, turned out in the storm by his cruel daughters, loses his reason. How could any *music* match this?[14]

But the main characters are very carefully portrayed, and Lear himself is taken through the play, in the metamorphoses of his theme, with an instinctive understanding of the inner meaning of the tale.

### NOTES ON CHAPTER 12

1. FB, pp. 81–82.
2. Glinka gave the theme to Balakirev on 26 April/8 May 1856, written in the key of C major in 2/2 time.
3. Balakirev's own word.
4. FB, p. 93.
5. I cannot trace this theme. It is not in William Chappell's collection (see note 6 below) and is not known at Cecil Sharp House, London.
6. K(3)B, p. 20. This theme is quoted in William Chappell's book (see note 16 to chapter 2). The title is 'When that I was a little tiny boy, With a heigh ho! the wind and the rain'. Chappell gives the following note about the song:
   WHEN THAT I WAS A LITTLE TINY BOY
   'The Fool's song which forms the Epilogue to Twelfth Night is still sung on the stage to this tune. It has no other authority than theatrical tradition. A song of the same description, and with the same burden, is sung by the Fool in King Lear, act III., sc. 2.'
7. Letter of Balakirev to Stassov, 25 July/6 August 1858.
8. K(3)B, p. 94.
9. FA, p. 45; this letter is without date.
10. The overture *only*.
11. K(3)B, p. 213. Balakirev, in the same programme, also conducted Schumann's Overture, *Julius Caesar*; the *Queen Mab* scherzo from Berlioz's symphony, *Romeo and Juliet*; and the march from Mendelssohn's *Midsummer Night's Dream* music.
12. Beethoven composed his *Egmont* Overture when he was forty, in 1810.
13. This punctuation is taken from the *New Temple Shakespeare*.
14. But the twentieth century may produce a composer able to portray this scene!

# CHAPTER 13

*Orchestral Compositions (2): Symphonic Poems*

## SYMPHONIC POEM *RUSSIA*

In the early 'sixties Balakirev planned a programme symphony in four movements entitled *Russ* (the old name for Russia). However, this plan was superseded and, instead of the programme symphony, he composed his Second Overture on three Russian Themes between 1863 and 1864, which was first performed on 6/18 April 1864 at a Free School Concert. This was revised and published by Johansen in 1869 with the title, 'Musical Picture, *1000 years*', and further revised and rescored in a new version entitled Symphonic poem *Russ* between 1882 and 1884. It is generally known (in the West) as Symphonic poem *Russia*. This second version was eventually published by Bessel in 1889, and new editions were published in 1894,[1] also by Bessel, and in 1907 by Zimmermann. The rather misleading preface (dated 11 May 1887) to the Bessel version seems to have been tailored to fit the overture rather than the music built round the ideas expressed in this preface. It is given in full in Chapter 3 (p. 51).

In fact, the three folk-themes are chosen for their variety and also for the infinite possibilities of juxtaposition and contrapuntal interplay which they afford rather than for any historical reasons Balakirev may have conjured up in his mind *after* the composition of the work.

There is no material difference between the 1869 version and the version published in 1889; there are occasional alterations in the distribution of parts, orchestration and unimportant details, but that is all. The 1894 and 1907 versions show slight and unnecessary changes in the preface, which are of no interest and give the impression of a mind fussing over one of its earlier inspirations.

The basic situation here is the same as in the first Overture on the Themes of three Russian Songs. A slow evocative theme is used as an introduction and epilogue, and two fast dance-themes are employed in the main *allegro*. But the difference between the two works is no less than that between the overtures *Fidelio* and *Leonora No. 3*. The first does not detract from any drama which is to follow, the second is a symphonic work in which all the drama is unfolded to the full.

Two wind and brass chords of B flat minor introduce the first theme (ex. 25), a wedding song, 'It was not the wind', which rises

Ex. 25

out of the depths on the violas, cellos and basses in octaves, answered by flutes, clarinets and harp, and ending with a plagal cadence of the *major subdominant* chord followed by the bare fifth of the tonic (without a third)—a most effective harmonisation. Repetitions of the theme culminate in a chord of B flat major, with rising arpeggios on the harp and held wind chords. These four bars are of particular interest, as they are also used as the four closing bars of the work, but with important additions on the strings.

The *allegro moderato* opens with four bars of introduction bridging the key of B flat to that of D major, the main key of the *allegro*, and the key of the second theme, (ex. 26), 'I'll go up', three bars in length, first announced on the clarinets and bassoon.

Ex. 26

At a change of time to 3/4, *l'istesso tempo*, the first theme (ex. 25) is given to the full brass with dashing semiquaver string passages in accompaniment, the whole being most effective and quite unexpected. It acts as a bridge passage leading to the third theme, 'Jolly Katya in the meadows', a peasant-dance song like its predecessor (ex. 27). A return of the key of B flat major does

Ex. 27

not introduce the development section but a new fourth theme in this key, ex. 28, accompanied by harp arpeggios.

Ex. 28

In an autograph of a score of *1000 years* given to him by Balakirev in 1869, Stassov has written against this theme, 'evoked in the valley of the Daryal',[2] and it is clear that it was composed by Balakirev during his holiday in the Caucasus in the summer of 1863.[3] It is used as an episodic bridge to the development, and is treated in a secondary capacity, not being used in the development of the other three themes, but only being re-introduced to quieten down the recapitulation, in order to regain the original atmosphere of the first theme (ex. 25) at the end.

The development proper starts after a repetition on the flute of ex. 28, the time changing to 4/4. This magnificent development-fresco employs every possible combination of all three themes. A full knowledge and understanding of it is only possible by studying the score, as the ear cannot pick up some of the delicate intricacy—not at a first hearing, at any event. Exs. 29 and 30 give some idea of this intricacy.

A tremendous accelerando is built up (at the end of the recapitulation) of the three themes of the *allegro*, the incessant anapaestic rhythm of the second bar of ex. 27 adding considerably to the exciting effect. Eventually the pace slackens, until only the figure (a) rhythm of ex. 28 is left, on the timpani, with low held chords on the wind and brass. These, and a single *mezzo forte* stroke of the tam-tam, re-introduce the first theme (ex. 25) as it first appeared.

This theme reappears only once, and the work ends as it began, but with this exception: in the last four bars the violin, descending, refers to ex. 26 and the cellos, ascending, hint at the augmented fourth used in the fourth theme (ex. 28, bars 5, 9, 11 and 13), while the harp and the wind have the same music as at the end of the opening *larghetto* (ex. 31).

Ex. 31

These additions, in the last four bars, make a most imaginative close, as if the experience of the *allegro* has been added to the bareness of the introduction to create, in the very end, a magic caught only for a moment before its elusive aural fragrance fades. These bars can hardly be forgotten if a full but necessary intellectual effort of the mind does not interfere with the clear classical ecstasy of the moment. And the effect is purely musical, and has nothing whatever to do with the prefatory note.

# Analysis and Criticism

## SYMPHONIC POEM *IN BOHEMIA*

The Symphonic poem *In Bohemia* was composed in 1866–67 as Overture on Czech Themes, and was published in a revised and rescored version in 1906. It seems, however, that Balakirev started work on his revision some years earlier. In a letter to B. F. Kalensky, a Czech writer on music and propagandist of Russian music in Bohemia, Balakirev wrote on 5/18 June 1902: 'Having finished my *King Lear,* I shall immediately begin preparing for publication my Czech Overture, which, because of its serious character and breadth, I consider to be a symphonic poem. I shall give it the title *In Bohemia.*'[4]

His revision was not completed until 12/25 November 1905. It can be assumed that the changes that Balakirev made were again not radical and that, except for clearing up points which had not satisfied his nice nature, the work remains substantially as it was when he first performed it at a Free School Concert on 12/24 May 1867. It was in a book called *Marriage among the Czech People* by B. M. Kulda that he found the three songs, in Vienna in 1866, and the overture was finished in Prague on 6/18 January 1867 and orchestrated by 2/14 May,[5] only ten days before the concert.

The three songs, Nos 57, 56 and 17 in Kulda's collection, are of quite different types: the first, slow and wistful; the second, fast and merry; and the third, medium-paced and rhythmically subtle. The overture is scored for the normal full orchestra, with a third flute or piccolo, a third clarinet, a tuba and full percussion section including three timpani, triangle, tambourine, side drum, cymbals and big drum; there is also a harp. In *Tamara* this orchestration is only exceeded by the addition of a second harp and a tam-tam for the main climax.

The first theme (ex. 32), is a two-fold one: the first four bars are similar to the original folk-song, but the second group of four bars is more or less of Balakirev's own invention, based on the rhythm of the original. The mixture of F sharp minor and A major (immediately repeated in C sharp minor and E major) is

Ex. 32

typical of Balakirev. This duality of key is a mark of his style, as are the ensuing restlessly shifting modulations. The orchestration is delightful; the *larghetto* and *piano* melody is given out on a solo oboe, answered by muted upper strings *divisi*. The theme gradually impinges on the consciousness, the second half slowly assuming more importance than the first. The harp, and arpeggios on the woodwind, are used in rather the same way as in the opening of *Russia*. A slow, upward arpeggio of the dominant ninth in C sharp major, scored for harp harmonics, horns and gradually added upper wind, introduces the first vestige of the second theme over a pulsating string figure.

The second theme proper, *allegro moderato* (ex. 33), is clearly a patter or dance song, and Balakirev treats it as both. It consists of only four bars, the second and fourth being repetitions of the first and third. The first bar starts with four consecutive upward semiquavers; the third bar has four descending semiquavers. This answer of ascent by descent is much used later, giving the effect of inversion. There is also a fundamental duality of key here (F sharp major and D sharp minor).

Ex. 33

The string exposition of the theme is followed by woodwind, while *pizzicato* violins and cellos have a syncopated figure:

and the violas play repeated semiquavers.

The addition of horns and trumpets heralds a key-change to two flats (G minor *and* B flat major). Over a slightly changed version of the theme in the wind, the strings introduce a new descending counter-subject (ex. 34).

Ex. 34

Ex. 35

The third theme, *allegretto* (ex. 35), though slower than its predecessor, has infinite possibilities as regards rhythmical accompaniment of which full use is made. Whereas in the first two subjects the full development has been left till later, this third subject is fully developed here—that is, if the constant repetition of the theme in shifting surroundings with changing keys and varieties of rhythmic background, can be called development. It *is*, of course, development in Balakirev's sense, the patterns of the mosaic fitting beautifully together, but each one differing from the last in quality, quantity and context of sound.

Ex. 35 is the second version of this theme—affording opportunity for a mixture of D major and B minor. Another fascinating harmonisation (ex. 36) occurs a few bars before a return to the

Ex. 36

*larghetto*, and is used as a codetta to the section. The reference to the first theme in ex. 36, on the horn and harp in unison, reintroduces the *larghetto* smoothly.

The recapitulation of the *larghetto* is considerably shortened and leads straight into the return of the *allegro moderato*. This serves not only as the recapitulation of the whole work but as the joint development of all three themes, which are played both separately and together.

There is an occurrence of the second theme here accompanied by a semiquaver figure to which certain figures of Mussorgsky bear a striking resemblance, particularly in *Pictures from an Exhibition* (figure (a) in ex. 37). A quotation is made of an exciting

Ex. 37

chromatic build-up (ex. 38) leading to a recapitulation of all three themes mixed up together with great ingenuity (ex. 39).

Ex. 38

Ex. 39

A melodic twist is introduced in a mixture of the opening of the third theme, with the close of the first theme attached to it (ex. 40); and the second theme, countersubject, and a reference to the third theme occur together in the following bars (ex. 41). Balakirev takes an exuberant delight in these intellectual manœuvres.

Ex. 40

Ex. 41

The pace increases, the dance becomes more and more frenzied before there is a syncopated passage similar to a passage towards the end of Borodin's famous choral Polovtsian Dance from *Prince Igor*. A version, *not* of any of the themes, but of Balakirev's own countersubject to the second theme brings the work to a triumphant conclusion.

*In Bohemia* points the way to *Tamara* in many respects—in its uses of the scale, of rushing semiquavers, sometimes in triplets, of fascinating rhythms and chromatic harmony. But, in the use of intellectual acrobatics, it is still in the world of the first movement of the C major symphony (which was abandoned in its favour in 1866) and even to some extent in that of the restrained *King Lear* overture. It therefore holds a unique position in Balakirev's music.

## SYMPHONIC POEM *TAMARA*

*Tamara*, by M. Lermontov (translated by the author)

In the deep gorge of the Daryal, where the Terek roars in the gloom, an ancient tower stood upon a dark crag.

In this tall narrow tower lived the Princess Tamara, beautiful as an angel from heaven, evil and cunning as a demon.

Through the rising mists of night there shone forth from the tower radiant, golden lights, attracting the traveller's eye, enticing him to find shelter for the night.

When he heard Tamara's voice, he was overwhelmed by passionate desire, as if an incomprehensible power, an unbreakable spell had been cast over him.

It was her voice, not a vision of her, which drew the warrior, merchant or shepherd: before him the doors were opened wide, he was received by a black eunuch.

Upon a soft, luxurious couch, dressed in brocade and adorned with pearls she awaited her guest. By her side were two sparkling goblets of wine.

Then fingers were warmly interlaced, lips fell upon lips, and strange savage sounds the whole night through echoed to the vaults.

Within this hollow tower it seemed as though a hundred ardent youths and maidens had come together on their wedding night to the sounds of the keening at a sumptuous funeral.

But as soon as the first light of dawn appeared over the mountains, in an instant an uncanny silence fell once more on that place.

Only the Terek in the gorge of the Daryal with its roaring broke the silence—the waves rushed and tumbled, wave upon wave.

They seemed to weep as a silent corpse was swirled past by their current: then, at the window a flutter of white, a wafted whisper of 'Farewell'.

So tender was the farewell, so sweet-sounding was the voice, that it seemed to promise an encounter of ecstasy, a caress of love.

A knowledge of Lermontov's poem is vital to the understanding of Balakirev's music. It is not so important to know *what* happens *when*, as to be soaked in the language of the poem, its exotic savagery, its romantic cruelty, its imaginative evocation of atmosphere. Without this knowledge the listener is more at a disadvantage than he would be if he did not know what the bleating of the sheep was in Strauss's *Don Quichotte*, or if he were ignorant of the words of the 'Erl-King'.

It is a very difficult work to place in a concert programme. *Tamara* does not make a happy bedfellow. Its music is so exceptional, its atmosphere so unique, at once banal, cruel, evocative, alluring, rhythmical, exotic but powerful, strong, almost demoniac in places, that either its companion would be paled by it, or else the companion piece would make *Tamara* appear too depraved, too exotic.

*Tamara* was presented as a ballet by Diaghilev, but it was not successful in this role. It might be quite well adapted to the kind of short film shown at film festivals; the producer, in full knowledge of the poem, could evoke the right atmosphere for the listener wholly to appreciate the music—it would make a truly epic, wordless fairy-tale film.

But the really imaginative listener who knows the poem, or

perhaps even a translation of it, is as well-placed as such a producer could be. My prose translation of the poem follows the original closely, and it may evoke something of the atmosphere, although no great poem may be adequately translated into another tongue. (Rosa Newmarch made a partial translation of the poem for a Queen's Hall concert.)[6]

Balakirev's first thoughts for an 'Eastern' orchestral work were for a piece entitled *Lezghinka*, like Glinka's piece of the same name (in *Russlan and Ludmila*). In 1867 the subject of Tamara had superseded this. *Islamey* was considered as a sketch for it. Between 1872 and 1876 all composition ceased, but in the latter year at Ludmila Shestakova's instigation he had started work on it again, and most of the main work was done between then and 1879, when Stassov wrote that, except for unessential details, it was finished (see Chapter 9).

It was actually finally completed on 14/26 September 1882; the first performance was on 7/19 March 1883, and it was published by Jurgenson in 1884. It may therefore be said that fifteen years of Balakirev's life, as far as composition was concerned, were devoted solely to the ripening, completion and perfection of *Tamara*—although the bulk of the work was done in three years. It is the only work of his most mature years—his middle period. Glinka's *Russlan and Ludmila* showed Balakirev the way to such writing, but he goes much further than Glinka and also than his successors in the field—Rimsky-Korsakov, Ippolitov-Ivanov and the like. There are no half-measures in *Tamara*.

The atmosphere of the 'deep gorge of the Daryal, where the Terek roars in the gloom' is created by a soft timpani roll and a triplet semiquaver repeated figure on the muted cellos and basses, with the flattened supertonic in a prominent though immediately contradicted position. The key is B minor, and the bass trombone and tuba add their ominously low tones, followed by the violas, also muted, in demi-semiquavers. The bassoons and horns give out a gloomy snatch, answered by the oboe, painting the picture of the ancient tower standing upon a dark crag, accompanied by the demi-semiquavers and triplet semiquavers of the Terek in the gorge below.

The first hint that the tower belongs to Tamara is given by the cor anglais, the oboe and the violins, in that order, playing the first five notes of what is eventually to be Tamara's siren-like love-song. It all dies away to the strain of harp arpeggios and held notes on the woodwind, only to start again a major third higher in D sharp minor. The spell is working—everything is coming to life. Besides material already used, a figure on the clarinet, and then on the flute, serves as an ever-livening background to the scene. No pains are spared to create a sombre atmosphere, the uncanny feeling which compels goose-flesh. (Rimsky-Korsakov, making very little alteration, used the clarinet melody (ex. 42) as one of the main themes of his *Sheherazade*.)

Ex. 42

Gradually the pace increases to the accompaniment of a sway-ing minim/crotchet figure and two harps, the mutes of the strings are removed and we are plunged headlong into an *allegro moderato ma agitato*, in D flat major, 12/8 time. The first few pages of the *allegro* are based on jottings in Balakirev's note-book after his visits to the Caucasus—but it is only the intonations, the *genre*, that Balakirev uses from outside—the actual themes are his own, except perhaps for one.

In the first eight bars, the rhythmical scene is set. The violas have an important figure, with bowing across the beat for synco-pated effect, and the strings in octaves usher in the main part of the first theme on the bassoon (ex. 43). In outline it sounds like a

Ex. 43

descending melodic minor scale in F minor, but in fact it is noth-ing of the sort, since the key is D flat major, with the prominent use of the sharpened subdominant (in this case, G natural). The abrupt finish on a chord of D flat (instead of proceeding to the expected C, which it would have done had the key been F minor) has a rather jolting effect. This, in combination with the high register of the bassoon, to which the theme is given, is most effective. According to Rimsky-Korsakov, he and Balakirev heard the first theme at the Petersburg Imperial Barracks[7]—but in a more primitive form than Balakirev employs, it would seem.

The pace increases, and at the tempo sign *poco più animato* another rhythmical pattern appears (ex. 44) which sounds like a

Ex. 44

poco più animato ♩. = 72

new theme with a similar harmonic basis to the first theme, ex. 43. The orchestra plays the transformed theme in octaves, punctuated by held chords on the brass and fierce percussion rhythms. But this passage merely serves as an introduction to Tamara's own themes, for it significantly gradually dies away, the grim exterior of the castle is expunged from the traveller's mind as he hears the insinuating strains of Tamara's song. This is a very long pair of melodies, seeming to portray two sides of the princess's nature.

Her first melody, in B minor, *meno mosso*, is given to the oboe with a held F sharp on the flute, plucked rhythm on the strings and a fascinating side-drum pattern (ex. 45). The theme is tortu-

Ex. 45

meno mosso (doppio movimento)

ously chromatic, and the general effect is oriental and pagan. A repetition of the first four bars of the theme is given to the bassoons in octaves, starting this time after a modulation to D major, but soon returning to B minor. This introduces the second melody, on the clarinet (the first five notes of which have already been heard in the introduction), *allegretto quasi andantino* (ex. 46).

Ex. 46

It adequately illustrates the luscious, voluptuous side of Tamara's nature, her passion for seeking the perfect lover, her depraved nature.

Although it is not a perfect slow melody, it can be treated unkindly with impunity. When the pace becomes more frenzied and it is finally proclaimed by an overwhelming brass section there is not the slightest feeling of horror at the composer's rough treatment of the theme. It is rather a lewd theme constructed with an eye to a crude climax.

Nevertheless the theme is not really beautiful enough for its purpose. Balakirev, searching for the perfect theme, must have found it very hard. For a really beautiful theme at this point (such as the slow movement of Borodin's second quartet) would not have produced the effect Balakirev desired later on, even if he had been capable of composing it. Balakirev was not the man to make the mistake which Khachaturyan makes in his piano concerto, of allowing a delightful little theme to be blazoned out by the full orchestra near the end of the work, thus hideously parodying its earlier form. Balakirev's theme *is* suitable for symphonic development. Nor does it lack subtlety; but the subtleties are often lost in performance, as Balakirev's metronome mark of sixty-three dotted crotchets to the minute is frequently exceeded. The effect of later increases in tempo is much enhanced if this theme is taken slowly enough in the first instance.

A partial repetition of this clarinet theme, *poco più mosso*, with different orchestration, is the cue for the rather considerable development of both Tamara's themes. A fugal build-up ushers in a *vivace* (*alla breve*) (ex. 47): the traveller has entered the castle, seen Tamara, and now the revelries have begun.

Ex. 47

The theme of this *vivace* is really a mixture of ex. 43, particularly the first rhythm, only very much chromaticised, and of the main purport of ex. 45—in fact, it grows out of previous material, and is used for development purposes. It is in D major, with the accustomed hint of B minor.

This development theme soon reveals its true colours by turning into Tamara's first theme with the rhythm straightened into continuous quavers. Everything subsides, and a march-like rhythm emerges, generated to begin with by the original viola figure (*poco meno mosso ma agitato*). The development theme, with altered rhythm, is answered by Tamara's second theme (ex. 46) hotted up to the march-rhythm; and a sentimentalised version of ex. 45 makes a gorgeous melody of this originally rhythmical tune:

Ex. 48

So Tamara displays new facets of her nature. Another slackening of time and pace precedes the final *poco a poco più animato*. This is, of course, the most exciting moment of all. As the pace is forced more and more, part of ex. 45 inverted (alternating with ex. 47) appears at enormous speed, Tamara's second theme following in frenetic form (ex. 49). This theme is soon blared forth on

Ex. 49

the brass in savage mockery, *ancora poco più animato*, and the horrid deed is done. Suddenly nothing is left but clarinet trills and the swaying figure of the introduction. The last guise of Tamara's clarinet melody, the sweetest and most sugary guise of all, is used, *andante*, for the tender whispered farewell. The strings are divided to play full-sounding chords in semiquavers, and the theme appears *tremolo* as the whisper is caught caressingly on the breeze.

Finally, with the lower strings' triplet semiquavers, the bass trombone and tuba of the introduction (but now in the key of D flat major) the Terek rolls on its way, bearing a corpse. The bitterness of the Terek's semiquavers are followed by the sweet arpeggios of the harp, which, with held woodwind chords, gradually die away as the fairy-tale picture fades into the distance.

NOTES ON CHAPTER 13

1. FB, pp. 130–133. The full score of this edition (lent to the author by Gerald Abraham), bears the date '11 August 1893'.
2. TA, No. vi, p. 61.
3. FB, p. 140.

4. Letter printed in *From the History of Russian-Czech Musical Relations*, 1915, p. 35, and quoted in the Moscow edition of the full score (1960), p. 2.
5. FB, p. 146, et seq.
6. Rosa Newmarch: *Concert-goer's Library*, Vol. V, p. 1. (Oxford University Press, London, 1938). The translation is inadequate.
7. FB, p. 170.

# CHAPTER 14

*Orchestral Compositions (3): The Two Symphonies*

## FIRST SYMPHONY

There is evidence that sketches of the C major symphony were made as early as 1864. The principal themes of the first movement and the general way in which they were to be developed had already been determined in a first rough manuscript dated 19 May 1864. Balakirev wrote to Cui at the beginning of August: 'I hope, but am not yet sure, that I shall bring the first *allegro* to Petersburg completed, introducing a Russian element of a religious nature, which is new . . .'[1]

It would therefore appear that Balakirev set to work on the symphony as soon as he had finished the Second Overture on Russian Themes in 1864, and set it aside again in 1866 in order to compose his Overture on Czech Themes. A guide to how much he had written by then is given by Rimsky-Korsakov in his autobiography:[2]

About one third of the first movement was already written down in score. As well as this, there were sketches for a scherzo, and also for a finale on the Russian theme 'Sharlatarla from Partarla', which I was responsible for bringing to his notice. It had been sung to me by Uncle Pyotr Petrovich. The second theme of the finale was intended to be the song 'We sowed the millet'.[3]

Subsequently this scherzo was incorporated in the *second* symphony, and a different theme of a more Eastern character was substituted for the second subject of the finale. But Rimsky-Korsakov's eccentric uncle was responsible for the first theme of the finale! It is doubtful how much of the first movement had been written by 1866. Rimsky-Korsakov's 'about one-third' would bring it as far as the change of time in the *allegro* from 2/4 to 2/2, and Gerald Abraham puts it either a few bars before this (where it reiterates the opening notes of the first *largo*) or about twenty bars after the 2/2, which must have been part of the original plan.[4] Dr Abraham inclines to the latter view, and in fact according to Balakirev's correspondence with Stassov and Cui he had already sketched out (though not written in score) about *two-thirds* of the first movement in 1864; but it is impossible to guess how much of this very early material was incorporated later.

The symphony was taken up again in the early 'nineties; it was finished in December 1897, and first performed on 11/23 April 1898 at a Free School Concert, which was also Balakirev's last appearance as a conductor. It was started, then, before Tchaikovsky had written any of his symphonies, and not finished until after his death.

The first movement opens with an introductory *largo*, twenty-five bars in length, which contains the seeds of the whole movement. Balakirev's idea, clearly, is to germinate a movement of symphonic proportions from material purposely kept as simple as possible, so that almost anything can be done with the material —and it certainly appears in innumerable different guises and shapes which, whatever the composer's intentions may have been, give much more the impression of an elaborately planned fresco than of a classical symphonic movement.

Ex. 50

The opening bars contain the germs of both the first (A) and second (B) subjects (ex. 50). The bare unison and octaves, sequentially rising quavers and simple diatonic harmonisation which follow, though looking so ordinary on paper, yet seem to have an atmosphere of unfulfilled mystery and of withdrawn contemplation—more than the *genus* of the Russian church chant from which it all springs. In the following bars, it gradually emerges and we are launched into the fascinating journey of the *Allegro vivo*.

Here, the first subject (theme A) starts in quavers in octaves (ex. 51), but very soon (at the fourteenth bar) as the theme goes on

Ex. 51

its continuously developing way, figure (a) is augmented to crotchets in an accompanying capacity (ex. 52). A rising semi-

Ex. 52

quaver scale (of D) on the strings derives from the rising quavers of the *largo*, and a short *fortissimo* passage, in which the brass play theme A, figure (a), again in *crotchets*, introduces the second subject (theme B), now still in exactly the same shape as in the *largo* introduction, but repeated in descending semitones (ex. 53). So, it seems to darken as it proceeds, as well as developing. Only a few bars later it appears in a form which, had it not been a constantly developing theme, might have been more suitably reserved for the development section (ex. 54).

Ex. 53

Theme B

Ex. 54

Theme B

It rises again to a climax on the full orchestra, followed by a chromatic rendering including a curiously twisting enharmonic change of A sharp to B flat and back. An effective *tutti*, to appear twice later, with a bass rhythm of two quavers followed by a crotchet (see figure (c) of ex. 60 p. 199), finishes the main exposition, except for a coda in which theme A, figure (a) appears in crotchets with triplet accompaniment, harking back to the later bars of the *largo*.

A change to 2/2 brings in what may be called a *second* exposition. This is, however, a continuous development of the first, which itself also contained much development. Ex. 55 gives a

Ex. 55

Theme A

Ex. 56

taste of the lovely atmosphere of this part of the movement. Theme A seems here, in the crotchet form and in canon, to be

going through the same chromatic process as theme B did in
ex. 53. A variant of theme A (ex. 56, theme AA) introduces a new
theme, perhaps a 'secondary' second subject, but based on the
falling figure of theme A, figure (a) and a variant of the rhythm
of figure (b) of the same theme (ex. 57, theme C). The *tutti* section

Ex. 57

which, except for a short coda, ended the first exposition, also
ends the second exposition, over a tonic pedal of B major.

The middle section of the movement—to call it *the* development would be futile—starts with theme B, now also in augmentation. It soon appears in a similar form to ex. 54, with notes of
twice the value (ex. 58). The continuous development and

Ex. 58

Ex. 59

Ex. 60

augmentation process cannot be divided up into ordinary symphonic sections. After a pause, a variant of theme B is introduced

as an episodic theme (ex. 59, theme BB). A fugato development of theme C bridges a change of key back to C major and
theme A is revealed for the first time in minims, getting gradually
louder until the *tutti* passage which ended both expositions is
reached, only this time with the addition of the minim version of
theme A, figure (a), on the trombones (ex. 60). If the word
'recapitulation' has any meaning in the context, then this is it.

Theme AA is used as a bridge, not to theme B, which has so
recently been fully exploited, but to theme BB, leading to the
coda, *più animato*. The passage work is a diminution of theme A,
figure (a), but the whole effect, in spite of the increased pace, is of
added spaciousness as well as excitement (ex. 61). The two

Ex. 61

quaver/crotchet figure is augmented to two crotchets and a
minim (figure (c) of ex. 60). Theme B is repeated in its most
prolonged form and then, considering the movement as a whole,
the only possible form of theme A is used for its last, grand
peroration—in *semibreves*, ex. 62, on the full brass. If, up till this

Ex. 62

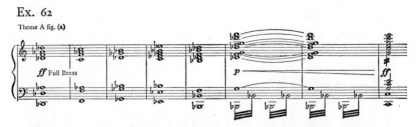

moment, the form has been in doubt, not so now. The continuous
mosaic pattern, based on a 'central' *largo*, blossoms in all directions, to the final fortissimo augmentation of all the parts, accompanied by fresco-like diminutions of themselves. As music cannot
proceed backwards, the *largo*, which is 'central' to the scheme,

comes at the beginning. The whole conception is unique, with impressive results, and worthy of the closest study.

The second movement, a scherzo, *vivo*, and trio, is not the one originally intended for this symphony. The scherzo eventually used in the second symphony was destined for the position, but was discarded in favour of this lively and interesting piece. It seems to have been composed in the same white heat as some of the first movement—perhaps as a result of the successful completion of a movement which had remained unfinished for so long.

It is a perfect example of a pithy symphonic scherzo, ideally suited to its place in the scheme. It does not play to the crowd, but its unobvious depth of feeling is on the same plane as the opening *largo* of the symphony. The flavour of what can only (incorrectly) be described as a Dorian mode transposed to a basis of A can hardly be missed, and is used to particular effect in the coda.

Four bars of repeated Es set up the rhythmic pulse for the first subject (ex. 63). The homogeneity with the first movement is further increased by the similarity of the second subject, announced on the cor anglais (ex. 64), to theme B of that movement—compare with ex. 53. p. 198. Its continual 'flattening'

Ex. 63

Ex. 64

course also proceeds quite similarly to the descent of that subject, though here it is a matter of key rather than pitch. Both themes recur before the start of the trio, the recurrence of the second subject being particularly interesting because of the use, on the brass, of B sharp going to C sharp. Although this is a chromatic decoration of a *tierce de Picardie*, it *does* give the effect of a minor chord (A minor) going immediately to a major (ex. 65), a similar effect to the middle section of the early 'Song of the Golden Fish'.

Ex. 65

The trio, in D minor, *poco meno mosso*, is tinged with a bitter-sweetness far removed from similar melodies in his weaker pianoforte compositions—they are merely pale reflections of a melody such as this (ex. 66). The scherzo is repeated exactly, with

Ex. 66

the addition of a coda, based on the trio melody, of exquisite subtlety, which starts *forte* and gradually rises, as it gets softer, to the high wind notes so typical of the composer, finishing on the piccolo (ex. 67), accompanied by a high chord of A major.

Ex. 67

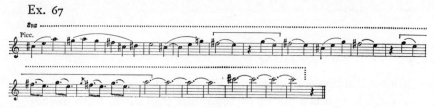

## Analysis and Criticism

The slow movement only partially lives up to the artistic preparation so carefully thought out for it at the end of the scherzo. Nevertheless, this poetic nocturne is, in many respects, an excellent third movement to the symphony. It is exotic, and the opening is comparable to the rather luscious chords near the end of *Tamara* as the princess waves 'farewell' to the corpse of her erstwhile lover. Compare ex. 68 (*Tamara*) with ex. 69 (the

Ex. 68

Ex. 69

opening of the first subject of the movement). Whereas in *Tamara* they merely give a fleeting glimpse of Tamara's rather affected nostalgia near the close of the work, here the accompanying chords in D flat are the whole basis of the movement.

A concluding codetta to the first (clarinet) theme, based on a figure used in the development followed by a rising octave figure, acts as a bridge to the second subject, in the contrasted key of E major. The opening of the first subject and the rising octave figure conclude the E major section, and the unusual form for a slow movement of 'Sonata-Rondo' reveals itself. The codetta figure just mentioned is now very beautifully developed, serving as a middle section before the return of the first subject in the original key, with semiquaver accompaniment. The second subject reappears in D major, followed by a variant of the codetta-development figure (ex. 70). The return of the first subject is

Ex 70

broken off in its penultimate bar by harp arpeggios on a diminished seventh chord. It starts again, accompanied by *tremolo* strings, but is again interrupted by the harp; a dominant chord in D flat becomes a French sixth in C major, followed by a dominant seventh in that key, and the finale follows without a break.

Such a nocturne as this might be unreservedly allowable in the position Balakirev allots to it, were it not for two rather important failings. First, the 'Sonata-Rondo' form of A, B, A, C (based on codetta figure of A), A, B, A, is too long for a slow movement in what is already a long symphony—he did not make the same mistake in his piano sonata a few years later; and, secondly, neither of the themes is sufficiently beautiful for the loving care which is lavished upon them. Even the length of the movement would be quite excusable if such a theme as that in the slow movement of Borodin's second symphony or of his second quartet were used in place of themes which just fail to be on the same plane. Balakirev found slow-moving themes difficult to compose —he was apt to find them over-sentimental or banal, as Rimsky-Korsakov discovered when he was trying to compose such a melody for his first symphony under Balakirev's supervision. Both Balakirev's themes here avoid banality, but they also just miss that supreme beauty which Borodin was able to attain.

The finale starts with Uncle Peter's 'Sharlatarla from Partarla' played in octaves on cellos and basses (ex. 71), theme A. The similarity of the outline of this theme to theme A, figure (a) of the first movement (ex. 51, p. 197), as well as its initial bare-octave treatment, *may* be coincidental, but it binds the whole symphony together. A subsidiary motif (ex. 72), is somewhat similar in rhythm to the opening fanfare of Tchaikovsky's fourth symphony.

Ex. 71

Ex. 72

Ex. 73

That the finale is going to be a superb symphonic study in rhythm is not in doubt by the time the second subject is reached (ex. 73), theme B. In the change to 6/8 time the dotted crotchet equals the previous crotchet, so that the basic tempo is unchanged. This theme is more oriental in nature. It is not dissimilar to the D major theme in *Tamara*—compare with ex. 47, p. 192—and may originally have been destined for that work. According to Tchernov[5] Balakirev was travelling third-class on the Finnish railway when a blind beggar boarded the train and sang this song in a loud voice, accompanying himself on an old harp which was out of tune, afterwards passing round the hat.

The transition to the relative minor over a tonic pedal of D by means of an A sharp, the sharpened dominant, a characteristic of Balakirev's style, is not neglected. This virile tune has hardly any melody to speak of, but is an ideal vehicle for Balakirev's overflowing vitality. A third episodic theme (ex. 74), theme C, using an accompaniment identical with that in Balakirev's second collection of thirty folk-songs, No. 22 ('There is a little tree on the hill'), possesses rhythmic punch of an unusual nature. The main accent is on the *fourth* beat, and the rest of the tune seems to

Ex. 74

work away from this beat, as Gerald Abraham has pointed out,[6] an accent on the penultimate note of the phrase being the only other discernible stress. Its rhythmic bite is enhanced by the melody's being allotted to the cellos in their upper register, accompanied by the violas (lower down), basses and harp. A crescendo leads up to theme B on the full orchestra.

The development section starts with theme A in B flat major on the cellos and basses. This is developed very fully, theme B occurring (just before a change to A flat major) as an *accompaniment*. It soon appears in its own right, however, alternating once or twice with theme C, and then being used in *fugato* over a G pedal—a more pedantic and less successful treatment. But its climax, the simultaneous appearance of themes A and B, is extravagantly exciting (ex. 75).

Ex. 75

Theme A is recapitulated on the brass, in octaves, accompanied by triplets on the rest of the orchestra, followed by the full orchestra version of theme B with percussive accompaniment, and theme C with the tonic, C, as its basis. Inevitably, themes B and C appear simultaneously (ex. 76) before a final *tempo di*

Ex. 76

*polacca*, which acts as a coda. Theme A is treated in diminution, while a broader effect is gained by the crotchet pulse lessening by more than one third (ex. 77). Once again, Balakirev achieves

Ex. 77

greater but at the same time *more spacious* excitement, making an admirable peroration to a symphony which would surely not have been so neglected in the past if it had had a more popular melody in its slow movement.

But, in a symphony of this sort, the public does seem to require a really good melody in the slow movement. Would Borodin's second symphony, or Dvořák's E minor symphony, for instance, have achieved such a favoured place in the concert repertoire without their slow movements? Would Borodin's *Polovtsian Dances* have become so well known and so much sung without the beautiful chorus of the female slaves singing of their home-land? Perhaps all the rhythmic vitality and symphonic dexterity in the world do not make up for a lack of this kind (in a mid- or late-nineteenth-century national-symphony) in the public mind. In the case of Balakirev's C major symphony, that is rather a pity, as it is a work of profound merit, full of clever and subtle touches not to be probed at a single cursory hearing.

## SECOND SYMPHONY

Balakirev began work on his second symphony in D minor in 1900. He finished it, however, only on 22 June/5 July 1908, and it was published by Zimmermann in 1909.[7] It was first performed at a Free School Concert on 10/23 April 1909 with Lyapunov conducting.

Balakirev wrote to Calvocoressi on 6/19 February 1908:

> You ask for news of my second symphony. It is progressing at the speed of a tortoise (as is always the case with my compositions) and up to now, three of the movements have been composed and orchestrated: 1st, *Allegro*, 2nd, Scherzo *alla cosacca*, 3rd, Romanza *(Andante)*: the finale has still to be finished, but I don't expect to complete it quickly.[8]

Balakirev was wrong! It was all finished four months later. And the following year, in another letter to Calvocoressi: 'I am happy to be able to write and thank you for being so good as to think of arranging a performance of my second symphony in Paris.'[9] He urged Calvocoressi, instead of continuing with this project, to organise a memorial concert to Chopin on the centenary of his birth in February 1910, and sent him the score of his newly-orchestrated Chopin Suite in this connection. The performance of the second symphony nevertheless took place in Paris. Its performances in Britain have been rare.

The first movement is short and pithy. It is in ordinary sonata form. Two abrupt chords at the beginning set the pace. Its basic emphasis is a cross-rhythm of 6/8 and 3/4 which occurs in both subjects. The first subject (ex. 78 (a)), based on the descending

Ex. 78 (a)

Ex. 78 (b)

melodic minor scale, seems to have its roots in the *deux-temps* rhythm of the second subject of the finale of Schumann's pianoforte concerto (ex. 78 (b)), and in the bassoon subject of the

Ex. 79

first *allegro* of *Tamara* (compare with ex. 43, p. 189). It is shortly repeated on the full orchestra, and a modulation to D flat major introduces the second subject (ex. 79), in that key. A comparison of the development passage of the first subject in the *slow* movement of the C major symphony (figure (a) of ex. 70, p. 204) with figure (c) ii, in ex. 79, will reveal an almost exact similarity of feeling as well as in actual notes. This augmentation into 3/4 is the result of figure (c) i, in 6/8, and makes the tempo of the passage as slow as the C major symphony *Andante*. Perhaps these undoubted similarities in both these subjects were subconscious. But Balakirev's habits of studying other works when deliberating on a new composition must not be overlooked.[10]

The second subject, very shortly afterwards, appears against a 3/4 cross-rhythm on the trombones, and its own version on three *fortissimo* trumpets destroy any misconception that the subject is too lyrical for its content in such a terse movement.

The development is short and neat. Figure (a) and the descending motif of figure (b) of the second subject are used separately and together, followed by a variant of the first subject (ex. 80).

Ex. 80

Towards the end of the development this same passage occurs, transposed a semitone down to the dominant of D minor, but with important new additions in the harmony (clashing false relations between F sharp and F natural, E natural and E flat; and figure (a) of the second subject played simultaneously with the first, ex. 81).

Ex. 81

The recapitulation modulates to allow the second subjects' reappearance in the tonic major. The addition of a short coda, *poco più animato*, based on both themes, ends a movement which is more conventional than its counterpart in the C major symphony, shorter, less profound, less experimentally interesting than its predecessor, but as incessantly modulating as most of Balakirev's music, and quite well suited to its place in the scheme of the symphony.

The scherzo *alla cosacca* is one of Balakirev's finest movements. The form, simple though it is, has much in common with the first movement of the C major symphony: the fresco-like effect of starting at a focal point and emanating from it, not with a rather Westernised idea of *getting* anywhere, but just from sheer joy and exuberance in the pleasure of the design. This is the type of development which suits Balakirev best, and the movement out-shines all its fellows in the symphony. It is almost as if Balakirev has thought that, though he required a shorter scherzo for his first symphony because of the length of the first movement, nevertheless this excellent flight of his youthful imagination was worthy of having a symphony composed *around* it.

The classical control which is exercised in this scherzo is remarkable. A six-bar introduction (of which ex. 82 is the start)

Ex. 82

"Scherzo alla cosacca" (2nd movement)

Allegro ma troppo, ma con fuoco e energico ($\text{♩} = 108$)

(Introduction)

is used again as a short development passage of thirty-six bars, as an introduction to the recapitulation of the scherzo (twenty bars), after the trio, and as a sixteen-bar coda to the movement.

The first six bars, though only setting the rhythmic pace in the first instance, are therefore not as innocuous as they seem. The main theme itself, in B minor (ex. 83), is full of pulsating

Ex. 83

Main subject

vitality. It is soon developed in a charming canon (ex. 84). A subsidiary theme (using the chord of B minor as the sub-dominant of F sharp minor) stems from the same creative flash—trumpets

Ex. 84

and trombones answered by flute and piccolo with attractive naïveté and freshness (ex. 85). The introductory figure serves as a

Ex. 85

short development and the recapitulation of the main theme is for full orchestra. Its canonic variant, ex. 84, appears in full and the subsidiary theme, now in the tonic key, is similarly orchestrated. The piccolo/flute figure becomes a cooling influence on the scherzo, which by this stage has already been worked out in *full sonata form*, without a single note being unnecessary or out of place in the development of the whole.

Rhythmic held notes on the horn make a bridge to a trio, which is based on the Russian folk song 'The snow is melting' (ex. 86),

Ex. 86

No. 33 of Rimsky-Korsakov's collection of 100 folk-songs. The continuous semiquaver accompaniment maintains the underlying excitement. An excellent example of development of this folk-theme which *achieves* nothing, and serves no *Western* purpose, but merely delights in its own exuberance, is given by ex. 87, where at figures (a), (b) and (c), the chord of the dominant seventh of E major occurs, setting out on a short journey and returning again to the starting point.

Ex. 87

In a compressed recapitulation of the scherzo, the trio theme appears as the second subject (instead of the original subsidiary theme).

The third movement, Romanza, is weak. Balakirev never allowed himself a really *banal* melody, but both the themes in the movement are devoid of interest, and afford opportunity for fake sequences to such an extent that one can only wonder how the same composer could have written this Romanza and the preceding scherzo. He could never have used such an Arensky-Glazunov movement in his early period (they were born in 1861 and 1865, respectively). The slow movement of the C major symphony is incomparably superior.

But a worse disaster is to come. A superb Polonaise follows the Romanza as the finale of the symphony. It is charged with rhythmic vitality. Both themes, ex. 88 and ex. 89, are epic and heroic in character, the second being the Russian folk-tune, 'We have, in our garden' (Rimsky-Korsakov's collection, No. 31). The idea

Ex. 88

Finale ♩ = 80 (Polonaise)

Ex. 89

Folk Song theme (Korsakov's Collection No. 31)

of a polonaise came naturally to Balakirev, and this particular example is much superior both to Mussorgsky's Polonaise from the Polish scene in *Boris Godunov* and to Tchaikovsky's Polonaise from *Eugene Onegin*. The return of the first subject after a full exposition of the Russian theme seems to imply a simple ternary structure but, before many more bars, the second subject of the Romanza has returned, its weak chromatic romanticism jarring horribly, *l'istesso tempo*, in the midst of the splendid Polonaise. It becomes more and more impassioned, with *forte* triplet accompaniment. A *poco più mosso* section brings relief in the form of further development of the folk-theme, but the Romanza theme appears again before a coda which is one of Balakirev's most successful efforts at adding a maximum of ripeness to his themes *without* romanticising them (ex. 90)! How curious is his superb treatment of both the main themes coming, as it does, immediately after the regrettably passionate relapse to the weakest section of the slow movement. Balakirev himself compared his treatment of the folk-theme here (ex. 91a) to a similar treatment in *In Bohemia* of the second theme there (ex. 91b).[11]

Ex. 90

1st theme
Coda

This magnificent Polonaise, then, is spoilt by its reference to the slow movement. True, Balakirev uses this device in his piano sonata, but there the innocuous *intermezzo* not only gives no

Ex. 91 (a)

Ex. 91 (b)

Balakirev's quotation from "In Bohemia" (letter to M. D. Calvocoressi 7/20 February, 1909)

offence but, rather, enhances the atmosphere of the finale. Also, his impassioned emphasis of Tamara's clarinet theme towards the end of that work has a specifically ruthless, cruel and extremely effective purpose. In this symphony he seems to have been trying to portray his idea of perfect womanhood—hence the title, Romanza—and to have wished to mix this up in his masculine and virile Polonaise. But Balakirev's 'ideal woman', not only here, but in his songs devoted entirely to the subject of 'love', falls very flat on twentieth-century ears.

## NOTES ON CHAPTER 14

1. FB, pp. 178–180.
2. *Record of my Musical Life* (*Letopis moei Muzykalnoi Zhizni*), Moscow, 1928, p. 39.
3. No. 8 of Balakirev's collection of forty Russian folk-songs.
4. A. F., *Music and Letters*, xiv, 1933, p. 355 et. seq.
5. K. N. Tchernov: 'Mily Alexeyevich Balakirev, recollections and correspondence', from *Muzykalnaya Letopis*, Coll. III. Leningrad, 1926.
6. See above, note 4.
7. FB, p. 196.
8. CC, p. 12.
9. Letter of 14/27 September 1909.
10. see chapter 9, letter to Tchaikovsky of 30 October/11 November 1884.
11. CC, p. 13.

# CHAPTER 15

---

*Original Pianoforte music, and chamber music with pianoforte.*

---

## EARLY PIANOFORTE MUSIC

Balakirev's first pianoforte composition was the Grand Fantasia on Themes from Glinka's opera, *A Life for the Tsar*, written in 1854–55, and revised in 1899, when it was published by Zimmermann. This fantasia is not an arrangement, but an original work based on Glinka's themes (from the trio, 'Do not torment yourself, my dear') and, on the whole, on Glinka's harmonies. It is pianistically dexterous, and shows how brilliant the young man Balakirev was; it already shows, too, a rare ability for spinning a web of sound around a melody. Three examples, 92, 93 and 94, show the first bars of the *andantino* theme, in B flat minor, in increasingly exciting forms. A six-and-a-half-page cadenza of great difficulty follows, based on the same theme, and the finale is a Polonaise in which almost every pianistic device is used. Like *Islamey*, this is hardly a piece for humble pianists. But its enthusiasm is infectious, and the final *tempo di polacca* is stimulating and exciting.

Balakirev was not unjustified in his later poor opinion of his Scherzo No. 1 in B minor, finished in March 1856, published by Stellovsky in the early 'sixties and re-issued by Gutheil. He imitates, rather weakly, Chopin's B minor Scherzo, and the work is full of vague meanderings; the use of chromatic scales, octaves and the like reveals a rather floundering technique. The first

Ex. 92

Grand Fantasy on Theme from "A Life for the Tzar" (1899 version)

Ex. 93

Ex. 94

theme, *allegro assai,* in B minor, is four-square. The first eighty
bars all consist of four-bar phrases answering four-bar phrases,
sometimes repeated without the alteration of a single note. The
second theme, *meno mosso,* in A flat, has little to recommend it.
The return to the first theme and original key and tempo is
achieved quite well, but the first part of the recapitulation is note
for note the same as the opening sixty-four bars, and is finished
off by a double bar, as if the young man were saying, 'Now, I
think I'll do something different.' One passage with a low rumbling bass is notable, being an element in his mature piano style.
There are other passages of interest in this way, especially in the

use of the augmented fifth, but with a much more Glinka-flavour than he later developed (ex. 95).

Ex. 95

After finishing his C major symphony in 1898, Balakirev no doubt looked over the score of this early Scherzo and found it wanting. But with the piano work contemporary with it, the Nocturne No. 1 in G sharp minor, he was better pleased, since he revised it (in B flat minor) for publication by Gutheil. The opening melody of this Nocturne is in a slow compound quadruple time with delightful lilt. But in the middle section, rather curiously, the time changes to *allegro non troppo ma agitato*, in D major and B minor. This naïve *scherzando* passage bears Balakirev's unmistakable imprints—the augmented fifth, and much use of a tonic pedal in D, and a dominant one in B minor. It is followed by a single return of the original *andante* melody. The *scherzando* passage is hardly very comfortably sandwiched between the B flat minor melody. The general effect is scrappy.

A Polka in F sharp minor was the earliest piano work of Balakirev to appear in print. It was published by Denotkin, to whom he sold his first twelve songs in 1859, and appeared in a later edition by Gutheil. Although, like the Scherzo, it is somewhat four-square, based entirely on one melody, it has a certain innocent charm and a very attractive coda. It owes much to the polkas of Rubinstein (particularly Op. 14, No. 6, 1854) and Smetana (1855).

Both the early edition of Balakirev's first two Mazurkas (Stellovsky, 1861) and the later Gutheil editions are extant, and throw light on the changes which Balakirev later made to his music written in the early 'sixties. In fact, the changes are very slight. The Mazurkas stand very well in their early form. The

original of the first, in A flat, is almost identical with its later
revision; the elimination of a double bar or two, the filling out of
the odd chord, the change of one quaver in the melody, these are
the only differences. In the second Mazurka his 'improvement'
consists in the changing of the key from B minor to C sharp
minor, the addition of a repeat, and the filling out of chords and
harmonies. A four-bar example of the two versions, a few bars
from the end, shows a section where rather more filling out has
been thought desirable (ex. 96a and 96b). But, in essence, the
two versions are the same.

Ex. 96a

## OCTET

Balakirev wrote the first movement of an octet for piano, violin,
viola, cello, double bass, flute, oboe and horn before Glinka left
for his final visit to Berlin in the spring of 1856. Sixty-nine bars of
a scherzo were also sketched out (later the basis of his second
Scherzo for piano). Glinka indicated to Balakirev various changes
he might make in the instrumentation—such as, for instance,
putting the oboe up an octave[1]—and was favourably impressed.
It is probably an arrangement of his earlier septet (1852), which
is not extant; 'Quatuor original Russe' also dates from this time.

Both these works were composed before his arrival in St Petersburg late in 1855.

The opening *allegro* of the octet is in the Beethovenian key of C minor, and it starts in a manner suited to the key (ex. 97). But,

Ex. 97

even in such an early composition, there is a predilection for a mixture of relative keys (C minor and E flat major in the first two bars)—this he derived from Glinka. The piano has much the most important part, blossoming into semiquavers and Schubertian triplets. The weak second subject shows signs of immaturity.

The working-out follows strict classical lines and is of some length. That Balakirev understood the meaning and use of sonata-form cannot be disputed. The main interest in the work, however, is the brilliant extemporisation of the pianoforte, for both the themes are juvenile and the development shows little of originality.

## *ISLAMEY* AND THREE SHORT PIECES OF THE EIGHTEEN-EIGHTIES

Discounting the piano compositions of the last decade of his life, Balakirev's Oriental Fantasy *Islamey* is his finest piano work, and, with no exception, it is his best-known composition. It was composed very quickly, between 9/21 August 1869 (in Moscow) and 13/25 September (in St Petersburg).[2] He had been forced to resign from the conductorship of the Russian Music Society, it will be remembered, and Nicholas Rubinstein had promised to come and play at a Free School Concert in the following season. The concert took place on 30 November/12 December 1869, when the Fantasy received its first performance. The audience were rather nonplussed—stunned—but it soon became popular, and in spite of its difficulty it was the only work of Balakirev, according to the publisher Jurgenson, to make a profit for the latter (letter from Jurgenson to Balakirev of 2/14 November 1886).[3]

Balakirev considered *Islamey* as a study for his projected symphonic poem *Tamara*. It is perhaps the 'ultimate' technical piece in the pianoforte repertoire. Pianists who can play it effectively are not numerous. There can be no point in such a piece unless it can be flung out as if it were a technical joke—an amusing ten minutes of exotic colour, insistent rhythm and pianistic exhibitionism. The notes are super-abundant, certainly, but not one is superfluous or unnecessary to the glittering, rippling, effect of colour. The build-up towards the end is not unlike the build-up in *Tamara*—but whereas the orchestral work is sombre, dark and haunting, the piano work, finished so much more quickly, is light, airy; superficial, perhaps, in a way, but fascinating, intriguing and thoroughly worth while.

There are three themes. The first two, ex. 98 and 99a, are dance rhythms, which Balakirev had jotted down on one of his

Ex. 98

Ex. 99a

Ex. 99b

visits to the Caucasus in the 1860s.[4] The first was known there as *Islamey*—a Kabardian dance. The two themes are developed side by side. The rhythmic impetus carries all before it, casts everything in its way to one side, relentlessly pushes onward with hypnotic power. The opening key is B flat minor. The repeated note figure and augmented second in the first subject and the consecutive fifths and flattened seventh in the second are important, adding considerably to the pagan and Eastern effect. Soon an appearance of the second theme in D flat major gives it the air of a lawful symphonic second subject (ex. 99b). The melody only is quoted. But in fact this occurrence of the theme is only a development of its first appearance. The continuous development and modulation is broken for the introduction of the third and central theme, in D major, *andantino espressivo*, which Balakirev heard an Armenian actor singing at Tchaikovsky's house in Moscow in the summer of 1869.[5] The first part is quoted as ex. 100.

Ex. 100

Already the themes have spread themselves out, mosaic-fashion, but the real development is left until all three have been established. The D major theme soon reveals itself, in a heightening of tension and increase of pace, to be as rhythmical as the other two. The first theme enters again in B flat major and, after various modulations, appears in repetition over an A flat pedal, *poco a poco più crescendo ed agitato*. After a climactic build-up, that innocuous seeming *espressivo* D major melody receives the following treatment: ex. 101.

Ex. 101

But this is not all—it occurs again, preceded by an octave *glissando*, with the semiquavers of the third bar of ex. 101 in double octaves. A *presto furioso* variant of the second theme seems to herald the end, but not until a final version of the D major melody has been blasted forth, *fff*, in bars of exceptional difficulty. It is surprising how well this theme lends itself to such forceful treatment. Indeed, these latter versions, crude though they are, seem to be no less characteristic of it than the initial presentation.

The general effect of startling vitality is difficult to resist, and none but the most academic of listeners would quibble at this piece of 'glorious pianorama'.

The only other new piano compositions of Balakirev between *Islamey* in 1869, and 1900, were two short Mazurkas and the Study-Idyll, *Au jardin*. This piece was sold to Jurgenson in 1884, when proof copies were passed between the composer and that firm.[6] It was dedicated to Henselt. Mazurka No. 3 in B minor and No. 4 in G flat major were published by Jurgenson in 1886. The third Mazurka was also arranged for piano duet. Both were dedicated to young ladies named Maria (Maria Volkonska and Maria Gurskalina). They are light and do not contain very much of interest—occasional pieces, and rather insipid.

*Au jardin*, in D flat major, owes something to the style of Henselt, a style Balakirev absorbed into his own, with widely spaced arpeggios in the left hand and a long, plaintive melody in the right which, unfortunately, in a middle section, is thumped out, *poco più mosso*, in broken octaves with a chordal accompaniment; but as the heat subsides a lovely passage (ex. 102), is heard. This hardly compensates, however, for the somewhat cheap *poco più mosso* passage, and the piece as a whole is not quite successful.

In 1899 Balakirev was considerably older than Borodin,

Ex. 102

Andantino quasi allegretto

Mussorgsky or Tchaikovsky were when they died. Had he died in that year, *Islamey* would unquestionably be his only—if not great—piano work, at any rate his only original piano composition worthy of a place in the regular concert repertoire of today. But Balakirev lived more than ten years longer. These years were probably more fruitful in piano writing than in any other form of composition.[7]

## LATE PIANOFORTE MUSIC

Balakirev met his new publisher, Julius Heinrich Zimmermann, in 1899. The first result of this was the publication of his early Fantasia on Themes from Glinka's opera, *A Life for the Tsar*. He then looked again at two earlier compositions: the incompleted scherzo from the octet and the first movement of his youthful piano sonata. Taking a theme from each, he composed his Scherzo No. 2 in B flat minor, one of his greatest compositions.

The Scherzo opens with a short introduction, based on the first subject marked 'quasi corno'. The main B flat minor theme is of the quality of the *King Lear* overture, mature and easily handled (ex. 103). The varying harmonies and distribution of the constantly

Ex. 103

recurring melody not only show a rare insight into all the hidden possibilities of the onward-moving theme, but show a quality of building up patterns around a theme almost unique in its variety. It is pianistically superb, like *Islamey*, but, unlike that piece, reasonably easy to play.

14. Autograph of the title page of *Islamey*

15. Autograph of the first page of *Islamey*

A subsidiary subject is in D flat major, over a repeated A flat pedal (ex. 104). But, just as the main subject modulated before long D flat, so this theme modulates soon to B flat minor. It is no

Ex. 104

to D flat, so this theme modulates soon to B flat minor. It is no less than thirty-one bars in length, the pedal changing to B flat at the modulation.

A recurrence of the introduction effects a modulation to D major, which is the key of the middle section, *l'istesso tempo* (ex. 105). The fact that it is in the same time affords opportunities

Ex. 105

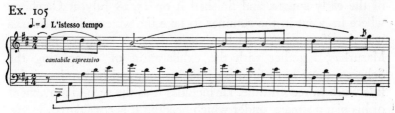

for this theme's later introduction during the recapitulation of the other two themes. Its shape is hardly changed from that of the second subject of his early sonata, from which it is taken.

After a recapitulation of the introduction, the main subject is repeated in virile fashion. The sixth bar occurs again with interesting harmonies (ex. 106). Another harmonisation of this subject is to be found soon after a return to five flats, introducing the central theme quite naturally, in D flat, without slackening off *tempo* or tension. It is the main subject, however, which ends the work, most beautifully (ex. 107).

Ex. 106

Ex. 107

The Scherzo was completed on 29 June/12 July 1900. Balakirev must have been pleased with it, for he went straight on to compose his D major Mazurka (the fifth), based on the second movement of the early sonata, and finished it on 15/28 July at Gatchina, where he went in the summer to take the waters. The Mazurka was therefore completed in sixteen days. A study of his early Mazurkas, together with the exhilaration of completing the Scherzo, must have fired his imagination, and he produced this fine work in record time. He includes it as the second movement of his piano sonata, under which heading it is considered.

When he had finished the Mazurka, Balakirev set to work immediately, at Gatchina, on his first two Waltzes. The *Valse di bravura* in G major he completed in less than three weeks, on 3/16 August. It has nothing so impressive or powerful to say as the Scherzo, and it is clearly meant to be in a lighter vein. But it is probably one of the best of Balakirev's lighter pieces, playful and amusing, with no sign at all of weak lyricism. Similarly the *Valse mélancolique*, finished in the following month (27 September/10 October), by which time Balakirev had returned to St Petersburg, is pleasantly nostalgic rather than deeply melancholic.

It seems that Balakirev felt that a waltz is not a type of piece which should have any particularly deep meaning. The darkening of the colours for the second subject, in D flat, which bears the familiar stamp of augmented fifth and pedal (ex. 108), arises from

Ex. 108

the use more of a somewhat richer water colour, perhaps, than of the bold strokes in oils of the Scherzo. But this is surely intentional, and there is no reason why the same artist should not feel himself free to use water colours as well as oils.

The third and last Scherzo was composed in the following year (9/22 June 1901). It starts ambiguously, in F sharp major–D sharp minor, with the latter predominating. Bare octaves add to the doubt of tonality. The first sentence of twenty-four bars is repeated exactly a perfect fifth lower, ending in G sharp minor. The main key is still in doubt. A dominant seventh of F sharp major for eight bars, is followed by the same chord in D major for another phrase. The G natural of this chord, however, suddenly becomes an F double-sharp, going to G sharp, which turns out to be the supertonic of F sharp major, and a quick crescendo ushers in the main theme *fortissimo*. In this way, the subtle feeling that one is hearing this theme for the *first* time only, after an introduction, is imparted by the composer, but in fact this is the third time that it as been exposed in its entirety.

A middle section, in D major, starts with another version of the theme which has a chromatic inner part over a short pedal (ex. 109). This is repeated over a moving bass. Before long a

Ex. 109

second subject, also in D, appears; it bears a harmonic relationship to the 'Song of the Golden Fish', but transformed here into a happy little ditty. After a repetition in D flat major, a return to F sharp brings now delightful variants of both themes, simple but effective, and a variety of 'cyclic' form is achieved by leaving the bare octaves until near the end, when they become broken octaves, which lead to an emphatic finish. This Scherzo lacks the power of its predecessor, but captivates, nevertheless, by its charm.

Besides the *Valse di bravura* and the *Valse mélancolique*, Balakirev wrote five other Waltzes between 1901 and 1906. They are all in an attempted lighter vein, and are weak watered-down versions of his great piano works. The *Valse-Impromptu* (No. 3, 21 August/3 September 1901) in D major, is pianistically interest-

Ex. 110

ing. Its second theme (rather Glinka-like, ex. 110) reappears in a form reminiscent of Liszt's *Valse Oubliée* in F sharp major. The fourth Waltz in B flat major (13/26 July 1902) bears the sub-title *Valse de Concert*. It is quite an extended work, but the contents hardly justify the length, both the themes being distinguished by their feebleness.

For the fifth Waltz in D flat major (14/27 February 1903), Balakirev has apparently run out of sub-titles. It has no distinctive features whatever. The sixth Waltz in F sharp minor (11/24 July 1903) is less disorganised, but is still uneven in quality. The second theme, *più animato*, in A major, forms the basis of an excellent coda with chords in the right hand accompanied by arpeggio triplets in the left. The last Waltz, in G sharp minor (8/21 July 1906), has a first theme which it would be kind to describe as nondescript and, unusually for Balakirev, effects a weak modulation to the relative major key, rather than hinting at it without modulation. It would be tempting—but quite untrue—

to consider that Balakirev's powers were falling off at this stage. The very next piece he wrote, after this watery waltz, was one of his greatest short piano pieces, *La Fileuse*.

Balakirev wrote two Mazurkas after the fifth in D major. The sixth, in A flat major, was completed on 13/26 September 1902; and the seventh, in E flat minor, on 24 August/6 September 1906. The sixth Mazurka opens with promise that is never fulfilled but the seventh Mazurka is a much more successful work, written as it was immediately after *La Fileuse* while Balakirev was still under the influence of the inspiration of that work. The first theme, in E flat minor, is a wistful melody of charm, and a D major theme has rhythmic impetus, even if the inevitable A sharp (augmented fifth) finds its way into the third bar.

Besides the early Nocturne, Balakirev wrote two others, both of which are more fully-flavoured than the weaker mazurkas and waltzes. In the second Nocturne in B minor (29 May/11 June 1901) the first melody is reminiscent of Glinka's song 'The Lark'. A lovely harmonisation of this melody (ex. 111) occurs just before

Ex. 111

the second theme, *l'istesso tempo, religioso*, which is lucidly and originally treated. (The first phrase is almost identical with the opening melody of Schubert's *Great* C major symphony!)

The only weak moment in the Nocturne is at a change of time to 12/8 (B flat major), but the coda (based on the *religioso* theme with a low rumbling bass in triplets, followed by the first melody accompanied by the triplets, now well-spaced in arpeggios, in the left hand) is very beautiful.

The first subject of the third Nocturne in D minor (25 August/ 7 September 1902) owes something to Glinka and Chopin, but is not by any means entirely derivative; a *poco più animato* (D major) theme (ex. 112a) bears Balakirev's imprint, not only in the A sharp of its second bar, but in the darker shades of its reprise (after the reprise of the first theme, ex. 112b).

Ex. 112a

Ex. 112b

All Balakirev's other piano works are short pieces with different titles, and for the most part they reach a higher standard than the waltzes, mazurkas and nocturnes, though not higher than the fifth Mazurka, nor than the second or third Scherzos. These remaining pieces will be divided into two groups, according to their speed.

None of the slower pieces is really weak, and some are of great beauty. The *Berceuse* in D flat major, for example, finished on 16/29 June 1901, is one of the most beautiful lullabies ever written for piano. Cradle songs seem to have inspired Balakirev with some fine, original melodies. The *Berceuse* is prefaced by the following note: 'A mother tenderly sings a lullaby to her son. The child sleeps, but a bad dream frightens him and he awakens, crying. The mother sings again and the child falls asleep, lulled by a delicious dream of golden butterflies fluttering around him to the tinkling of little silver bells.'

The preface allows of a piece in ternary form, starting with the lullaby, interrupted by the bad dream, and after the recapitulation of the lullaby a delightful coda based on the butterflies and silver bells which lulls the listener into the dream of the child.

The melody, twenty-two bars in length, with two bars of introduction, is too long to quote complete, but the first phrase reveals some of the beauty (ex. 113).

Ex. 113

The middle section, *adagio misterioso*, owes something, perhaps, to the rhythm of the slow movement of Chopin's B flat minor piano sonata. Gradually the dream rises from the depths and the child wakes up with a cry. The tears of the child subside in a cadenza and the lullaby starts again, with varied harmonies after the first eight bars. The bell-butterfly coda consists of very high notes over held chords in the middle register, and widely-spaced arpeggios in the bass.

Another lovely piece, *Dumka, (Complainte)*, (7/20 June 1900), is reminiscent of *Balakirev's arrangement* of Glinka's song, 'The Lark'. After a short introduction in Dumka style, a melody in E flat minor is exposed, simply harmonised. The second, contrasting melody is spiced with G flat major, but the joy of that key, though it contrasts well with the first melody, is not without its own wistful tinge. Both melodies, on their reappearance, are decorated with triplet semiquavers. The second theme is imperceptibly darkened towards the end (ex. 114) and the tonality of E flat minor is finally established, though an extended series of arpeggios

Ex. 114

with a G natural *tierce de Picardie* gives an impression of the major mode.

*Gondellied* in A minor (20 April/3 May 1901) is probably not called a *Barcarolle* on purpose. It owes something to Chopin, certainly, but is on a much smaller scale, more easily comparable with Fauré's A minor Barcarolle. When the gondola has been gently pushed out from the bank a theme in A minor is played by the right hand, interrupted by ripples towards the end of the melody, which closes delicately (ex. 115). The second theme, in Ex. 115

F major, provides a suitable contrast, but rather lacks distinction. It is at *this* point in its comparable design that Chopin's *Barcarolle* becomes more and more interesting, but Balakirev soon falls back on the second half of his first theme, which works itself into a climax, subsiding in fluid triplets to the reprise of the first melody, with tasteful accompaniment. The second half of the melody is particularly well done (ex. 116). A coda on a tonic pedal is based Ex. 116

on the F major theme, and the whole dies away in the topmost register of the piano. Tonic major harmony alternates with the added sixth of the flattened seventh (ex. 117); or it could be taken Ex. 117

as a French sixth on the flattened super-tonic, with G in place of G sharp.

Two pieces whose exact date is not known, but which are mentioned in letters of 1903, are *Rêverie* in F major, the last slow piece to be considered, and *Chant du Pêcheur* in B minor. The *Rêverie* is rather sentimental, but does not lack expressive feeling. It is based entirely on one melody, whose development culminates in a cadenza, *vivo agitato*, and the recapitulation brings some additional attractions; but only in the harmonies of the coda does the melody achieve its *round* timbre and the dream its mellow depth. Finally, all sinks into a dreamless slumber on a low F.

*Chant du Pêcheur* is a brilliant enough piece, an excellent example of Balakirev's pianism, with fast octaves of the melody in the right hand and a difficult, flexible motion of swinging up and down the keyboard in the left. The colouring is similar to that in the third Scherzo, and it is a good example of a Balakirev waterpiece (in the literal sense).

Instead of adding further to his Scherzos, after the third (in 1901) he turned his hand to fast and brilliant pieces of various sorts. The first of these was a *Tarantella* in B major (1/14 August 1901), which consists of fifteen pages of *allegro vivo* quavers, in 6/8 time, and demands, like many of Balakirev's quicker-moving pieces, a prodigious technique. Chopin and Liszt are again the influences at work. Two themes are exposed in the first section, the second being in D major (ex. 118). The whole piece is more

Ex. 118

(opening of 2nd theme)

derivative and less interesting than *Islamey*, without being much easier.

*Capriccio* in D major (14/27 April 1902), may have been composed as a result of Balakirev's reading the D minor Prelude of Chopin. There is no holding the right hand in the introduction, which flutters about the keyboard while the left hand sits on a double pedal a tenth apart (of the root and third of the chord) with varying notes in between, all in *agitato* quavers. The first chord is evidently one of D sharp minor seventh with various decorations, which proceeds at the seventeenth bar to a chord of C sharp minor seventh. The introduction ends *andantino sostenuto* and the first subject still leaves dubiety about the key which, however, turns out to be D major. A centre-theme in B flat, *l'istesso tempo*, later (ex. 119) belies its initial nondescript appearance.

Ex. 119

Agitato assai (a tempo)

In the Toccata in C sharp minor (2/15 August 1902), the first subject is in Balakirev's clearest and most classical style—but it does *not* look back, nor is it derivative. Towards the end it is treated chromatically (ex. 120). Unfortunately a sentimental middle

Ex. 120

Più animato

subject, *l'istesso tempo*, provides too great a contrast, and its sugary sweetness is not very happily sandwiched between the pungent crusts of the first subject.

Very soon after the composition of his Toccata, Balakirev produced what is probably his most successful light piece, the *Tyrolienne* in F sharp major (22 November/5 December 1902). The first subject is carefree in its abandon, and the second subject, in D major, is wholly delightful, both in its initial simple presentation (ex. 121) and in all its subsequent development. Both themes

Ex. 121

Risoluto

are surrounded by triplets, and the work is not too long for its content nor too difficult for its worth. (The first subject ends rather attractively, ex. 122.)

Ex. 122

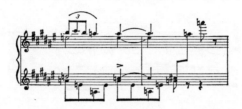

On the other hand, the *Humoresque* in D major (19 March/ 1 April 1903) is more obviously but less engagingly amusing. It is in a similar strain to the 'Ballet of the Unhatched Chickens' from Mussorgsky's *Pictures from an Exhibition*, but if it is more pianistic than that picture, it is also more derivative, less inventive. Similarly, *Phantasiestück* in D flat major (17/30 September 1903) lacks fantasy or any distinctive feature; it probably owes its title to Schumann's works of the same name.

A *Novelette* in A major dates from 21 February/6 March 1906. It is quite unworthy of its composer. The feeble first melody, reminiscent of Lyadov or Glazunov, is matched by the second, which derives from Balakirev's own better works.

But Balakirev's powers were not failing beyond hope of revival. One of his last piano pieces, *La Fileuse* (2/15 August 1906) in B flat minor, is also one of his best—a Russian 'Gretchen' for solo piano, perhaps, but quite original. The first melody is of the type of the fugal subject in the piano sonata. Every accompanying semiquaver is as important as in the accompaniment of 'Hebrew Melody', its nearest equivalent from Balakirev's own earlier works. The same type of spark has inspired the old man as inspired the young man forty-seven years before, and with results whose white-heat of creation is no less remarkable. The same augmented second and accented passing notes are discernible. The second subject, in G flat major turning to E flat minor (ex. 123) is darkened in exceptional fashion near the end (ex. 124).

235

Ex. 123

Ex. 124

It is most extraordinary that the same composer who wrote this could also write the following passage (ex. 125), which is the open-

Ex. 125

ing of his *Esquisses*, or Sonatina in three movements. The rest of this work (25 September/8 October 1909) also shows signs of extreme poverty of invention.

From the early nineteen-hundreds date some sketches and fragments of pianoforte compositions by Balakirev, now in the State Public Library, Leningrad. They are quite graceful, and the worked-out fragments include a Ballade in D flat major and a

*Child's Song* in G minor. The music of the Ballade is rather reminiscent of the pieces *Au Jardin* and *Rêverie*, while that of *Child's Song* is more of the Dumka-Nocturne type.[8]

## SONATA IN B FLAT MINOR

Balakirev's biggest piano work of the last years was the Sonata in B flat minor, a work in which none of the weaknesses of those years is apparent. The Sonata is Balakirev's most remarkable composition for the piano. His first sketches of the work date from 1855, when a fugal epilogue in memory of Lermontov was planned. The earliest version was in four movements. Three movements of a sonata in B flat minor were written in the 1856–57 period[9] and were dedicated to Cui. This second version was first published in 1951.[10] The first movement might have been written by an immature Liszt, and in fact starts in almost exactly the same way as the Liszt sonata. But the second subject (D flat major *meno mosso*) is used in Balakirev's B flat minor Scherzo (1900). The third movement, *Andante*, is not very original but the Mazurka is excellent, and its form and shape are very little changed in the later sonata.

The third and final version of the sonata, dedicated to Lyapunov, was completed on 12/25 September 1905; the revised Mazurka (second movement) had been finished in July 1900.

The first movement, Andantino, takes the place of the originally intended 'fugal epilogue', but it is much more than a fugal introduction. Here, Balakirev's peculiar gift for building patterns is effectively employed by using a fugue subject of a slim, wandering, elegant nature as the unitary basis of the whole movement. To understand this movement, Bach and Hindemith must be forgotten, preconceived ideas eliminated, and mosaic patterns of the Eastern Orthodox churches called to mind, where mosaics spread themselves out in a magnificent plethora of delicate vision. (The harsh sunlight and pagan voluptuousness of *Islamey* is quite foreign to the classical serenity of this movement.)

The main subject (ex. 126), is fugal and has a variety of rhythm

Ex. 126

and a delicacy in outline which achieves suppleness at the outset. This, if developed on too academic lines, would sink into a stodge which would destroy lightness and frailty. The answer is in F minor (very correctly), and the subject, in the bass, returns to B flat minor once again. A turn is immediately taken to the relative major, where a secondary theme (ex. 127), has the two-

Ex. 127

fold function of acting as a foil to the first subject, while at the same time mating fugue and sonata-form.

Opening outwards from triplet semiquavers to demi-semiquavers, it woos the fugue-subject, which answers by showing off various angles of its figure (a) accompanied by the demi-semiquavers of the secondary subject, mounting to a climax, and dying away.

The exposition is completed; the vision returns to the starting-point of the pattern, whence it sets out on a new journey, in F sharp minor. A mild *stretto* is achieved by using only figures (a) and (b) of the subject, and the pedal-like accompaniment of the secondary subject soon enters; the keys are changed and all is repeated, starting with a semiquaver staccato accompaniment to the subject. A cadenza, in 12/16 time based on the triplet semiquaver figure and figure (c) of the fugue-subject—a figure that has not yet been used in the middle section—rises to a climax, *più vivo, brillante,* and falls away again to a return of the exposition, a recapitulation, in which the eye, starting again from the focal point, wanders slowly towards colours of a deeper hue. The answer is in E flat minor, the subdominant; and the secondary subject, in G flat major, opens its arms wide to embrace a coda of remarkable loveliness, where a closer *stretto* is achieved over a tonic pedal (ex. 128).

Ex. 128

A last *poco animando* produces, in demi-semiquaver arpeggios, a major ninth chord based on D flat, followed by the final chord of B flat major rising *pianissimo* to the top of the piano—an exceptional close to a movement which, by its very nature, avoids being as episodical as it would at first appear. As well as being constructed of patterns, it has an over-all pattern ideally suited to its content.

The second movement, Mazurka in D major, shows even more clearly than the B flat minor Scherzo in how many ways Balakirev was capable of dressing up a theme to its advantage.

To facilitate comparison, a few different versions of the two themes are quoted together (examples 129–134).

If this virile, masculine mazurka, one of the greatest of its species, acts as an excellent counterweight to the suppleness of the

Ex. 129

Ex. 130

Ex. 131

Ex 132

Ex. 133

Ex. 134

first movement, the intermezzo (third movement) is an ideal interlude between the mazurka and the finale, as well as being an
admirable introduction to the latter. It performs the same function
as the slow movement of Beethoven's *Waldstein* sonata. It will be
remembered that Beethoven rejected his *Andante in F* as being
too long, and too important melodically, in comparision with the
size and power of his other movements, to be suitable for the
sonata.

In the same way, Balakirev's intermezzo, in constant modulation with triplets in the left hand, avoids any form of sentimental
melody (ex. 135); the climax is short, and can be compared in type

Ex. 135

16. Title page of the first edition of 'Thirty Songs of the Russian People'

with the second theme of the third Nocturne. A cadenza based on the dominant of B minor falls away and the whole is repeated a semitone lower, ending on the dominant chord of B flat minor which introduces the finale without a break. The intermezzo has the function of darkening the colours, a gradual clouding over of the spirit from the mood of the mazurka towards the more stormy but equally virile and masculine finale.

The finale is as unitary in design as the first movement; both the main subjects are based on the same material. The first theme, characteristically, has a repeated phrase, the first time staying in B flat minor, the second modulating to the relative major (ex. 136). A short secondary subject (ex. 137), leads to a return of the first

Ex. 136

Ex. 137

theme with brilliant semiquaver accompaniment. The second version of the main subject (which takes the place of the second subject) is not in the relative major key but in D major (ex. 138); a darker version is used as a coda of the exposition (ex. 139, *poco a poco più tranquillo*). The little melody from the intermezzo makes

Ex. 138

Ex. 139

an unexpected appearance, gradually dying away (*poco a poco ritenuto e morendo*).

No new material is subsequently used. No development in the usual sense takes place. The next sixty bars, from *a tempo*, are merely a repetition of material used earlier on, only all a semitone higher. By a deft change two bars before the re-introduction of the second version of the main subject, the whole is transposed one tone down, so that this theme appears a semitone *lower*, that is in D flat major (instead of D major), which is the relative major key. The recapitulation of the main subject (first version) takes the following form; it follows the outlines of the theme and harmony of the exposition exactly (ex. 140):

Ex. 140

The intermezzo theme is not again introduced; the tension decreases (*poco a poco più tranquillo* as before) through harmonies based mainly on the flattened super-tonic and the mediant ninth to the closing bars, *poco meno mosso*. The penultimate chord, *ppp*, is out of the ordinary (ex. 141). It could be considered as the

Ex. 141

minor chord on the flattened leading note (A flat, C flat, E flat), with the added sixth (F natural) in the bass. A *tierce de Picardie* on the equivalent of a high held wind chord, with a *quasi-pizzicato* bass note, brings the sonata to a characteristic conclusion.

The effect of this sonata on the wary listener is of a remarkable unity of design coupled with diversity of treatment which admirably displays its material. The unity may not only be ascribed to the single main themes in the two outer movements, but to similarity of rhythm and type. Consider, for instance, the rhythm of (i) the first three notes of figure (c) in ex. 126; (ii) the three notes in the mazurka, ex. 132, marked (a); (iii) the notes marked (a) in the finale, ex. 136. These identical rhythms are each at such important places in their respective melodies that it surely cannot have been entirely by chance that they were placed in such positions in three out of four movements. Further, it would not be stretching the point too far to say that in ex. 135 from the intermezzo the first three notes are a syncopated version of the same rhythmical idea—quick-quick/slow.

The general result in the sonata as a whole is of the composer leading up to a *rhythmical* climax in the finale, while the essence of his musical *thought* has gone into the first movement, his exuberant facility for dance variations into the second, and his quality of lucid contemplation into the third. The sonata is compelling, and structurally logical. As it is the only great sonata to have been composed by one of Stassov's 'mighty handful', it is rather sad that it has found its way into the regular repertory of so few pianists.

### NOTES ON CHAPTER 15

1. M. Balakirev, Octet, ed. I. Iordan, Moscow, 1959, pp. 6 and 28.
2. See chapter 7.
3. Balakirev published a new edition of *Islamey* with the Hamburg firm D. Rahter in 1902. This edition (the one invariably used today) differs in some respects from the 1869–70 version (see also chapter 7). There are two particularly important differences:

   (1) A new transitional passage (*tranquillo*) is introduced between the first *allegro agitato* section and the middle *andantino espressivo* (D major

subject). This passage is similar to the introduction to Konchak's aria in Borodin's *Prince Igor*.

(2) Balakirev, dissatisfied with the plain chords of D flat in the first edition at the end, has substituted other chords in the 1902 version:

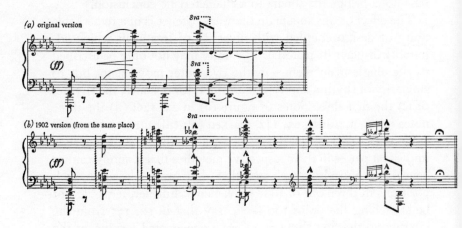

The Rahter edition was reprinted by Jurgenson in 1909.

4. See Chapter 7, note 1 (p. 99).
5. See Chapter 7, p. 89.
6. See Chapter 10.
7. Two early incomplete works for piano were a polonaise in D major and a 'Witches' Dance', now in the State Public Library, Leningrad.
8. K(4)A, pp. 264–265. The dates of all Balakirev's piano works are taken from K(4)A, pp. 246–264.
9. See appendix to Chapter 1.
10. SA, Vol. I, pt. 2.

# CHAPTER 16

*Pianoforte transcriptions and arrangements. Suite for Pianoforte Duet, and* On the Volga *for pianoforte duet.*

Balakirev's arrangements and transcriptions for pianoforte fall under various headings and are of different types. They will be considered in three main groups: original compositions based on the themes of other composers, included here because they very often are based on the harmonies also of these composers; pianoforte transcriptions of the works of other composers with added embellishment, so as to make a virtually new composition; straightforward pianoforte transcriptions of the works of other composers. In addition, Balakirev published, with Zimmermann, a group of selected compositions by K. Tausig (whom he had met on his visit to Prague) under his own critical editorship; reissued in 1895, a Berceuse by Odoyevsky, previously published by Bernard in 1849; and edited a new version of Count Vyelgorsky's song, 'I loved him', transcribed for pianoforte by Liszt. Balakirev gave this version to Jurgenson in 1886, its first publication having been by Bernard in 1842. In these three instances he has merely acted as editor and they cannot be considered as transcriptions. In his last years, too, he edited a number of other compositions for publication.

The Fantasia on Themes from Glinka's *A Life for the Tsar* comes under the first heading, but, being his first big pianoforte composition, has been considered in Chapter 15. Other original compositions of this type are *Spanish Melody* (26 April/9 May 1902), *Spanish Serenade* on a theme given to Balakirev by Glinka

(24 May/6 June 1902) and an Impromptu on the Themes of two Preludes by Chopin (1907).

The *Spanish Melody* has the same type of left-hand accompaniment as the 'Song of the Golden Fish' and the secondary subject of the first movement of the sonata. A simple exposition of the melody over a pedal is followed by its more elaborate accompaniment by triplets, similar to Balakirev's Dumka. This is a type of decoration in which Balakirev's imagination especially revelled, and its effect here is particularly fine in the repetition of a slight variation of the theme. An excellent taste of this occurs near the end of the melody (ex. 142).

Ex. 142

Allegretto quasi andantino

*Spanish Serenade,* based on a theme given to him by Glinka, is a revision of the early 'Fandango-Étude' (see page 31). This piece captures some of the elements of the Spanish guitar in the accompaniment. Its use of the augmented second is faintly Spanish, too. But a weak *passionato* passage at a change of key signature from five flats to two sharps rather mars the result, and the deliberately Spanish effect is less happy than his simple treatment of the *Spanish Melody.*

In the last three years of his life Balakirev was much occupied with centenary celebrations of Chopin's birth, and preparations for them. He arranged a Suite of four of Chopin's piano pieces for orchestra (a Study, Mazurka, Nocturne and Scherzo),[1] a Mazurka for string orchestra and for unaccompanied chorus (to words by Khomyakov). Balakirev also arranged the slow movement of Chopin's E minor concerto for piano solo, re-orchestrated and partly re-wrote the orchestral score of the whole concerto, and composed an original impromptu based on the themes of two Chopin Preludes (E flat minor and B major). Balakirev may not intend to be trying to improve Chopin's preludes, but the impression he gives in mixing up these two separate preludes (even using the term *delirando* six bars before the end) is inappropriate to Chopin's music. Apparently Tchernov persuaded him to write down this improvisation.[2]

Balakirev's transcriptions in the second category also number four. Of these, the most beautiful and effective is his arrangement of Glinka's song, 'The Lark', originally a setting of words by N. Kukolnik in 1840, and issued in a group entitled, *Farewell to St Petersburg*. Balakirev transposed the song from E minor into B flat minor, and afforded it exactly the same treatment as his later *Spanish Melody* and *Dumka*, only here he does not use triplets, except in the last bars, but semiquavers and demi-semiquavers, for his decoration. This piece attained a degree of popularity and was reissued a number of times. Stellovsky first published it about 1862, and not only Gutheil but a French publisher (Hayet), and the English publisher Augener, printed it in later years.

Balakirev introduces the introductory figure (ex. 143), into the accompaniment at the decorated repeat of the melody (ex. 144).

Ex. 143

Ex. 144

The *cadenças*, of the same sort as he later used in the Berceuse and the first movement of the sonata, have a particular freshness and appositeness here, soaring skywards over very different country to the much later violin of Vaughan Williams in *The Lark Ascending*. Balakirev's work is romantic but not contemplative, and it has the classical purity of the original Glinka song, with many of the original harmonies unchanged. Balakirev's lark, however, bursts out from Glinka's bonds into a song of fantasy, but at the same time of classical simplicity and restraint.

'Do not speak' was one of Glinka's last songs, a setting of words by A. Delvig in 1856. Balakirev finished his arrangement on 1/14 January 1903. Jurgenson held the copyright, and wrote to Balakirev[3] that he had no objection to the latter's publishing a pianoforte transcription of the work, which Balakirev sold to Zimmermann, as a note on this letter shows. The sub-title of the arrangement reads: 'Arabesque for concert performance'. It would appear to be a rather feeble song into which Balakirev almost manages, in his later arabesques on the theme, to inject some form of lyrical life. But the weakness of the song is manifest throughout. The melody is as poor, as the melody in 'The Lark' is rich, in possibility.

Balakirev's arrangements of *Rêverie* by Zapolsky and two Valses-Caprices of A. S. Taneyev (in A flat and D flat major) follow the same lines, but here again the original music is of an exceptionally tame order. Zapolsky's pretty little piece is passionately (*passionato*) triplified to little effect, and Taneyev's Valses-Caprices have difficulty in attaining the standard of Balakirev's own lesser Waltzes and Mazurkas.

All Balakirev's other works in this field fall more or less into the category of straightforward transcriptions for piano. Seven are for piano solo, three for piano duet, and one for two pianos. Three of these, all works of Glinka, the *Jota Aragonesa* (first edition c. 1864), *Night in Madrid* (1864) and *Kamarinskaya*: Fantasia on two Russian Folk-songs (20 January/2 February 1902) have been so lovingly transcribed that Balakirev seems to have added something to them while the spirit of the original score is strictly observed. The other transcriptions are more interesting for the insight they give into Balakirev's tastes than for the result, which is as good or bad as such arrangements usually were—necessary, perhaps, for the greater spreading-abroad of the works involved in pre-wireless and pre-gramophone days.

Cavatina from Beethoven's string quartet Op. 130 (May 1859), and *Allegretto* (including the well-known folk-song, 'Slava') from the second *Rasumovsky* quartet, Op. 59, No. 2 (28 June/10 July 1862) for piano solo, and the whole of the F minor quartet Op. 95, for two pianofortes, four hands, are all transcriptions of Beethoven quartets. The two-piano version of the F minor quartet was first performed by Balakirev and Canille at a musical morning at the A. A. Alexandrov Hall (St Petersburg) on 22 April/4 May 1864, and was published by Bessel in 1875.[4] Both the others were published by Stellovsky.

Two Berlioz transcriptions, of the Introduction to *La Fuite en Égypte* (piano solo, January 1864) and *Harold en Italie* (piano duet 1876) are unremarkable, as is his version of Liszt's arrangement of Chernomor's March from *Russlan and Ludmila* (1890).

Balakirev's version of Lvov's Overture to *Undine* (piano duet) reveals that the music has some merit, and the arrangement of the Romance from that old favourite of Balakirev, the E minor concerto of Chopin, incorporates without much difficulty the thin orchestral score in the solo piano part.

Balakirev's harmonisations of thirty folk-songs for piano duet are considered in Chapter 20. His only original works for piano duet were a Suite, and a piece called *On the Volga*.

The first sketches of the suite are attributed to the 'fifties, and the manuscripts are preserved in the State Public Library in Leningrad. They consist of a Polonaise-Fantaisie in the form of an incompleted orchestral score; a 'little song without words', completed for piano duet in a slightly different version; and a fragmentary scherzo. The polonaise was possibly intended as part of the programme of an orchestral suite on the subject of *Taras Bulba* by Gogol. The project was apparently not realised and subsequently Balakirev included the polonaise in this suite, which he finished on 23 May/5 June 1909.[5]

The polonaise, in C sharp minor, is masterly, and is one of Balakirev's greatest conceptions. Short, vigorous, clear, classical, purposeful, tinged with humour, it makes its point clearly, with no recourse to any of Balakirev's later idiosyncrasies. A short introduction of six bars, based on a repeated note figure and a typical polonaise rhythm, is followed by the main subject, very much in the style of the *King Lear* music—particularly the processional polonaise. After a short middle modulating passage the subject returns in unaltered form.

A trio, in A major, *l'istesso tempo*, introduces another vigorous melody in Balakirev's most classical style, the tune in bare octaves over a double rhythmical pedal. The music sweeps on to a development of the introductory repeated note figure, sparsely and effectively harmonised, and the trio theme occurs in G major in thirds. A chromatic passage over a bass tremolo pedal and a repetition of the repeated semiquaver figure precedes the recapitulation of the polonaise, which is exact, and is followed by an exquisite coda, on the trio subject over a tremolo tonic pedal, concluding as at ex. 145. This polonaise is worthy of a place at the head of polonaises by Russian composers.

Ex. 145

The second movement, 'Little Song[6] without Words', is a piece in the folk idiom, in a Borodinesque style—or was Borodin acquainted with the earlier version? It is not quite in the same style as Balakirev's folk-song arrangements for piano duet—though it starts off as though it might well be.

The third and last movement is a long and brilliant scherzo and trio. Although not up to the superb standard of the polonaise, it is ideally arranged for piano duet, which, perhaps, the more orchestral polonaise is not. The scherzo is also vigorous and harmonically interesting. In the trio Balakirev seems to be indulging in a rather trite little tune, as indeed he is, but after the recapitulation of the scherzo its appearance in the coda is delightful (ex. 146), though it lacks the freshness of the coda in the polonaise.

Ex. 146

The Suite shows how Balakirev, just before his death, has tried to recapture his youthful simplicity. This has not been difficult in the polonaise which was mostly written in his early days in St Petersburg, but the scherzo perhaps only appears to possess such a simplicity.

Amongst the manuscripts of Balakirev, in the possession of A. S. Lyapunova in Leningrad, is a short original piano duet called *On the Volga*, not published during his lifetime.[7] It is very much in the style of his folk-song arrangements. His piano duet arrangements are of the *second* group of thirty folk-songs (1898), the first group of forty songs having been arranged for voice or voices and piano only. It is possible that this piece dates from the earlier period (1866), which includes most of Balakirev's Volga collection. It is tasteful and simple, but contains no unexpected harmony, nor is it nearly as interesting harmonically and rhythmically as his 1898 arrangements for piano duet.

### NOTES ON CHAPTER 16

1. In this, the extraordinary situation arises of Lyapunov 'arranging', for piano duet, Balakirev's orchestral arrangement—thus Chopin's piano pieces are

rather superfluously arranged for piano duet through the second-hand medium of Balakirev's score.

2. K(4)A, p. 264.
3. Letter of 4/17 January 1903 (L(1)C, p. 165).
4. SA, Vol. III, pt. 1, p. 273.
5. ibid, p. 274.
6. Russian *pesenka*, French *chansonette*.
7. It was first published in 1948 by the State Publishing House, Moscow, and reissued in SA, Vol. III, pt. 1, p. 288, in 1954.

# CHAPTER 17

*Music for Pianoforte and Orchestra. 'Grande Fantaisie' on Russian Folk-songs (1852), Concerto movement in F sharp minor (1855–56), and Pianoforte Concerto in E flat major (1861–62, 1906–09, completed by Lyapunov).*

Balakirev wrote two works for piano and orchestra, both unfinished, in the 'fifties, and a piano concerto in E flat major, begun in 1861–62, and resumed in 1906, was completed after his death by Lyapunov.

The first part of a 'Grande Fantaisie' on Russian Folk-songs, Op. 4, was finished on 12/24 December 1852. At the end of the score Balakirev wrote 'Finis del prima parte'[1] indicating that he intended to add to it—but he never did. It is an uncoordinated piece, based on the two Russian folk-songs 'The sun is not eclipsed' and 'Down in the vale' showing brilliant piano passage work and a rather flimsy orchestral part which nevertheless has most of the thematic material.

On 12/24 February 1856, he performed the first movement of a piano concerto in F sharp minor at a University concert—his début in St Petersburg. It was praised by Serov. This concerto was also not completed, and it is therefore somewhat misleading to call it his 'first' concerto. Balakirev never considered it in this light, and he discarded it in favour of the E flat concerto soon afterwards. As it is called 'Op. 1' on the title page, it may have been the first composition he embarked upon, but the main body of the movement was composed and the rest revised in 1855–56.

It is an extended movement of little originality, owing much

253

to Mozart, Beethoven, Schumann and Hummel, with piano technique of a virtuoso order. The second theme in A major, (ex. 147), is interesting in its Mozartian connotation, and in its orches-

Ex. 147

tration, which is for wood-wind with *pizzicato* string accompaniment. The shape and style of the music are classical, with the usual opening *tutti*, and the piano has a great deal of thematic material, and not just an *extraneous* virtuoso part.

The E flat major concerto was started in 1861. In the summer, Balakirev wrote to Stassov from Nizhny-Novgorod asking him to send the score of Litolff's fourth concerto and Rubinstein's second. He was also examining Liszt's E flat major concerto at the same time. He intended to write a Requiem also, and both the slow movement of the concerto and a movement of the Requiem were to be based on the Russian church chant *So svyatymi upokoi*, the equivalent of *requiem aeternam*. By the end of 1862 the first movement was finished, the second (based on the above melody) outlined, and a plan and sketch of the finale were made.[2] In October, Balakirev wrote to Stassov: 'I played to Korsinka[3] the whole of my concerto, and he declared emphatically, banging his fist on the table, that it was better than *Lear*.'[4]

By this time, therefore, Balakirev was able to extemporise the whole concerto, but unfortunately he could not be prevailed upon to write down the second and third movements until 1906, and then only on the insistence of Zimmermann. He interrupted the composition of the finale to arrange his 'Chopin' Suite and died without finishing it. It is certain, however, that Lyapunov completed it in accordance with the composer's wishes, which he must have known well enough.

In the first movement, *Allegro non troppo*, Balakirev does not make the mistake of employing a long orchestral *tutti* to introduce all the themes, as he did in the F sharp minor concerto movement. The first theme, in E flat major, is clearly destined for a heroic role (ex. 148). It has a certain affinity with the opening of the

Ex. 148

*Eroica* symphony of Beethoven, and also with Schumann's E flat symphony, of which Balakirev was very fond, as has the next theme, introduced by the orchestra, which proves to be a secondary subject at the entry of the piano (ex. 149). The piano leaps

Ex. 149

away to glittering arpeggios, the orchestra adding a corollary to the theme (ex. 150). A *cadenza* leads to the main second subject, introduced by the piano (ex. 151). This passage, except for a

Ex. 150

Ex. 151

central *fugato*, is almost the only other place where the piano has any melodic significance.

A return of the opening *tutti*, in the dominant key, is the signal for an extended development based initially on the start of the exposition, but the second subject soon asserts more authority, and is treated to a *fugato*, starting on the piano (ex. 152). This

Ex. 152

piano passage, dry and school-masterly though it at first seems, in fact leads to an effective fugal climax on the orchestra. But it is repeated with additional accompaniments, perhaps rather annoy-ingly—for its propriety as the *main* basis of the development is questionable.

The first subject *fortissimo* on the trombones (a characteristic appearance of this theme), allows no doubt about when the recapitulation starts. The piano's entry, on a variant of the sec-ondary subject, is not very well done: a rather weak sequential passage is allowed to intrude. The second subject is allotted to the orchestra, thus producing a balancing effect (it first appeared on the piano), but because of this the piano is relegated to a purely decorative role until the end of the movement, which is perhaps rather flashy.

The second movement, based on the *requiem* theme, is most beautifully conceived. The melody is one of the loveliest of Russian Orthodox chants, and its treatment is impeccable. Here, indeed, is the starting point of the first movement of the C major symphony—compare ex. 155 and ex. 156 with the opening *largo* of that work, ex. 50 (p. 196). As this movement was originally conceived in 1862, two years before he started his symphony, it is reasonable to assume that the first form of this *adagio* movement in the concerto had considerable influence on the symphony.

Ex. 153

The theme, (ex. 153), is quoted in full. The piano has bell-like arpeggios as if, at the end of the chant, the funeral bells have rung for a time.

The piano gives out the theme in widely spaced chords, and thereafter, except for four bars of a second theme in octaves, is assigned (as in the first movement) a role as commentator on the proceedings rather than as a participant. But here, the sound of the piano in imitation of bells adds considerably to the effectiveness of the theme, and its frescoes and arabesques, exuberant as they are, increase the solemn majesty of the whole.

The second subject (ex. 154), the equivalent of *lux perpetua*,

Ex. 154

sheds its ray of hope in distinguished opposition to, or rather coexistence with, its neighbour. The exposition ends with a beautiful motif (ex. 155), accompanied by harp-like arpeggios on the piano.

Ex. 155

The development is based entirely on the *requiem* theme, which is treated contrapuntally (ex. 156), in a way which adds to the

Ex. 156

listener's insight into the melody rather than artificially playing with the theme, as in ex. 152 of the first movement.

The recapitulation, on the full orchestra, with blaring brass and brilliant piano chords, is very moving; a low E on the bass tuba is particularly magnificent. The second subject starts in C major, modulating to the tonic key (B minor) only at its conclusion. Gradually, in a coda, the *requiem* theme dies. The first theme of the first movement is used as a bridge to the finale—this device is not entirely convincing.

The introduction to the first theme of the *allegro risoluto* finale shows a typical facet of Balakirev's tortuously chromatic (but *not* cloying) harmony and melody (ex. 157). The first theme is

Ex. 157

Ex. 158
1st subject

announced by the piano (ex. 158). It is full of rhythmic vigour, but the real interest lies in the second subject—not a theme, really, but just a set of patterns. The whole concerto was planned, and this movement was in an 'extempore' state by late 1862, if the letter of Balakirev to Stassov quoted above (p. 254) is to be believed. Therefore it may be that the bell-like tones of this subject were played to Mussorgsky as well as to Rimsky-Korsakov, and if so, then the similarity of the second subject (ex. 159), with

Ex. 159

the ringing of the cathedral bells from the Coronation Scene of *Boris Godunov,* which can hardly be missed, is of exceptional interest.

And yet, Balakirev uses this idea quite differently from Mussorgsky. With Balakirev the effect is gay, effervescent, after the solemnity of the slow movement; but with Mussorgsky (in his own orchestration, not Rimsky-Korsakov's) the effect is solemn and full of foreboding. Balakirev's bubbling joy is always close to a key, whereas Mussorgsky's orchestral chimes are more forthright, freer from any distinct tonality.

Of course Balakirev *may* have borrowed the theme from *Boris;* Mussorgsky may have thought of the idea first. For Balakirev (as we have seen) did not actually live to write this finale— that was left to Lyapunov. Also, it seems that Balakirev had originally planned the finale differently,[5] though *how* differently it is impossible to say.

A third, episodical theme (ex. 160) closely resembles the fourth

Ex. 160

Episodical theme

original theme in *Russia,* adds to the general jollity, and the only effect which fails in the remainder of the bustling, high-spirited movement, is a *fugato* passage in the development, again started by the piano but, even so, it is much better placed than the *fugato* in the first movement; and, immediately preceding this *fugato,* the trumpets, *nobile,* play the first theme of the first movement.

This theme also occurs in B major, just before the end of the movement, but it is rather dragged in, and neither of its occurrences in the finale quite achieve as noble a result as seems to have been intended. Nor is the effect one of cohesion. In fact, the first movement is the weakest of the three, melodically and from the point of view of development. The whole concerto is bound to suffer as a result, but the second and third movements are surely interesting enough to warrant its being performed now and then.

# Analysis and Criticism

## NOTES ON CHAPTER 17

1. S.A., Vol. III, pt. 2, p. 274.
2. ibid, pp. 269–270.
3. Rimsky-Korsakov.
4. Letter of 11/23 October 1862.
5. K(4)A, p. 222.

# CHAPTER 18

## *Choral Compositions and Choral Arrangements.*

Six of Balakirev's original choral works were written for the Polotsky College for Girls in Vitebsk, a large town in White Russia about a hundred miles north-east of Smolensk. The Headmistress of the college was Maria Samochernova, Balakirev's first cousin (daughter of his uncle Vasily Yasherov), who was aided by her sister Anna Yasherova.[1]

At this college much time was devoted to music. Both choral and solo singing were encouraged. Some of the girls learned to play the piano and violin, conducted the choir, and attempted to write music—Balakirev published a Polka-Mazurka by O. Orlova in a supplement to *Nuvellist*.[2] The most gifted singers performed songs by Glinka and Balakirev which the latter had sent to them, and the choir learned Balakirev's hymns and songs.

In 1891 Balakirev visited his relations in Vitebsk. His reception at the college was enthusiastic. Everyone was amazed by his piano playing and delighted by the simplicity of his manner. The fact that Balakirev composed so many works for Mrs Samochernova and the college shows how warm were his feelings towards them. Her frequent requests to him to write songs or hymns were always met, though naturally, being occasional pieces, they were written speedily. They are all for women's voices in three or four parts.

The texts of these pieces, too, cannot be considered as the flower of Russian poetry, although one is set to an early poem of Pushkin originally written in honour of Tsar Alexander I.

The words of the others were by Mrs Samochernova herself, A. Yasherova, N. Zabelina-Bekarevich, a pupil at the college, and the poet Vladimir Likhachev. The verses express gratitude to the college and teachers, and to the 'most august patroness' (the Empress herself), and a salutation to the 'beloved bishop', the immediate head of the college.

In the first 'Leaving Song of the Pupils of the Polotsky Ecclesiastical Girls' College' the harmony is simple, and the melody straightforward but somewhat uninspired. It is in three parts, unaccompanied. Mrs Samochernova, in a letter to Balakirev of 30 November/12 December 1891, had requested Balakirev to write the work—the first he wrote for the college. The words, by A. Yasherova, start as follows: 'The golden time has flown away, the season of carefree childish years. Farewell, dear college! We send you our warmest greetings.'

The 'Second Leaving Song of the Pupils of the Polotsky Girls' College', 'Farewell our unforgettable haven' (words by N. Zabelina-Bekarevich) is Balakirev's last choral composition. It was written in July 1908, and is also in three parts, unaccompanied. The sweet nostalgia of the words of the young former pupil is not echoed in the music.

In March 1898 Balakirev composed music for a 'Hymn in honour of the most august Patroness of the Polotsky Girls' College, the Empress Maria Feodorovna', in four parts with piano accompaniment. The words are again by A. Yasherova, but it is more sentimental than either of the 'leaving songs'. According to Mrs Samochernova it 'produced a *furore*',[3] and she took the liberty of sending a copy to the 'most august lady' herself. A 'Hymn for women's choir' (four voices, unaccompanied), to words by Likhachev ('Beneath the shadow of Thy overflowing mercy'), published in 1899, belongs to the same category; in a reference to the 'two crown-bearing Marys', Balakirev divides a word by a pause. He was not always very careful in his setting of words, and neither of these hastily composed hymns is musically in the front rank.

The opening of a hymn in four parts, unaccompanied, to words by Mrs Samochernova herself, 'Praise to Almighty God', is solemn and purposeful. But sentimental touches similar in character to those in the hymn to Maria Feodorovna appear in the repeats. This hymn is dedicated to the opening of a new building in the Polotsky College.

Now that the 'most august Patroness' had been suitably honoured, it only remained to sing the praises of the Tsar himself. For this purpose, Balakirev was asked to set 'The Prayer of the Russians' by Pushkin, whose jubilee was celebrated in 1899. Balakirev set it in four parts, unaccompanied, and also published an arrangement for mixed voices. The opening words are identical with those of the old Russian National Anthem. Pushkin wrote the poem in 1816 when he was seventeen.

In 1902, for the twenty-fifth anniversary of the primary schools of St Petersburg, Balakirev composed a School Hymn for a women's or children's choir in four parts, unaccompanied, 'We sing you a hymn, O dear school' (words by P. Lebedinsky). The sugariness of the words are unfortunately reflected in the music. This is Balakirev's least successful choral work. Writing for small children did not perhaps inspire him to the greatest heights—this is quite distinct from his beautiful cradle songs.

Nizhny-Novgorod may have forgotten Balakirev at the time of his concert there in 1870, but in 1889 the Nizhny-Novgorodians invited the Director of Music of the Imperial Chapel to write a hymn in honour of the Grand Duke of Vladimir, Georgi Vsevolodovich, the founder of Nizhny-Novgorod. They were celebrating the seven-hundredth anniversary of the birth of this remote prince. The hymn was sung in Nizhny-Novgorod on the 4/16 March 1889 at a public meeting of the Archive Commission, and on the next day at a public meeting of the Society for the Propagation of Literacy.

The epic and heroic nature of the words, by Likhachev, inspired Balakirev to a greater degree than any of his other choral works except for the Glinka-Cantata. It follows the style of Russian folk-song closely, and its movement is like a solemn processional hymn.

It is written for unaccompanied mixed chorus in seven parts, only the altos not being divided. It starts with an episode per-

263

formed first by the tenors and basses in four parts (ex. 161) which
is later repeated by mixed voices. The basis is a simple melody,

Ex. 161

rather reminiscent of the chorus of welcome to Ivan the Terrible
in the *Maid of Pskov* (Rimsky-Korsakov) and the archers' theme
in Mussorgsky's *Khovanshchina*. Its character, though, is perhaps
that of an ancient Russian battle-song. It is severe, unhurried,
controlled, creating a noble and manly picture of a Russian
warrior from ancient times.

At the words 'to the heavens' the melody moves upwards in all
the parts in masterly fashion. A central *andante* is followed by a
short conclusion to the hymn in which praise is proclaimed 'to
the lowlands of Novgorod' and to Prince Georgi.

Balakirev wrote six anthems for unaccompanied voices for
performance in the Imperial Chapel; and one anthem for women's
or children's voices, also arranged for mixed voices: the Easter
anthem, 'Christ is risen' on a traditional orthodox melody,
which he also used to such great effect in his song, 'Starless midnight coldly breathed', No. 3 of his last group of ten songs. This
anthem was sung by the chapel choir when the monarch was in
residence during ceremonial religious processions.[4]

Of the other anthems, perhaps the most interesting is 'Rest
with the holy ones' (*Requiem*), the theme of which is used in the
slow movement of the E flat piano concerto. This is also a traditional melody of great beauty, treated in a manner suited to its
solemnity. It is very difficult to translate religious titles into
another language, but rough translations of the titles of the
remaining anthems are: 'From Heaven the prophets', 'Thy soul is
regenerated', 'All flesh is silent', 'It is worthy' and 'Song of the
Cherubim'.

Balakirev frequently starts in homophonic style, even if only
for a bar or two, then proceeds to contrapuntal imitation of the

voices, returning again to the homophonic style when the imitation has played itself out. So it is in 'Song of the Cherubim', which is in a ternary form of this kind. Or it may happen a number of times, producing a type of rondo form. He does not deny himself the full use of chromatic harmony on occasion (dominant thirteenths being rather prominent in the major key); his treatment of voices is adequate and the effect is never cloying.

But for the most part the writing is austere. A particularly interesting feature is the occasional use of a second bass part doubling the first bass an octave lower, sometimes producing a very low note indeed—these Russian basses must have sounded magnificent if they could sing such notes effectively.

Balakirev's most important choral composition is the 'Cantata for the Unveiling of the Glinka Memorial in St Petersburg', completed on 10/23 February 1904. Balakirev had already invited friends to hear it in a piano duet version. But as he wanted the first performance in Russia to be at the inauguration of a monument to Glinka commemorating the centenary of his birth in 1904, he refused to allow it to be performed at a Free School Concert.[5]

For political reasons the monument was not unveiled until 3/16 February 1906, by which time the work had been performed twice in Paris.[6] Miss N. Friede of the Opera sang the soprano solo (she was a mezzo-soprano, but the part is not high), and the chorus and orchestra of the Maryinsky Theatre directed by Napravnik performed the cantata in the Grand Hall of the Conservatoire. This was the last public appearance of the elderly Balakirev (he was heartily applauded).[7]

The cantata is in three distinct sections, which follow one another without a break. In the first part there are similarities with Russian folk-songs, but no actual quotations from any of Glinka's works, although a thorough knowledge of these works has brought about a closeness of feeling. The second movement, for soloist and orchestra, is rather of the character of Glinka's romances. But in the finale, quotations are made both from *A Life for the Tsar* and *Russlan and Ludmila*—the quotations conclude the cantata, which turns out to be rather a hotch-potch. The

central Romance for soprano solo is out of place in a work which
starts in the folk style, and finishes in the same way, with quotations from the more exciting moments of the two operas.

The words, by Vasily Glebov, are also curious. The first verse
tells of the 'song of the Russian people' which is sung through
the whole land—in forests and fields. But the second part, sung
by the soloist, is devoted to words of this sort: 'You created our
school . . . in all its glory—its rays shine brilliantly, thanks to
you, in the same way as the sun, king of the world, shines in the
sky . . .' The third part: 'Life for the Tsar and immortal Russlan
are the foundations of our music: to Michael Ivanovich Glinka,
GLORY' ('Slava, slava, slava' in Russian),

Like the overture to *A Life for the Tsar* the cantata starts in
G minor. The first theme, in its leaps of fourths and fifths, is
typical of Russian folk-song, and bears a certain resemblance to
'Mir, v zemle siroi . . .' ('Peace, in the damp earth') from the
epilogue of *A Life for the Tsar* (ex. 162). Compare it also with

Ex. 162

ex. 185, from the group of songs written at the same time (1903–
1904). It is introduced by four tenors and continued by four-part
male voice choir, unaccompanied. An orchestral answer is not
unlike the famous song, known in the West as 'Song of the Volga
Boatmen',[8] (ex. 163). After a repetition in D minor, this time by
altos and tenors, the orchestra, *poco animato*, embarks on a
peasant dance type of theme (ex. 164). The full choir, in four parts,

Ex. 163

Ex. 164

sings the first theme with orchestral accompaniment, and the orchestra leads directly to the entry of the soprano solo. A short *recitativo*, concluding with a passage reminiscent of Glinka's *Valse-Fantaisie* is followed by an aria which is rather typical of Balakirev's weaker type of lyrical melody.

The third part of the work starts in D flat major, with an *ostinato* bass on the bassoons. The peasant dance theme is re-introduced, *allegro animato, come sopra*, while the basses sing, over a pedal, of the glory of the sublime Bayan, a character in *Russlan* (the archetype of 'the Bard'). A general crescendo ushers in the full chorus, singing in unison 'Life for the Tsar', on a motif from the introduction to that opera, and 'immortal Russlan', while the orchestra plays the opening bars of the overture to *Russlan and Ludmila* (ex. 165). The glory to Glinka part is also

Ex. 165

sung in unison, on an arpeggio of B flat major. The soprano soloist adds her voice to the general clamour here, while the orchestra, *più stretto*, plays almost note for note the same as at the *più stretto* at the end of the introduction to *Russlan and Ludmila*.[9]

Balakirev made a number of arrangements of the works of other composers for chorus. Of two arrangements of songs by Glinka, the 'Cradle Song' from the cycle *Farewell to St Petersburg*, published in 1900, is more important than 'Venetian Night' (*c.* 1887). Both are for an unaccompanied mixed chorus. The 'Cradle Song' is in seven parts, all the parts being divided except the soprano. The second basses sing an octave below the first, but

are marked *non obligati*. The effectiveness of this arrangement
may be seen from ex. 166. (It is just as well, perhaps, that the
bottom A in the second bass part is not obligatory.)

Ex. 166

His own 'Cradle Song' to words by A. Arsenev (No. 4 in the
early group) Balakirev arranged for two-part women's or
children's choir with accompaniment on a small orchestra or
piano. He has slightly altered the interlude and conclusion, with
the results of added colour and less simplicity which such an
arrangement must betoken.

'Mazurka', arranged, from two Mazurkas of Chopin, for unaccompanied mixed chorus in six parts (two tenor and two bass
parts) to words by Khomyakov, is Balakirev's biggest choral
arrangement. The two Mazurkas are Op. 6, No. 4 in E flat minor
and Op. 11, No. 4 in A flat major, starting at bar 16. He has
transposed them into F sharp minor and A major, and the work
is in ternary form, the first mazurka being repeated after the
second. The melody remains, for much of the time, in the soprano,
except in the second section, where it is sometimes given to the
altos. The first tenors also have an interesting part to sing, and
again the second basses sing an octave lower than the first basses.

This 'Mazurka' was published in 1898, but its first performance,
together with the arrangement of Glinka's 'Venetian Night', was
given on 17/29 March 1887 by the choir of the Imperial Chapel at
a concert in aid of the disabled.[10]

Balakirev made three other choral arrangements, all of folk-
songs from his second group, *Thirty Songs of the Russian
People*.[11] They are for unaccompanied mixed chorus in four

parts. The titles are 'Nikita Romanovich', 'The King's Son from Cracow' and 'Oh! My Heart'. The first two were published in 1902 as *Two Legends,* and the last exists in manuscript form only.[12] All use basically the same harmonies as in the arrangement for voice and pianoforte, though the keys of 'Nikita Romanovich' and 'The King's son from Cracow' are both changed to G minor from G sharp minor and F minor respectively.[13]

Nearly all Balakirev's choral works, then, were composed either for his own choir, or for the Polotsky College, or for special occasions. They are compositions, more than any of his others, of a working musician composing as an artisan rather than seeking 'inspiration' in the more 'romantic' meaning of that word. As such, they achieve a remarkably high standard, but the feebleness of the words and the general context and style of most of them, as occasional pieces, will hardly secure a lasting platform for them.

## NOTES ON CHAPTER 18

1. RA, p. 342 et seq. Extensive use has been made of this article.
2. 1899, No. 6.
3. RA, p. 345.
4. TA, No. vii, p. 72.
5. RA, p. 349.
6. See chapter 11: letter to M. D. Calvocoressi, of 10/23 February 1906.
7. *Russian Musical Gazette* (Findeisen), 1906, Nos 7–8.
8. No. 40 in Balakirev's 1866 volume of arrangements.
9. Balakirev uses the time-signature 6/8, whereas Glinka's time is 6/4.
10. RA, p. 359.
11. Nos 6, 8 and 27.
12. Institute of Russian Literature, f. 162.
13. RA, p. 360.

# CHAPTER 19

## Songs

### EARLY SONGS, 1855–65

Balakirev's first three songs date from 1855, and were written in Kazan. They were not published until 1908, as *Three Forgotten Songs*: 'Thou art so captivating' to words by A. Golovinsky, 'The Link' to words by V. Tumansky and 'Spanish Song' to words by M. Mikhailov. Of these songs, 'Thou art so captivating' is the most interesting in that it is the first early work of Balakirev that he later considered worthy of publication. It is in 6/8 time with a very simple crotchet/quaver accompaniment, and owes much to Glinka. The song might, indeed, have been written by Glinka, and even the charming little coda is in Glinka's style (ex. 167). Nevertheless it is from these beginnings that Balakirev's

Ex. 167

fondness for writing poignant bitter-sweet codas over a pedal sprang.

All Balakirev's other early songs, twenty in number, were written between 15/27 January 1858, by which time the first in the group (Brigand's Song) was completed, and 16/28 June 1864, when he finished writing down 'Dream', No. 20, though he had played it to Stassov on the piano in November 1863.[1] The last songs in the group were published by Stellovsky in 1865.

The first eleven of these songs were composed in 1858, and two of them are masterpieces, No. 4, 'Cradle Song', and No. 11, 'Selim's Song'. 'Cradle Song,' to words by A. Arsenev is masterly in its two-verse simplicity, the second verse being identical to the first. In this song, Balakirev shows himself to be a miniaturist of the first order. This is the song which Sir Henry Wood orchestrated so delicately.[2] The slow running semiquaver accompaniment and the voice part turning frequently within itself have a lulling and soothing effect (ex. 168).

Ex. 168

Both the song written before the 'Cradle Song' and the one written after it are as delightfully simple as that song. In No. 3, 'Barcarolle', the accompaniment gives the required lilt; the second half becomes more passionate and agitated, subsiding into a semi-quaver low B flat and A natural rumbling bass to a *pianissimo* finish. No. 5, 'The Bright Moon' (words by M. Yatsevich) is almost as beautiful as 'Cradle Song'. It is in ternary form, and the simple running quaver accompaniment in the first section

Ex. 169

(ex. 169), and at the end, bears a strong resemblance to the semi-quaver accompaniment in 'Cradle Song'. The melody is well constructed, the middle section being in the relative minor key, and the coda shows some advance from ex. 167 ('Thou art so captivating'), though still remaining essentially uninvolved (ex. 170). The song ends as it began, with four chords.

Ex. 170
(conclusion)

A different type of song is 'The Knight' (No. 7, words by K. Vilde). This is a subject which has not remained unexplored by other composers. The tale is of a bride left for five years by her knight, whom duty has called to the wars, and her cry of 'O pain past bearing, bereft I remain' is repeated by the knight himself at the end of the song when he hastens home only to discover that the grave has closed over his loved one. The crushing chord used to denote the 'pain past bearing' is only an inversion of a German sixth, and the rhythm used for the galloping horse is rather commonplace.

At the point of the saddling of the steed by the 'young man, bold and free' in the next song, there is a similarity to 'The Knight'; but this song, 'I'm a fine fellow' (to words by A. V. Koltsov) has more to recommend it than its predecessor. It bears these familiar marks of Balakirev's style at the beginning: the augmented fifth, and the mixture of major and relative minor keys (ex. 171). The introduction of semiquavers in the second verse

Ex. 171
Allegretto

Should I young and brave fel-low that I_ am_

is economical and effective. At the close the augmented fifth has turned into a minor sixth (ex. 172).

Ex. 172

Numbers 9 and 10 may also be treated as a pair, both being love-songs to words by Koltsov. But neither of them is quite able to obtain the effect which Balakirev was aiming for. 'Come to me', No. 10, dedicated to Cui, is rather longer than 'My heart is torn', No. 9, and perhaps the means used to illustrate the palpitating heart in the latter, and the continuous triplets in the former are of some interest.

It is quite another matter with the last of the 1858 group, 'Selim's Song', the first poem of Lermontov which Balakirev set to music. This song is a masterpiece of economical beauty, perhaps only surpassed in the same sphere by the 'Song of the Golden Fish'. The only means Balakirev uses for an Eastern effect is an augmented second melodically employed between B natural and C double sharp. The eight-bar introduction is in a mixture of B major and G sharp minor, but the duality is not obtained by the sharpened dominant of the major key in this case, but by switching directly from one chord to the other. Here, as in the 'Cradle Song', *it is not only* the accompaniment but the melody which is of haunting beauty, and only means which could almost be called 'naïve' are used. The effect, though, is masterly.

In the powerful and sad melody, *allegretto con bravura*, the singer tells how, by the light of the moon, the young warrior sets off to battle, exhorted by his loved one to be pious and brave (*amoroso, poco allargando*) and faithful to the prophet. In a middle section, *agitato*, based on the original melody with a triplet quaver bass on the piano, the singer foretells that he will perish shamefully if he betrays his love. The music slows down to a shortened version of the opening, with semiquavers in the accompaniment (ex. 173). The harmonies at figure (a), the modulation to B major at figure (b), which had not occurred in the

Ex. 173

first verse, the immediate return to G sharp minor at figure (c), and the simplicity of the chord structure at figure (d), are a few of the more interesting points in the song.

The next three songs (Nos 12–14) were composed in 1859. In neither 'Lead me, O night!' dedicated to Mussorgsky, a short song in F minor to words by A. N. Maikov, nor 'Rapture' (or 'Exaltation'), to words by Koltsov, is the melodic line of much interest; but in 'Rapture' the accompaniment is quite assured.

The finest of these three songs is 'Hebrew Melody', No. 13, set in B flat minor to a poem of Lermontov after Byron. The melody admirably fits the words: 'My soul is very sad. O hasten, singer, and take your golden harp, and let your fingers straying over it awaken sounds of blessed Paradise . . .' Balakirev uses a *largo* introduction for 'My soul is very sad', followed by a passionate *allegro* with a most lovely semiquaver accompaniment; the last two lines of the first verse give an idea of how lovely the setting is (ex. 174). The delightful use of an *appoggiatura*, an auxiliary note, an accented passing note and an A natural followed by an A flat at figure (a), the beautiful rising part in the left hand at figure (b), and the chords including the use of the flattened supertonic and the naturalised leading note at figure (c), are of particular interest.

Balakirev composed only a pair of songs in 1860. Both are

Ex. 174

settings of words by Lermontov. The first, 'Why?', affords a good
opportunity at the end for a juxtaposition of F minor and A flat
major: 'That is why I mourn; while you are full of joy.'

Probably the greatest song he wrote, the second to be written
in 1860, was the 'Song of the Golden Fish'. The fresh, passionately frigid enchantment of Lermontov's words, of the mermaid
enticing her victim to the soft sea-bed, where the years and
centuries will glide past in marvellous dreams, is perfectly caught
in the music, with the softly lapping waves and the lilt of the
siren-like seduction in the accompaniment, and the melody turning in upon itself bewitchingly. The clean, cool, chromaticism
of the harmony is an enchantment in itself, with its bold simplicity.
Particularly fascinating is the mixture of minor and major at bar
10 (ex. 175). The middle section, starting at bar 40 (ex. 176), shows

Ex. 175

Ex. 176

clearly that this is no E sharp chromatically decorating F sharp,
but an F natural making a chord of D minor in its own right. The
use of triplets in the right hand of the accompaniment for the
'noiseless dance' (ex. 177), is a delightfully simple addition. At bar

Ex. 177

64 (ex. 178), towards the end, things become more impassioned
at the words (transliterated) 'lyubyu kak volnuyu struyu'—'I

Ex. 178

love thee as the rippling wave' and continuing, 'my love, *my life*,
come to me'. The top A, at bar 71, on the word 'life', is the climax

(at the very end of the song), and after this the coda on the piano gradually subsides into the frigidity of the opening bars.

'The Song of the Golden Fish' must surely be counted among the world's greatest songs. It is a perfect miniature of impeccable loveliness, of restrained passion, of frail brittle beauty. Of its kind it is unsurpassed. Balakirev never wrote again anything quite like it in innocent boldness. The boldness perhaps remained, but the innocence was lost.

The last four songs, 'Old Man's Song', words by Kolstov, 'When I hear Thy Voice', words by Lermontov, 'Song of Georgia', words by Pushkin, and 'Dream', words by M. Mikhailov after Heine, were almost completed towards the end of 1863. Of these songs, Balakirev's later song 'Dream' (1904) to words by Lermontov is better than this one; 'When I hear thy voice' is quite charming in its unsophisticated way, but weak in comparison with its successor in the series. It is based on the rhythm at figure (a) of ex. 179; the last bars of the accompani-

Ex. 179

Love, if I on - ly might clasp thee in greet ing

ment have the equivalent of a held wind chord on the left hand, and a *quasi pizzicato* note in the right at figure (b). The song is dedicated to L. I. Karmalina.

But the gem of these last four songs, a result of the composer's visits to the Caucasus mountains, is undoubtedly the 'Song of Georgia' dedicated to N. N. Karmalin. Balakirev had met the Karmalins at Tiflis in the summer of 1863. The song he dedicated to the husband, then, is much better than the lyrical love-song he dedicated to his wife!

In 1873 Balakirev sent the score of the orchestral version of the accompaniment (together with other scores) to Ludmila Shestakova at her request,[3] and it was performed with orchestral accompaniment at a Free School Concert on 27 February/11 March 1884. This song is perhaps one of the turning points in Balakirev's career as a composer, being the first really successful attempt at what must be called an 'oriental' style for want of a better term. It is also probably one of his best attempts at a sad, wistful melody, beautiful on its own account, regardless of the words (by Pushkin) and the accompaniment which together, however, add up to a song of considerable merit. It may be wondered, though, how many sopranos would like to leap up to a high A flat on the third note of a melody (ex. 180); there are few sopranos too, who

Ex. 180

could give a ravishing enough effect to the A natural, B flat, A flat at ex. 181.

In form the song is again simple, the first verse being repeated at the end with the same melody and accompaniment, while there is a *recitando* and *agitato* middle section to conjure up the ghosts which the haunting melody brings to the mind of the listener, the song of that distant land of Georgia which the singer will never see again. The 'Song of Georgia' is the prototype of the chorus of

Ex. 181

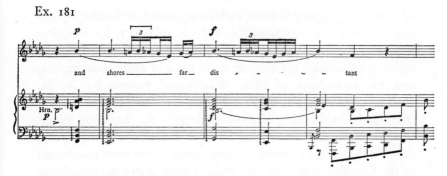

slaves from Borodin's *Prince Igor*; the melody here is not quite as exceptional as Borodin's, but it is doubtful if Borodin could have written his lovely chorus had this song never been written.

But it stands up very well on its own, though not quite on the same level as the 'Song of the Golden Fish', the 'Cradle Song' or 'Selim's Song'.

Balakirev did not publish a single other solo song for the next thirty years.

## LATE SONGS, 1895–1909

Two sets of ten songs were composed after Balakirev's retirement from the Imperial Chapel. The first was written in 1895–96 and published by Jurgenson, the second, in 1903–04 and published by Zimmermann. In addition, in 1909, he composed two songs, published as *Two Posthumous Romances* after his death.

The 1895–96 group are not comparable with his first twenty songs finished thirty years earlier. There are flashes of inspiration, certainly, and in some cases subtle and fascinating effects, but it is all much more contrived, more obvious and at the same time less naïve, less fresh and less interesting. There are touches of lyrical weakness he hardly allows himself in other published compositions, except in one or two of the latest piano works, and were no other works to have followed, a biographer might have been pardoned for alleging that the sixty-year-old man had lost for ever the inspiration of the thirty-year-old.

The accompaniments are stylistically faultless, the knowledge of romantic harmony is surer, and the comment of the accompaniment upon the words is still well done. In No. 1, for instance, 'Over the Lake' (words by A. A. Golenishchev-Kutuzov), at the mention of ripples the pianoforte is allotted *scherzando* triplets, and the monotony of 'The Wilderness' (words by A. M. Zhemchuzhnikov) is obtained by a rhythmically reiterated C sharp pedal in the bass, which also denotes the 'trudging along' of the singer. The mirage of an oasis tempts the composer to fuller harmonies, rather in the same style as the slow movement of the C major symphony (composed soon afterwards) with the inevitable augmented fifth, (ex. 182).

Ex. 182

The third song, 'The sea does not foam' (A. K. Tolstoy) attempts again to return to the simplicity of the early days; but, excellent though the piano coda is, the general effect is rather spoiled by a tendency to go to the flat side (the key is G major) in an obvious way (ex. 183). Yet another augmented fifth manifests

Ex. 183

itself here. In 'When the yellow cornfield waves' (Lermontov), No. 4, the augmented fifth occurs in the third bar, but the melody is singable, and the accompaniment pianistic when it changes to triplet semiquavers at the mention of a bubbling brook. In 'I loved him' (Koltsov), No. 5, a certain preoccupation with double flats does not raise this song above the commonplace.

The next two songs, 'The Pine-Tree' (Lermontov after Heine) and 'Nachtstück' (Khomyakov) bear certain resemblances to 'Song of Georgia' and 'Song of the Golden Fish' which cannot be ignored. When dreams of far away lands are evoked in 'The Pine-Tree', a *tremolo* accompaniment and *agitato* voice part are used in the same way as visions are conjured up in the middle of 'Song of Georgia'; while in 'Nachtstück' there is a syncopated accompaniment in D major, with a sudden change to D minor; and triplets, used in the 'Song of the Golden Fish' for the dancing episode, are here introduced at the mention of beautiful rivers. Although the climax is quite well contrived in the later song, the magical effect of the earlier songs is lacking in these two.

No. 8, surprisingly, is a tippler's song—'The Putting Right' (L. A. Mey). The interesting *acciaccatura* effect, however, fails to raise this song to the heights of Mussorgsky's achievements in the same field. In the 'Siege of Kazan' from *Boris Godunov*, to mention only one instance, Mussorgsky achieves brilliantly and unforgettably a result which eludes Balakirev.

The weakest of this set of songs is 'Mid Autumn Flowers' (I. S. Aksakov). Balakirev allows himself a number of feeble sequences and the 'greeting of past youth' at the end occurs in the key of F flat major with a return through a chromatically approached augmented sixth to B flat minor. Sweet nostalgia, indeed!

But the last song in the group, 'The rosy sunset fades' (V. G. Kulchinsky), employs both the augmented fifth and the more chromatic harmonies much more effectively. It seems as though, in this song, Balakirev is again finding his feet as a composer, and his added dexterity in the use of chromatic harmony, instead of being used as a gimmick, incorporates itself fully into the body of the song. He does not make the mistake of endeavouring to recapture the lost simplicity of the earliest songs. The pleasing harmonies and superb piano writing in ex. 184 give a clear indication of the difference between this and the other songs in the group.[4]

The ten songs composed in 1903–04 show a decided advance on the intermediate set, sometimes approaching a distinguished grandeur quite different from the first group, and a suppleness of

Ex. 184

harmony less innocent and bold, but more mature than in those early songs.

Only two may be considered as rather weak, both songs to do with love: 'Look, my friend' (V. I. Krasov, No. 6) where the melody is hardly memorable, and 'Under the mysterious mask' (Lermontov, No. 9) which contains, unfortunately, nothing much of mystery for the present-day listener. In this song, again, a middle section *parlando* with *tremolo* chords in the accompani-

Ex. 185

ment is used, as in 'Song of Georgia' and 'The Pine-Tree' from the two previous groups. He rather falls back on a formula here, somewhat feebly.

Two other songs bear such a close relationship to folk-songs that they are hardly distinguishable from them. No. 1, 'Prologue' (Mey), is simple and sad throughout, with as judicious an accompaniment as he allotted to genuine folk-songs in his arrangements (ex. 185.) The characteristic folk-song descending leap of a perfect fourth is used both here and in ex. 186 from 'Song' (Lermontov No. 8). The two quotations give a clear picture of the style of the two songs.

Ex. 186

Balakirev only attempts one song of a studied simplicity, and this is much more successful than the 'The sea does not foam'. In 'I came to thee with greeting' (A. A. Fet, No. 5) he has contrived a rather charming little melody, (ex. 187a)). It is hardly

Ex. 187a

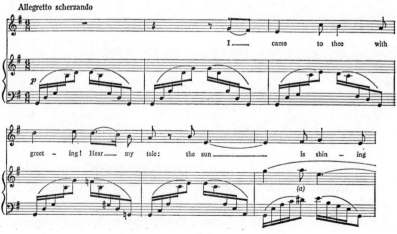

necessary to point out the augmented fifth at figure (a), and the typical accented passing note at (ex. 187 b), figure (b). The device

Ex. 187b

of echoing the voice (bar 5 of ex. 187 (a)) in the piano part (bar 6) is effective.

One of the best songs of the set is 'A whisper, a timid breath' (Fet, No. 7), written for Olenin's sister. His fondness for the young lady and belief in her artistry is apparent in this lovely, evocative, almost impressionistic song. Snatches of melody are accompanied by subtle and imaginative harmonies (ex. 188). This

Ex. 188

is a little masterpiece. It lives up to the imaginative beauty of his early accompaniments ('Cradle Song', 'Song of the Golden Fish', 'Song of Georgia'). The 'lulling' feeling is delicious, and the trill at the word 'nightingale', though by no means original, is beautifully done. Can this, it might not be out of place to wonder, have originally been a 'Fire-Bird's' song, from the unrealised opera of that name, adapted to new words by Fet?

Three of the remaining four songs are epic and heroic. All have magnificent piano accompaniments, and require no small, timid voice. 'Dream' (Lermontov, No. 2) is the song of a man lying wounded in a gorge in Daghestan (B minor and C minor) burned by the hot sun, who dreams of feasts and revels (D flat major) and brilliant nights in his beloved homeland, and of gay women—but of one in particular who in her turn (D minor) dreams of him, lying in the desert with a black wound in his breast, the blood flowing in a stream that was growing cold . . . The song is an advance on 'The Wilderness' from the previous group, but the very urbanity of the accompaniment perhaps tells against the realism Balakirev was clearly aiming at. In fact, it does not quite come off.

It is otherwise with 'Starless midnight coldly breathed' (No. 3), a setting of a 'Slavophile' poem by Khomyakov. The singer describes, with aid on a Wagnerian scale from the piano, the dark, frosty night, the whistling wind, his imagined flight, swifter than the eagle, soaring through the clouds ever higher and higher (ex. 189). In a middle *maestoso* section, with only one

Ex. 189

Moderato fantastico

more swift-ly than e-ver the sab-le wing'd ea-gle did fly thro' the air

or two chords in a bar, he sees Prague in her glory shining before him. This leads to a final section in B flat minor, *allegretto religioso*, where a solemn majestic scene in the cathedral is described to the tune of the old Russian Orthodox Easter chant, 'Christ is risen from the dead' (ex. 190). Prague cathedral is Roman Catholic. The point is therefore, that the poet dreams of an *Orthodox* chant being sung in a *Catholic* cathedral.

Ex. 190

The most dramatic song Balakirev ever wrote was '7th November' (Khomyakov, No. 4). In its Russian-Lisztian way, this is as gripping as 'Gruppe aus dem Tartarus' and requires a tremendous sense of dramatic power on the part of the singer. It describes the opening of Napoleon's tomb at St Helena. The original key is E flat minor. In 6/8 time, it starts with the piano giving out a march rhythm while the voice sings in tones of hushed excitement (ex. 191a). At the words 'furious ocean would raise towering waves' some magnificent chromatic semiquavers heighten the tension, and the climax in the accompaniment occurs just before the opening of the coffin, while the voice is silent. The key changes to B minor as the voice sings, very softly: 'The coffin stands open', the piano pivoting on an enharmonic E flat–D sharp. The semiquavers (less chromatic here) start again very quietly to the words 'not a cloud has risen, the forests and mea-

Ex. 191a

Ex. 191b

dows are still, the waters are silent and peaceful', with rippling accompaniment (ex. 191b).

The finish is similar to the opening, but the *marziale* rhythm has slowed down as the lid is set back on the coffin. The voice ends with the leap of a diminished seventh, resolved by the piano, whose opening *ritornello* is repeated, concluding with a *pianissimo* upward resolving *appoggiatura*. The march has ceased for ever. Balakirev is sure of his effects and has produced a song in the grand manner with a really effective accompaniment. In this type of song, only snatches of melody are required, and of this Balakirev is eminently capable.

The last song of the group, 'Sleep' (Khomyakov, No. 10), combines power of evocation with dramatic comment upon the words to produce quite a telling and artistic result. Every nuance of expression is written down by the composer. The long piano introduction creates a poignant atmosphere which is to be enhanced later. The song contrasts, in haunting strains, the sleep of the child, the man and the ancient, and Balakirev has achieved greatness in accompaniment, atmosphere, harmonic originality, tasteful stress of the Russian words—but not, unfortunately, in melodic line.

The piano introduction consists of continuous semiquavers, chromatic and light, seeming to waft us along the wings of sleep. In the last eighteen bars of this introduction a rhythmic tonic pedal is effective (ex. 192). At the first entry of the voice the piano

Ex. 192

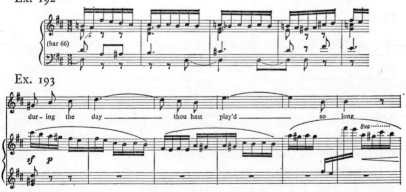

Ex. 193

is reduced to semiquavers only. The effect of the child's playing is sparingly produced by the cross-rhythm (ex. 193). At the end of the first (and each ensuing) verse, it seems as though the tonic pedal of ex. 192 is transferred to the voice on the repeated word 'Sleep! sleep!' while the piano has pivoting harmonies (ex. 194.)

Ex. 194

For the second verse the key changes from D major to G minor *poco meno mosso*, as the life of the little child flits by in a dream to its future working days. Towards the end of this verse there is a momentary excursion into B flat, with immediate return to G minor, again followed by the pivoting harmonies on 'Sleep' now a perfect fourth higher.

In the last verse the modulations are frequent, getting darker in conjunction with the words, passing through D flat at 'thy deep sleep' (referring to the death of the old man), seeming, when the words 'The dawn of everlasting life' are reached, as though it will return to D major at 'the dawn', but instead passing through B minor at 'everlasting life'—a variant of the sharpened dominant harmony, ending on a tonic pedal in lovely fashion (ex. 195)

Ex. 195

before reintroducing the words 'Sleep! Sleep!, as in the first verse. Finally, the piano gradually rises and finishes on the high held quasi woodwind chord of which Balakirev was so fond.

The general impression of these songs is of a mind which has emerged from the premature senility of the middle group into a renewed and youthful vigour, coupled with mature thought and distinguished, well controlled inspiration.

In 1909, shortly before his death, Balakirev composed two songs—'Dawn' to words by Khomyakov, and 'The Rock' to words by Lermontov. 'Dawn' may have been intended to be the first of a new series, but if so, then the plan is not known. It is the only setting of words by Khomyakov in which there are no religious connections (in 'Sleep', these were apparent in the final 'everlasting life' of the old man). The poem was written by the Slavophile poet as a young man, and is a meditation on the contradictory nature of man. This song is of the impressionistic type (like, 'A whisper, a timid breath'). Unlike the long, epic songs, 'Dawn' is intimate and near to the chamber music Balakirev so heartily despised, not only in size and scope, but in the polished and precise manner of its expression.

Actual descriptive passages are reduced to a minimum, being present only in the middle section ('When the blue sky')—one of Balakirev's most poetical passages. A choral sequence at a high register creates a sense of space and freedom, which is completed by 'vacillating' harmonies not unlike those in 'A whisper, a timid breath'.

Balakirev's last song, 'The Rock', is rather a mixture of elements. It was finished in 1909, but was evidently begun at a considerably earlier date. A. Vukhenskaya writes of this song:

It may be deduced from the handwriting that the work was composed in stages, with considerable intervals. The first version was written in the key of G sharp minor. The manuscript ended with the phrase: 'Gaily dancing through the sky'. Thus this fragment already contained more than half the whole piece. Unlike the printed version, it did not include the passage for piano dividing the first and second parts; the other differences are insignificant.

This early version already contained heterogeneous elements both of style and genre. It began in the style of Russian folk song ... The vocal melody, continuing and developing the music of the piano introduction, is entirely of the folk-song type. Thanks to the wide sweep of the melody Balakirev succeeded in creating an image of space without resorting to special descriptive methods. At the end of the first part, from the words 'Gaily dancing through the sky', the melody gradually loses the simplicity of a folk song, while in the accompaniment the form of supporting the voice is exchanged for that of chords. In the second part which follows ('But a damp trace remained . . .') the expression becomes more restrained, severer, because of the declamatory type of recitative employed.

It was here that the composition at one time came to an end. It was, evidently, considerably later that the composer finished writing, *on the other side of the paper*,[5] a passage (in the key of G minor) which was used as the conclusion of the piece when it was published. Of this new passage only three bars can be felt to be a continuation of the previous profoundly sad and spontaneously expressive music. From the words 'Quietly he weeps' the listener finds himself faced with a sentimental drawing room song, full of false, superficial expression . . . in the melody and feeble improvisations in the accompaniment.[6]

So, in one comparatively short song, his last, Balakirev manages to cram his folk-style, his declamatory style, and his lyrical love-song style, with disastrous results. And yet it is far more amazing that any revisions and completions of earlier works until this time bear no trace of apparent joins or obvious differences, than that this song, written only a year before he died, should bear such signs of its protracted and delayed growth.

## NOTES ON CHAPTER 19

1. *Russian Musical Gazette*, 1910, No. 30–31, and Institute of Russian Literature, f. 162, quoted in VA, p. 274.
2. See Chapter 2 (Note 25) (p. 46).
3. See Chapter 8. It is now thought that the orchestral version came *first*.
4. Compare ex. 184 with ex. 70 from the *andante* of the C major symphony.
5. My italics—E.G.
6. VA, pp. 326–327.

# Style, Harmony, Form and Influences

# CHAPTER 20

*Style, harmony, form and influences (1). Folk-song arrangements, 1866, 1897–98.*

Balakirev collected a number of folk-songs during his summer journeys on the Volga between 1860 and 1865. These, together with some from previous albums published by Práč, Kashin and Danilov, he harmonised in a most original fashion, and Johansen published them in 1866. In this first group there are forty songs.[1] No. 1, 'It was not the wind', No. 2, 'I'll go up', and No. 20, 'Jolly Katya in the meadows' were used in the Second Overture on Russian themes (*Russia*) in 1864. The first group is particularly interesting, taking into account how early these arrangements were made. Belyaev outbid Jurgenson for them when they were sold by the Johansen estate in 1884, but did not issue a second edition until 1895, and one with French words in 1898.[2]

Balakirev became a member of the Folk-song Commission of the Imperial Russian Geographical Society in 1897. He harmonised, on their behalf, Thirty Folk-songs from the Arkhangel and Olonets Governments from the 1886 collection of G. O. Dyutsh and F. M. Istomin. These were published by the Society in 1900. He also made arrangements of them for piano duet (in this case, sometimes producing two stanzas differently harmonised), which were published by M. Bernard in 1898. Jurgenson later published a second edition.[3]

The choice of keys or modes for these songs is well varied. As far as the types of song are concerned, they fall into four main categories: wedding songs, as 'It was not the wind'; peasant dances, as 'I'll go up' and 'Jolly Katya in the meadows'; laments (to use the familiar *Scottish* term for the type, which is probably its best translation into *English*), as 'Beyond the farmstead' (No. 4, first group) and 'Oh! My heart, woe is me!' (No. 23, first group); and peasants' or boatmen's songs—for example, the song popularly known as 'Song of the Volga boatmen' (No. 40, first group). (Balakirev was the first to publish this song.) There is also the occasional religious song, usually of the lament type, and street song of the towns ('Under the green apple tree', No. 29). It is not only choice of keys but the order of the songs which makes for variety in the collections.

In the first group, Balakirev has not apparently intruded his own personality on the songs, but, as far as possible, has harmonised them very simply, with concise care. As they are entirely free from the contemporary text-book methods of Western theorists, their freshness is extraordinary for 1866, and even today they show an originality combined with suitability which few arrangers of, for example, Scottish folk-songs have been able to achieve a hundred years later[3A]. Certain particular aspects are dealt with in detail, since much of Balakirev's early output of orchestral compositions is to some extent influenced by the kind of treatment he allots to such tunes as these. The translations of the titles of the songs, which are in very colloquial Russian, can only be rough.

'It was not the wind', No. 1, is remarkable for its use of what would be called in Western terminology the Dorian mode— D to D with no flats or sharps (ex. 196). No B flats or C sharps are used, even at cadences. The flat leading note, at figure (a), and
Ex. 196

Larghetto ♪=112 (No. 1)

the major subdominant chord, at figure (b) seem to give just the right flavour to the song.[4]

Another frequent harmonic trait is the use of the bare fifth, with no third. No. 14, 'Young, young girl' (ex. 197) shows the remarkable use of such a bare fifth at figure (c).[5]

Ex. 197

If, as so often in a folk-tune, any harmony at all seems to be inappropriate, then Balakirev uses only bare octaves and attempts no strait-jacketing of the tune. Ex. 198, No. 7, 'Long Hours',

Ex. 198

provides an excellent example, and so also does the opening of the famous 'Yo! heave, ho!' (No. 40) which is left almost entirely unharmonised.[6] The repeat of the tune here (Ex. 199) is treated

Ex. 199

with a barbaric bareness so much more suited to the sweating hauliers than Tchaikovsky's later version of the same theme.

Sometimes Balakirev uses an inner pedal to great advantage. Take, for instance, the theme (used as the first theme of the *allegro* in *Russia*) 'I'll go up', No. 2, (ex. 200), where an inner

Ex. 200

repeated pedal of C, at figure (d), produces exactly the right humorous effect—to describe this as a double accented auxiliary note on the F and D would be futile as well as incorrect.[7]

In No. 8, 'We have hired the land', the swinging, dance-patter theme is used in canon with the piano (ex. 201); this is not

Ex. 201

the same kind of effect as *podgoloski*.[8] Balakirev was not interested in the *form* of folk-melody. On this subject Olenin wrote:

Then, as now, a passionate lover and student of Russian folk-song, I was very curious to see what Balakirev thought about it. I introduced the subject fairly often, but he always seemed to be deaf to my inquisitive questions and never committed himself to a detailed opinion, but usually got out of it by answering in monosyllables. I came to the conclusion that Mily Alexeyevich valued Russian song so far as it could serve as material for musical development. He was not interested in any of the peculiarities of its structure, such as *podgoloski* [folk polyphony based on the simultaneous performance of the air of the folk-song and its variants].[9]

Perhaps it would be fairer to say that Balakirev had a composer's rather than a musicologist's view of folk-song. For none but a composer could have harmonised these songs so appropriately. (The second group of songs, however, do fall into a rather different category.)

One of Balakirev's favourite accompanimental devices is an *ostinato*. In some songs,[10] as in No. 29, 'Under the green apple tree' (ex. 202), the *ostinato* provides a bass throughout the song,

Ex. 202

Allegro vivo ♩ =100 (No. 29)

while in others,[11] the *ostinato* is an inner part with a moving bass below it. These are dance-songs, either from the country, or (No. 29) a 'street-song'. In other songs of the same genre,[12] with a bare *ostinato* accompaniment, Balakirev fills out the melody by using *two* voices, mostly in thirds.

Balakirev always uses suspensions, accented passing notes and appoggiaturas with great care. A notable suspension occurs in No. 12, 'Our Hostess' (ex. 203), figure (e), and an accented passing

Ex. 203

Larghetto ♪-88 (No. 12)

note in No. 17, 'Ivan's top-coat' (ex. 204), figure (f). Both these resolve on a very bare chord, of the plain octave in ex. 204, and of the octave with fifth in ex. 203.

Nor does Balakirev scruple to change the time-signature whenever it is necessary—neither Tchaikovsky nor Rimsky-

Ex. 204

Korsakov, in their arrangements, are so free, but impose unnecessary restraint on the songs. In No. 17 (ex. 204), 2/4 alternates with 7/4 and 4/4 to follow the natural accent of the tune. Other variations of beat can be found in No. 20, 'In the meadows', (5/4, 3/4, 4/4) and No. 32, a religious ballad (3/4, 5/4).

There are two interesting cases of the imitation of a strummed accompaniment—probably the balalaika: No. 24, 'Come let us play', and No. 38, 'Near the gate' (ex. 205). No. 10, 'The sun is

Ex. 205

Ex. 206

setting' gives another extraordinary instance of the composer's freedom from all preconceptions (ex. 206). Who else, in 1866, would have thought, in the second bar of ex. 206, of leaving alone the A flat, G flat and F in the melody, and merely accompanying it by a bare chord of F and C? The listener's ear does not have to cope with unnecessary embellishments; it takes in the unusual note (G flat) without difficulty and, if it is sympathetic, with enjoyment.

Of the two versions of the second group of Thirty Folk-songs, the arrangements for piano duet are slightly more extended than those for voice and pianoforte, the second occurrence of the theme often being varied and the harmonies being fuller. It is therefore the duet arrangements which will be considered, and only the number and key of the song will be given.

This second group of songs is stylistically less simple than the first. Many of the particular aspects of style in the first group also apply to the second, such as the rhythmical *ostinato* accompaniment (which is usually more varied here), frequent changes in time-signatures, starting in one key and finishing in another, strummed accompaniment, imitative effects and use of bare octaves where harmonisation would be unsatisfactory.

But his knowledge and use of harmonic idiom has undergone a change. There is nothing in the second group so radically simple as ex. 206 (see p. 298), so barbaric as ex. 199 (see p. 295), so essentially 'modal' and uninfluenced by the scale-system as

Ex. 207

Ex. 208

ex. 196 (see p. 294); and the use of the bare fifth is not nearly so frequent, nor so basic, as in ex. 197 (see p. 295).

Certain aspects of style in the first group are used more frequently in the second to *fuller* effect. Two short examples (207 and 208) from one of the most beautiful settings, No. 7 in B minor, show the lovely use of an accented passing note at figure (g), and exciting imitation, at figure (h). Ex. 208 is not only interesting on account of its imitation, but because of the varied treatment of the threefold repetition of the end of the tune. It is as if Balakirev has made the tune his own; as if the implications of the tune are taken in their original direction, certainly, but much further, to a conclusion of wonderful beauty. The chromatic decoration at figure (i) does not seem at all out of place—an *appoggiatura* a semitone either side of the fifth of the chord, falling (and rising) into the fifth is evidently quite in keeping with the style of the tune, as well as fitting into the (free) canon.

Ex. 209

Balakirev occasionally employs that favourite idiom of his, the augmented 5th, but never forces it unnecessarily on the melody. Ex. 209 from No. 14 in A major, illustrates its appropriate use (figure [k]).[13]

Altogether, then, the second group may be considered as *fuller* than the first, more Balakirev's own. They are really original compositions in miniature which almost make some of the folk-songs more beautiful than they originally were, while in no way detracting from their essential flavour.

### NOTES ON CHAPTER 20

1. Thirty-six songs and four variants (Nos 9, 20, 28 and 39).
2. G(1)A, p. 268.
3. SA, Vol. III, pt. 1, p. 323.
3A. With the notable exception of Kenneth Elliott.
4. Particular use of the flat leading note also occurs in No. 18, 'Assemble, comrades' (a recruiting song), No. 21, 'Go away, bad weather', and No. 36, 'Ah! that this world of bitterness'.
5. Further examples are to be found in No. 4, 'Beyond the farmstead', No. 13, 'My little strip of ground', and No. 34, 'She has taken flight'.
6. A further example is found at the end of No. 15, 'A gentleman rode'.
7. A similar pedal occurs in No. 22, 'At the end of the street'.
8. *podgoloski* = under voices.
9. A. A. Olenin: *My Reminiscences of M. A. Balakirev*, FC(x), p. 343.
10. Also No. 9, 'Lade, the sun-god', and No. 35, 'Speak, then, my cock'.
11. No. 24, 'My little duck', and No. 38, 'Near the gate'.
12. No. 15, 'A gentleman rode', No. 38, 'The length of the meadow', and No. 37, 'The girls have sown'.
13. A further example occurs in No. 3 in G flat major.

# CHAPTER 21

*Style, harmony, form and influences (2). Some special harmonic and stylistic features and influences, and some formal aspects of Balakirev's work.*

B alakirev uses some of the same harmonic and stylistic features of his folk-song arrangements in his overtures and symphonic poems based on folk-themes, and they also influence his work in other fields. An *ostinato* accompaniment is to be found, for instance, in ex. 6 from the Overture on three Russian Songs, ex. 26, from the symphonic poem *Russia*, ex. 86, from the trio of the scherzo *alla Cosacca*, the second movement of the second symphony (originally intended for the C major symphony), and ex. 74 from the finale of the C major symphony. Tamara's oboe theme, too, is accompanied by an *ostinato*-like figure, though it is not a folk theme, ex. 45.

'Modal' harmony, sometimes with a chord of the root and fifth (omitting the third) is, of course, employed in the first theme of *Russia* (the same theme as No. 1 of the first folk-song collection), ex. 25. The last bar of ex. 156—the slow movement of the piano concerto—also falls naturally into a chord minus its third. The very particular atmosphere of ancient orthodox church chants is admirably captured in Balakirev's treatment either of the themes themselves (ex. 153, Requiem theme, and ex. 190, 'Christ is risen') or of the flavour Balakirev reads into them (ex. 155, from the end of the exposition of the slow movement of the E flat piano concerto). This is the atmosphere, exactly, of the opening of the C major symphony, ex. 50.

'Modal' influence on Balakirev's original melody can occasionally be found. A good example is the piccolo's melody at the end of the scherzo from the C major symphony, ex. 67. There are instances, too, of Balakirev's composing themes which might very well have been folk-tunes. Their direct influence cannot be missed in examples 162, 163 and 164 from the Cantata in honour of Glinka, and in ex. 185 ('Prologue') and ex. 186 ('Song') from the 1903–04 groups of songs. The words in all these cases make the imitation of folk-song quite appropriate.

Balakirev's mind, then, was not harmonically stereotyped. From the very beginning his treatment of a melody, folk or original, is dictated solely by the appropriateness of the accompaniment to that melody, though the effect is never as uncompromising as with Mussorgsky.

Clever contrapuntal interweaving of themes occurs in all his overtures and symphonic poems on folk-songs. Sometimes the theme is played together with its own second half (ex. 9), sometimes with one or even two other themes (examples, 8, 29, 30, 39, 41 from Overture on three Russian Songs, *Russia* and *In Bohemia*). His contrapuntal dexterity in the first movement of the C major symphony can probably be partially attributed to his earlier work on the overtures on Russian themes.

Chromatic decoration in the accompaniment, very often weaving a web around one or two notes, is an interesting feature of style used both in dealing with folk-song (examples 35 and 36 from *In Bohemia*) and in original melodies. Of the many examples perhaps the most interesting are from the piano works— ex. 103 and 106 from the second Scherzo, and the bass of ex. 120 from the Toccata; and from the songs—ex. 174, figure (c) ('Hebrew Melody') and ex. 194 ('Sleep'). The last example shows the decoration of one note, on the word 'sleep', in the accompaniment, which does not progress in any one direction, but very happily finishes up where it started. Balakirev is fond of these short, circular trips. It would be rather futile to assert that he might as well have stood still, or, better, have proceeded from A to B. Instead of doing either his sole object has been to penetrate deeper, to put it on another plane.

Sometimes the chromatic interest is in the melody itself. What could portray the tortuous quality of Tamara's mind, as well as her siren-like seductiveness, better than her oboe theme, ex. 45?

Another favourite developing device is the chromatic contra-puntal build-up of a theme over a pedal. Ex. 38 from *In Bohemia* shows admirably how this is done. A more intimate and at the same time more intellectual example is ex. 54 from the C major symphony and the *alla breve* version of this theme, ex. 58.

Balakirev uses harmonic pedals a great deal. His music pro-bably has more pedal basses than that of any other composer. Nearly one third of the total number of musical examples in the present volume contain pedals. Although this is proportionately more than is to be found in most whole compositions of Balakirev, (much of his most interesting music is written over a pedal), yet it is true to say that one has not to turn over many pages of any Balakirev score before coming across a pedal. At times when he is not using a pedal, Balakirev skilfully employs his bass to the greatest advantage, always making it an interesting part and frequently keeping it moving quite rapidly. Nor are his pedals by any means similar in type. Only a cursory glance through the quotations is needed to show how they differ. Compare ex. 38 (*In Bohemia*), a static pedal, with ex. 45 (*Tamara*), a rhythmical one; or ex. 55 with ex. 60, from the C major symphony; or ex. 104 (B flat minor Scherzo for piano) with ex. 113 (*Berceuse* in D flat). And there are countless other varieties.

This fondness for pedals probably springs, in the main, from two sources: first, Glinka was also fond of pedals, much of his more inspired music, particularly of the 'Eastern' variety, being written over a pedal; and secondly, his early overture on Russian songs shows that he considered from the start that a pedal was an eminently suitable bass for a folk-song. But the variety of Balakirev's pedals, their distribution among the instruments in the orchestral works, and the well-contrived movement of the bass part at other times cannot be stressed too strongly. It would be quite erroneous to suppose that there is a certain sameness about Balakirev's music because of the number of pedals.

The same is true of his fondness for five flat (B flat minor and

D flat major) and two sharp (D major and B minor) key signatures. His music does not lack variety as a result of his obsession with these keys. A further reference to the examples will show not only how often he uses these keys, but that they extend over his whole output, fast and slow movements, orchestral and piano music, folk-themes and original melodies. Even if the original key of the movement is not one of the four relative to these key signatures, the chances are that there will be a modulation to one of them before very long. Even in the first movement of the C major symphony, the grand peroration, in semibreves on the full brass, is, in fact, in five flats (ex. 62, theme A, figure (a))! Both Chopin and Glinka are fond of these keys, but use them less frequently than Balakirev.

Perhaps Balakirev's constantly shifting modulations save him in this respect. He is seldom happy in the same key for more than a bar or two, and many of his themes modulate incessantly during their frequently lengthy course. This means that the key of the movement itself is not of any particular importance, but is only a basic tonality to be used as a spring-board for deeper waters.

One of the most important of Balakirev's characteristics, in developing a theme or in concluding a piece, is to darken it, to probe its depths in deeper shades, perhaps shades of purple and crimson rather than of duller greys and blues. It could be described as a ripening process of what may initially be a luscious fruit, or just a rather ordinary berry.

Compare the first appearance of the main theme of the polonaise from the second symphony, ex. 88, with its treatment in the coda, ex. 90; ex. 123 with ex. 124 in *La Fileuse*; ex. 129 with ex. 131 in the mazurka of the piano sonata; ex. 112 (a) with ex. 112 (b) in the third Nocturne; and, a particularly good example, ex. 138 with ex. 139 in the finale of the piano sonata.

Balakirev's cadences are sometimes of great interest. They are often painted in dark colours, though the last chord is usually major. The last two chords of ex. 62 (first movement of the C major symphony) show a chord based on the flattened leading note and flattened supertonic, a chord which would make a perfectly ordinary added sixth in F minor, or a chromatic one in F major, but which goes instead directly to a chord of C major as a *tonic* chord, in its own right, and not a dominant of F. The same pair of chords, but in A major, is used at the end of the piano piece *Gondellied*, ex. 117; and again, a semitone higher, in the piano sonata, ex. 141.

Balakirev occasionally alters the rhythm of a theme itself when developing it. Tamara's oboe theme, ex. 45, becomes more passionate and lyrical at ex. 48 and more frenzied at ex. 49. The lilt of the centre theme of *Islamey*, ex. 100, is transformed into the square-cut fury of ex. 101. But perhaps the most fascinating of all the metamorphoses of any one theme are those of King Lear's own theme in Balakirev's incidental music to that play. According to the stage in the play reached, the theme becomes pompous, tragic, ridiculous, pathetic, heartbreakingly sad. Examples 13, 17, 18, 19, 21, 22 and 24 are a few of the changes it undergoes in the course of this brilliant study in Shakespeare's drama.

A favourite method of decoration, derived from Glinka (particularly from the Persian chorus in *Russlan and Ludmila*) is the use of sometimes elaborate triplets to play around a theme. Naturally, both the 'Eastern' works *Tamara* and *Islamey* are full of triplets, and as early as the 'Song of the Golden Fish' they are used, Glinka-like, to accompany the words 'I call my sisters from the deep, in noiseless dance we glide', ex. 177. But Balakirev employs such triplet decoration in other types of composition also, with a chromatic depth and a ripe spontaneity. The elaboration in the first subject of the first movement of the C major symphony in ex. 55, in the repetition of *Spanish Melody*, ex. 142, and in the first mazurka subject in the piano sonata, ex. 130, show them in not necessarily Eastern dress. Two similar folk-themes are accompanied by lighter and more airily brilliant triplets at the end of the second symphony, ex. 91 (a) and in *In Bohemia*, ex. 91 (b).

The chromatic decoration of the major third of a triad by the semitone below it sometimes promotes a delicious tingle in the listener. This minor/major feeling is naïve and spontaneous in the 'Song of the Golden Fish', ex. 175, and in ex. 176 the mixture of major and minor has an indescribably lovely effect. Other later examples can be found in *In Bohemia*, ex. 36 (at the end of the quotation), in the C major symphony scherzo, ex. 65, blared forth on the brass, and in the Suite for piano duet, ex. 145 (4th bar).

Cross rhythms over the beat, or bar line, are effective too. Ex. 138, from the finale of the piano sonata, shows its delicate use in a left-hand accompaniment. It shows up to particular advantage in the song 'Sleep', ex. 193.

The beautiful pianistic decoration of themes, and well-spaced arpeggios in the left hand are aspects of Balakirev's piano writing which are not only of pianistic interest. The decoration in the Fantasia on Themes from *A Life for the Tsar*, ex. 94, the second piano Scherzo, ex. 107, the *Gondellied*, ex. 116, and The Lark, ex. 144, are of interest for the appoggiaturas, accented passing notes and chromatic grace notes in which they abound. Similarly, left-hand arpeggios have their harmonic effect—either fairly static, as in *Berceuse*, ex. 113, or gradually revealing new harmonies over a pedal bass, as in *Au jardin*, ex. 102, and the second Scherzo, ex. 105. The song '7th November', ex. 191 (b) gives an almost impressionistic result, the left hand arpeggios being supplemented by repeated semiquaver-figures in the right hand. The accompaniment in this song shows the influence of Liszt's late piano music.

Balakirev favours augmented intervals rather than diminished ones, on the whole. He uses a melodic augmented second for a Moorish effect in the Overture on a Spanish March Theme, ex. 1, and as a main feature of his fugal-arabesque melody at the beginning of the piano sonata, ex. 126, figure (c).

Occasionally the augmented fourth is employed as a chromatic embellishment, but it is of far more interest when it becomes an integral part of the scale. Balakirev seems most to enjoy this in the scale of B flat major—with an E natural instead of an E flat. It can have either a rather droll effect (ex. 28 from *Russia*) or a pathetic one (ex. 18 from the *Lear* overture), or a tragic one (ex. 24 from the *Lear* music).

One of the most important idiosyncrasies of Balakirev's style is his continual and unashamed employment of an augmented fifth from the tonic to give a quasi-modulation to the relative minor. This is not an original idea. Schumann, Chopin, Glinka and others use the device, but less frequently. On the other hand, there is hardly a work of Balakirev in which it is not to be found, at some stage. In ex. 95 from the early Scherzo in B minor, it is hardly distinguishable from Glinka; nor is there much difference between Glinka's and Balakirev's use of the idiom in ex. 150 from the first movement of the E flat piano concerto. It becomes far more important, playing a major role in the harmonisation of the melody, in the centre theme of *Islamey*, ex. 100, and the slow movement of the C major symphony, ex. 69. A nostalgic effect is gained in the *Valse mélancolique*, ex. 108, which quite suits the mood of the piece, but in some of the later piano works and songs the augmented fifth becomes more of a mannerism, which seems to be dragged in sometimes for want of anything more original. Ex. 118 in the piano *Tarantella*, and examples 182 ('The Wilderness'), 183 ('The sea does not foam') and 187 (a) ('I came to thee with greeting') from the last two groups of ten songs reveal a rather feeble repetition of what had previously been an intensely-felt idiom.

Balakirev only finished his works with a loud flourish if such an ending seemed to him to be eminently suitable. His reaction to the close of Tchaikovsky's *Romeo and Juliet* was one of horror at such an inartistic burst of loud chords.[1] In his own orchestral music, only the symphonies, *In Bohemia* and the Overture on a Spanish March Theme end in such a way as to court the applause of the public. The imaginative and artistic closes of *Russia*, ex. 31, the Overture on the themes of three Russian Songs, *Tamara* (the wafted whisper of 'farewell') and of the piano sonata, too, show his inability to play up to a less distinguishing audience, and at the same time his unerring instinct, in this respect, for what is in good taste, for what will enhance, to the discerning musician, the inner value of his work.

One of the most illuminating passages on Balakirev's methods in formal development—methods which Rimsky-Korsakov also used—has been written by M. F. Gnessin.[2] That suitable treatment of folk-themes influenced this type of development is evident. The Overture on the themes of three Russian songs (1858) is an early foretaste of what was to come in this direction, while the *King Lear* Overture reveals beyond cavil that Balakirev *could* write in perfect sonata-form if he so desired. Gnessin writes:

> [He] starts with the careful choice of a rich and expressive central idea (or ideas) which is the first and essentially vivid link in a series of vivid links, from which the artistic whole is gradually built up. Thematic repetitions, constant reminders of the idea, ensure against the introduction of elements which have no direct relation to the plan ... Melodic-rhythmic variations on the theme in different sections of the work, by enriching it with important and sometimes unexpected details, make the chief features and idea of the theme all the more strongly felt. The surrounding of the theme by constantly changing harmonies illumines it on all sides. The variation of exposition plays its part in the interpretation of the theme. The moments when the theme is transposed into different tonalities intensify its apprehension and make it felt as it were in different surroundings, while at the same time they *quantitatively* intensify the impression created by the theme. These are all ways of *analysing* the theme which is being impressed on the listener ... This analysis is deepened by contrasting the theme with another theme or other themes, also vivid and significant, in their turn submitted to a melodic-rhythmic or harmonic-polyphonic analysis ...[3]

There is a central point, or there are central points, from which a fresco of great elaboration can be drawn. The first movement of the C major symphony has but one central point—the statement of the theme in the opening *largo*—from which a fresco of intense feeling immediately emanates. With the gradual augmentation of the whole movement (corresponding to the increase in tension), Balakirev paints his pattern in ever widening and broader strokes —a brilliant example of this manner of intensifying an idea rather than indulging in a process of thematic development. In all his works based on folk-songs, too, Balakirev analyses them, and puts them together contrapuntally in shifting surroundings. What he does *not* do is to take a short figure and develop it, and then take another and develop that and so on.

Nor does he restrict himself to developing in a so-called development section. His development usually starts almost as soon as the theme itself. In the first movement of the C major symphony much of the development has already been heard by the end of the double exposition. This is not because Balakirev is unable to resist the temptation to play with his theme too early. On the contrary, it is the very basis of the particular form which, probably without knowing it, he invented; certainly it is unique to Balakirev's circle in the particular way in which they use it. The basis is not usually an extra-musical idea; as often as not, it is folk-song: Overture on the themes of three Russian Songs, symphonic poems *Russia* and *In Bohemia*, Finale of C major symphony and *Islamey*, for example. The Russian orthodox church chant atmosphere of the second movement of the E flat piano concerto, and the opening *largo* of the C major symphony come very close to this.

But to say that Balakirev uses folk-songs in these works, and to think of them in derogatory terms *for this reason*, would be to misunderstand the nature of the problem. He never makes the mistake of choosing a folk-song which is *in itself* and *by itself* already a really great melody. It is what he does with the folk-song, how he deals with it, which makes it great, as well as always being suitable to its original character. If we think the folk-songs by Balakirev in his works are great, then they are great because we have seen them through his eyes, mind and heart. As a scale might have been a basis for another man's fancy, so was a folk-song to Balakirev, and the folk-song is often no more to him than a scale in which he can work and from which he can modulate to another if he so inclines.

Balakirev's 'fresco-form' then, whether it is based on a folk-theme or not, is not produced by a lack of balance or a feebleness in the composer's grip of his material. The pattern of the fresco is as formal in its way as any Western form.

Two examples are sufficient to show how well Balakirev understood orthodox sonata form and composed in that form if he considered it appropriate to his material. The *King Lear* Overture (1859), and the first movement of the second symphony (1908), to take an early and a late example, provide perfect instances, showing that Balakirev understood the essential classical conciseness of the form (conciseness has nothing to do with length in this sense, but treatment), a form which he rightly did not use unless he felt that his inspiration matched the essential genre of the form.

The dramatic nature of sonata form was not lost on Balakirev. His use of it in his one overture to a stage work shows that the lessons of Beethoven's *Leonora No. 3* are clearly in his mind. Just as Beethoven's overture tells the whole story of his opera, so does Balakirev's tell, in synopsis, that of Lear. The dramatic contrast between the first and second subjects (intentionally avoided in the first movement of the C major symphony and in the piano sonata with its fugal-unitary conception) and the metamorphoses of Lear's theme provide an onward-moving account of the tale which, had Balakirev been writing this overture for an opera on the subject, might, like *Leonora No. 3*, have detracted from the ensuing material. The drama progresses inexorably to its tragic conclusion.

But, in the C major symphony and the symphonic poems, Balakirev did not want to move *on* anywhere. If any direction could be indicated, outwards would be a much more suitable word to describe the way the central ideas are fanned: upwards, downwards to a greater depth of chromatic shade, sideways; and always with the greatest clarity of delineation, revealing a clear, analytical, imaginative and clever mind at work, but perhaps too clever, too fussy over detail at times.

Balakirev's fussing over and testing out every note may have been why he composed so slowly, and why he found it very difficult to finish compositions already planned in outline. Every line of his pattern must be exactly right, in precise perspective. And so, very often the work was laid aside and left for leisure to finish it, and another was planned and started.

# CHAPTER 22

*Style, harmony, form and influences (3). A short survey of Balakirev's music, his development as a composer, and some further conclusions.*

Balakirev's symphonic writing lacks that monumental quality which is always connected with the idea of epic style, and is simultaneously an expression of the greatness of the folk spirit and the result of a great art of musical generalisation. It lacks also the capacity to pour the folk melody intonations into a musical form of great breadth.[1]

Enough has been said, both in the analyses themselves of the C major symphony and the symphonic poems, and in the chapters on the form and style of these works, to show that this conclusion of E. Fried shows a lack of appreciation of features of Balakirev's form and style which has for the most part been characteristic of many writers on Balakirev who have written about him in anything more than general terms. His continuing, 'All this, however, cannot detract from the enormous historical significance of Balakirev's work as a composer', is in no way a compensation for his earlier misunderstanding of the nature of Balakirev's work and its formal significance. Nobody has ever disputed the *historical* significance of Balakirev's work. But the timeless quality of all great creations has been denied to his compositions, and it is this quality which, it seems to the present writer, a few of his greatest works possess, regardless of their undoubted historical significance.

## Style, Harmony, Form and Influences

Of the orchestral works, the C major symphony, the symphonic poems *Tamara*, *In Bohemia* and *Russia*, and the incidental music to *King Lear* come into this category; the Overture on the themes of three Russian Songs and the Overture on a Spanish March Theme, though considerably lesser in conception, ought not to be passed over entirely. The same cannot be said of the second symphony whose fatal weakness, the slow movement, dates the work and takes away much of its significance. Similarly his orchestral arrangements (the Chopin Suite, Chopin's seventh Mazurka arranged for strings, and Lvov's Overture to *Undine*) are of little significance.

Balakirev revised all his completed earlier orchestral works after he had finished *Tamara*.[2] The revisions are mostly in orchestration—he considered his early orchestration to be somewhat poor and primitive. The revisions are in some cases slight, but the orchestration is vital to the interplay of contrasting colour-effects. He knew the effect he *wanted*, and was not satisfied until he eventually achieved it *exactly*.

While he was guided by Glinka's discoveries of the rich possibilities of the orchestra, particularly in *Russlan*, the Spanish Overtures and *Kamarinskaya*, Balakirev was not content with the classical simplicity of Glinka's instrumentation, and drew on the resources of a large 'romantic' orchestra. The study of the scores of Berlioz and Liszt led him to make wide use of particular instrumental timbres to produce vivid effects. The character of folk-song also influenced his orchestration—for example, a leading role is often given to the woodwind, *pizzicato* strings are used in imitation of peasant 'plucking' instruments, and pedal ('piping') basses, as has already been noticed, are employed.

The symphonic poem *Russia* is Balakirev's first work to use the harp (one of his favourite instruments) significantly. Its use is two-fold: as a striking instrument in pastoral episodes and in order to create a spirit of epic antiquity (Glinka also used it in this way, and, later, Borodin and, of course, Rimsky-Korsakov; in England, Vaughan Williams is the prime example). Other features are his use of the brass to convey a heroic figure; various ways of playing the tambourine (alternate blows on the skin and on the hoop); complex interplay of rhythms in *Tamara*, the first *allegro* perhaps evoking sounds of peasant stringed instruments and Tamara's oboe theme (with a pedal on the flute and *pizzicato* string accompaniment) imitating, remarkably, the sound of a Caucasian *zurna* (a type of bagpipe).

The orchestral devices and rhythmical subtleties used in *Tamara* are later employed in his re-orchestration of the Overture on a Spanish March Theme and the 'Czech' Overture (*In Bohemia*). They are employed, too, in the polonaise (finale) of the second symphony.

Much of Balakirev's most original creative thinking was done in the later 'fifties and in the 'sixties. A curious feature in his development is that his peak as an *orchestrator* was not reached until after this. Many of his orchestral problems were solved in *Tamara* and his experience there was made use of in his later revisions of earlier works which, from an absolute creative point of view, were *already satisfactory*.

Similarly his piano writing, from the technical point of view, did not become entirely assured until his later period—for example, the early form of his D major Mazurka (used in the piano sonata) is immature.

Balakirev's piano music shows well how difficult he found it to compose without first being given a 'kernel', a centre upon which to base his composition. When he did not have a folk-song or folk-songs, or an outside flavour such as old church chants, Caucasian rhythms or the works or themes of other composers, or even an extra-musical idea such as *King Lear*, upon which to build his own original work, he found it difficult to fill even a moderately large piece with emotional content. On his *own* account, he often did not have the necessary concentration of feeling and thought. There seems to be a compromise between breadth of content and comparative narrowness of ideas, in works which have as their basis only his own themes and thoughts, though there are, naturally, exceptions to this, notably in the piano sonata, a shining example of original style and thought.

Sometimes 'contrived' themes, when found side by side with others that are truly inspired, spoil a number of his works. Remembering that Balakirev was a brilliant improviser, and at times found it very hard to complete his works, it might be concluded that in his music the emotional predominates over the rational. This is not so. The crux of the matter is that Balakirev's emotions were short-lived outbursts of feeling which, as Rimsky-Korsakov put it, required 'chronic' inspiration, capable of burning long and evenly, to bring them to maturity. So, a continuous darkening of the theme, when it is well done, is wonderful in effect, but if there is mere padding of a short idea, then the effect is lifeless.

It would be naïve to say that the original idea requires emotion, and its fulfilment reason. Without emotion of a strong, creative kind it is impossible to carry through an idea. Balakirev sometimes lacked this quality of strong enduring emotion when the original idea was his own. The best results are achieved when he supports his idea by imposed energy from outside. But it was still in strengthening and perfecting *what was already there*, thus making it his own by force of personality, that his real genius lay, rather than in himself being inspired by *his own* original idea.

Balakirev's particular method of treating his ideas in shifting surroundings is responsible for the restlessness of his modulations. His desire to give variety is understandable, but too frequent changes can lead to confusion, the danger of too much variety resulting in a kaleidoscope which produces an effect, in the end, of greyness. His later stereotyped emotions are clearly seen in the typical quirks of harmony—particularly the augmented fifth and pedals—which he keeps on repeating in place of deeply felt emotion. But, even in the last years, he is still capable of fiery, strong, convincing outbursts of emotional energy (*La Fileuse* and part of the Toccata for piano, for instance) in treating original musical ideas.

In the later years, too, he was sometimes moved to imitation and stylisation by the richness of his impressions of the music of other composers, accurately registered by his extraordinary memory. This trend seems to struggle with his own originality without, often, achieving a decisive result.

But Balakirev claims special attention as the only composer of the Russian National School to achieve really successful piano writing. A few of his piano works are of outstanding merit: the B flat minor Sonata, Scherzo No. 2 in B flat minor, *Berceuse* in D flat major, *La Fileuse* in D flat major, *Tyrolienne* in F sharp major and *Dumka* in E flat minor. Other good piano works are Scherzo No. 3 in F sharp major, the first two Waltzes, *Islamey* (of its type), *Gondellied* in A minor, and Toccata in C sharp minor. Many of the other works are good in places, but some are weak more or less throughout: Mazurkas 3 to 6, Scherzo No. 1 in B minor, Waltzes 3 to 7, *Phantasiestück* in D flat major, *Novelette* in A major and *Esquisses* (Sonatina).

Balakirev's piano style developed from Hummel, Clementi, Weber and Field to Chopin and Liszt,[3] but he did create an original style of his own quite remarkable for the nineteenth century, more common in the twentieth. His transparency and clarity, lightness and flexibility are inherited from Glinka. But specifically his own is a quality, demanded in the interpreter, of an 'extremely highly developed technique of strong fingers full of initiative, capable of executing fast ornamental passages with the accuracy and assurance of engraving instruments in the hand of a master', as U. Kremlev writes.[4]

The pedal draws a gentle veil over the engraving, but does not blur its clear outlines, which reveal the powerful will of a remarkable musician. In his texture Balakirev shows a striking sensitivity to timbre, avoiding anything accidental, loose, summary or cloying. He endeavours, sometimes successfully, to combine the subtle and elegant with the weighty and powerful.

In his best piano music Balakirev subtly enriches and enlivens the outline with colour in a way unequalled by any other Russian composer, and in a way unique and unparalleled by other composers of any nationality. His best music is more intellectual than Chopin's, less showy than Liszt's (excluding *Islamey*), more vigorous than Lyadov's or Glazunov's, less effeminate than Scryabin's, less solid and heavily sentimental than Rachmaninov's, and in a more refined and transparent style than Brahms's. Such comparisons do not necessarily mean that his work is greater than any of these composers. In the small number of really great piano compositions he produced, he is vastly inferior to Chopin at one end of the scale, and equally superior to Glazunov at the other. In the intellectual quality of his emotion he is unique for his time.

In his songs, too, when he is not inspired by the outside elements already discussed, he is rarely at his best. Sometimes the quality of a poem will inspire him in the same way as these other factors. Just as Lermontov, in *Tamara*, inspires the most extraordinary originality of the orchestral poem which so exactly achieves the underlying atmosphere of the words, so, for instance, in the 'Song of the Golden Fish', 'Song of Selim' and 'Cradle Song' from the first group of twenty, Balakirev's imaginative insight into the poet's feelings is deep and powerful. But in some of his songs, notably those about love, a subject which he was never happy to embark upon (except for the evil love of Tamara!), and in which he was, no doubt, inexperienced, a weak salon element can be discerned at the very moment of the composer's striving to reveal the deep emotions of love without banality. Very often, too, the melody itself is rather insignificant, and the piano part assumes too great an importance.

Balakirev's facility in orchestration and technical writing for the piano improved with the years. What of his development as a composer? He cannot be said to have developed continuously, like Beethoven. To label 1837 and 1867 as period one, 1867 to 1882 (completion of *Tamara*) as period two, and 1882 to 1910 as period three would be too easy. It is true that *Tamara* occupied him from 1867 to 1882, and that he revised, in the last period, some of the works completed in period one. But Balakirev developed in much the same way as his own 'fresco-form'—in any direction but straight along. His occupation with *Tamara* in the whole of the middle period of his life was really a dead end as far as artistic development was concerned. Having achieved such mastery in this direction, he could not but return to the point of departure, first to revise earlier compositions, and then to complete some of them which remained unfinished, such as the C major symphony and the E flat piano concerto,[5] writing down former extemporisations and composing new works. His experience in *Tamara* is of practically no use to him in the C major symphony, which was taken up in the 'nineties where it was left off in the 'sixties. Any difference in style between the two periods is negligible. It is slightly fuller, perhaps, but Balakirev, in dealing with the same material, inspired by the same influence, writes almost the same kind of music. For him, any development away from such treatment, though he was thirty odd years older, would have been development in the wrong direction.

Consequently, any creative experience he has in one work does not necessarily move him onward to another, as with most composers. On finishing a work, he more or less goes back to his original point and starts out afresh on another tack, usually not allowing himself to be weighed down by experience gained in a previous and therefore irrelevant work.[6] It shows a lack of appreciation of this point to say, without qualification, that his style in 1866 is the same as his style in 1893 and has not materially changed, because he completed the first movement of the C major symphony as if no gap in time had existed in its composition. Compare the styles in the opening of the C major symphony and the opening of *Tamara*, or the opening of *Russia* with the opening of the second symphony; by the same composer, clearly, but different subjects and emphases, and so different ways of dealing with them.

Nor is it really profitable to wonder, if he had not been occupied with *Tamara* in his most mature years, whether he would not have been developing his 'symphonic' side and producing masterpiece after masterpiece. What has been written about his style and the conclusions that have been drawn make it clear that ordinary, even, consistent creative development seems to have been foreign to the very nature of the man; and it would have been much more surprising if such a man, inspired in volcanic phases of incredible but short-lived emotional power, were to have developed away from the central peak out of which the lava-like flow of his creations was produced. Whether it was folk-song, Caucasian music, church chants, poems or anything else which started the eruption, varied as it was, it all came from that same colourful source on the borders of European and Asiatic, ancient and modern, Russia; of borrowed and of original music; of the impassioned classical and controlled romantic; of poetry and of analysis; of heat and of coolness; of light and of shadow; of the intellect and the fancy.

### NOTES ON CHAPTER 22

1. FB, p. 202 et seq. I have made free use of this article by Fried.
2. The Overture on the themes of three Russian songs was revised just *before* he finished *Tamara*.
3. *Islamey* is, of course, based entirely on Lisztian technique.
4. K(4)A, p. 269.
5. Lyapunov completed the finale of this concerto, which Balakirev never finished.
6. The experience he gained in *Tamara*, in the light of which he later revised earlier compositions, was *orchestral* rather than *creative*.

## Appendix I

## BIBLIOGRAPHY

ABRAHAM, Gerald
1. AA    'Balakirev', article in *Grove's Dictionary of Music and Musicians*, 5th edn. (London, 1954), p. 362.
2. AB    'Balakirev: a Flawed Genius' in *Studies in Russian Music* (London, n.d.), p. 311.
3. AC    'Balakirev's Music to *King Lear*' in *On Russian Music* (London, n.d.), p. 193.
4. AD    'Balakirev's Piano Sonata', ibid., p. 205.
5. AE    *Rimsky-Korsakov* (London, 1945).
6. AF    'Balakirev's Symphonies' in *Music and Letters*, xiv, 1933, p. 355.
7. AF    'Balakirev's Symphonies' in *On Russian Music* (London, n.d.), p. 179.

CALVOCORESSI, M. D. and ABRAHAM, Gerald
8. CA    'Balakiref' in *Masters of Russian Music* (London, 1936), pp. 97–146.

CALVOCORESSI, M. D., ed. ABRAHAM, Gerald
9. CB    *Modest Mussorgsky, His Life and Works* (London, 1956).

CALVOCORESSI, M. D. (ed.)
10. CC    M. Balakirew; 'Lettres Inédites à M. D. Calvocoressi' in *Société Internationale de Musique, Revue Musicale Mensuelle*, No. vii (Paris, 1911).

FRIED, E.

11. FA    'Mily Alexeyevich Balakirev' in *Balakirev: Issledo-vaniya i Stati* (*Balakirev, Analyses and Articles*) (Leningrad, 1961), p. 5.

12. FB    'Simfonicheskoe Tvorchestvo' (Symphonic Compositions) (ibid., Leningrad, 1961), p. 76.

13. FC    (gen. ed.) 'Mily Alexeyevich Balakirev: Vospominaniya i Pisma' (Recollections and Letters) (Leningrad, 1962). This volume includes:

    (i) S. M. Lyapunov, A. S. Lyapunova, *Molodye gody Balakireva* (pp. 7–71).

    (ii) *Pisma k ottzu* (ed. A. P. Zorina), (pp. 72–93).

    (iii) *Pisma k V. M. Zhemchuzhnikovu* (ed. A. S. Lyapunova), (pp. 94–114).

    (iv) *Perepiska s P.I. Chaikovskim* (ed. A. A. Orlova), (pp. 115–203) (see also bibliography No. 27).

    (v) *Pisma k Louis-Albert Bourgault-Ducoudray* (ed. R. I. Zaritskaya), (pp. 204–221).

    (vi) *Pisma k T. I. Filippovu* (ed. B. B. Granovsky), (pp. 222–236).

    (vii) *Perepiska s S. K. Bulichem* (ed. M. K. Mikhailov), (pp. 237–276).

    (viii) *Pisma k G. N. Timofeyevu* (ed. A. N. Kryukov), (pp. 277–297).

    (ix) *Pisma k K. N. Chernovu* (ed. A. N. Kryukov), (pp. 298–305).

    (x) A. A. Olenin, *Moi Vospominaniya o M. A. Balakireve* (ed. L. Z. Korabelnikova), (pp. 306–366).

    (xi) S. N. Lalayeva, *Vospominaniya* (ed. A. S. Lyapunova), (pp. 367–377).

    (xii) V. V. Yastrebtsev, *Materialy 'Vospominany o Balakireve'* (ed. A. A. Yazovitskaya, V. N. Rimsky-Korsakov; introductory note by E. L. Fried), (pp. 378–425).

(xiii) V. G. Kulchinsky, *Vospominaniya* (ed. R. I. Zaritskaya), (pp. 426–431).

(xiv) *M. A. Balakirev: Zapisi kavkazkoi narodnoi muzyki* (ed. B. M. Dobrovolsky), (pp. 432–453).

(xv) *Bibliografiya epistolyary M. A. Balakireva* (compiled by V. A. Kiselev), (pp. 454–456).

GHIPIUS, E. V.

14. G(1)A *M. Balakirev: Russkie Narodnye Pesni* (*M. Balakirev: Russian Folk Songs*) (Moscow, 1957).

GOSENPUD, A.

15. G(2)A 'Neosushchestvlenny Operny Zamysel' (Project of an Opera Unrealised) in *Balakirev, Issledovaniya i stati* (Leningrad, 1961), p. 362 (including photostat of an unfinished song for the opera *The Firebird* with commentary by B. Dobrovolsky).

GRODSKY, B.

16. G(3)A *M. A. Balakirev: Kratky ocherk evo zhizni i deyatelnosti* (*M. A. Balakirev: a Short Essay on his Life and Works*) (St Petersburg, 1910).

KALMYKOV, V.

17. K(1)A 'Poyezdki M. A. Balakireva v Varshavu, 1891, 1894, (Balakirev's Journeys to Warsaw, 1891, 1894) in *Balakirev, Issledovaniya i stati* (Leningrad, 1961), p. 422.

KARATYGHIN, V.

18. K(2)A 'M. A. Balakirev' from *Apollon* (1910) (in Russian)

KARENIN, Vladimir

19. K(3)A 'M. A. Balakirev', obituary in *Russkaya Mysl* (1910), p. 191.

20. K(3)B *Perepiska M. A. Balakireva s V. V. Stasovym* (*Correspondence of M. A. Balakirev with V. V. Stassov*), Vol. I, 1858–69 (Moscow, 1935).

## *Appendixes*

Kremlev, U.
21. K(4)A 'Fortepiannaya Muzyka (Piano Music) in *Balakirev, Issledovaniya i stati* (Leningrad, 1961), p. 205.

Lyapunova, A.
22. L(1)A 'Glinka and Balakirev' in *Sovetskaya Muzyka* (1953), No. 2.

23. L(1)B 'Iz Istory Tvorcheskikh svyazei M. Balakireva i S. Lyapunova' (On the creative relationship of M. Balakirev and S. Lyapunov) in *Balakirev, Issledovaniya i stati* (Leningrad, 1961), p. 388.

24. L(1)C (ed.) and V. A. Kiselev, M. A. Balakirev: *Perepiska s notoizdatelstvom P. Yurgensona (Correspondence with the music publisher P. Jurgenson)* (Moscow, 1958).

25. L(1)D (ed.) *N. Rimsky-Korsakov: Polnoe Sobranie Sochineny (N. Rimsky-Korsakov: Complete works).* This includes the complete correspondence between Balakirev and Rimsky-Korsakov (Moscow, 1963).

Lyapunov, S. M.
26. L(2)A 'M. A. Balakirev' in *Ezhegodnik imperatorskikh teatrov (Year Book of the Imperial Theatres)*, Nos. vii and viii, 1910.

27. L(2)B (ed.) *Perepiska M. A. Balakireva s P. I. Chaikovskim (Correspondence of M. A. Balakirev with P. I. Tchaikovsky)* (St Petersburg, 1912).

Muzalevsky, V.
28. M(2)A *M. A. Balakirev: Kritiko-biografichesky ocherk (M. A. Balakirev: Critical-biographical Essay)*, Leningrad, 1938).

Newmarch, R.
29. NA 'Mily Balakireff' in *Sammelbände der Internationalen Musikgesellschaft*, 1902–3 (4th year) (in French).

Romanovsky, N.
30. RA 'Khoroviye Proizvedeniya' (Choral Works) in

*Balakirev, Issledovaniya i stati* (Leningrad, 1961), p. 341.

SOROKIN, K. S.

31. SA    (gen. ed.) *Polnoe Sobranie Sochineny dlya forte-piano* (*Complete Piano Compositions*), Vol. I (pts 1 and 2), Vol. II, Vol. III (pts 1 and 2), (Moscow–Leningrad, 1949–54).

TIMOFEYEV, G. I.

32. TA    'M. A. Balakirev' in *Russkaya Mysl*, Nos. vi and vii (1912).

33. TB    'M. A. Balakirev in Prague', in *Sovremenny Mir*', No. vi (1911).

VUKHANSKAYA, A.

34. VA    'Romansy i Pesni' (Songs) in *Balakirev, Issledovaniya i stati* (Leningrad, 1961), p. 271.

## *Appendix II*

## CHRONOLOGY

In each case, the first date given is the Russian one, 'old style', and the second is the equivalent according to the Western calendar.

| | |
|---|---|
| 1836–37 | Born at Nizhny-Novgorod (21 December 1836/ 2 January 1837). |
| 1853 | Enters the University of Kazan as an unmatriculated student. |
| 1855 | Ulybyshev takes him to St Petersburg. Meets Glinka and Ludmila Shestakova. Plays Fantasia on themes from *A Life for the Tsar* to Glinka, who is impressed. |
| 1856 | Glinka gives him three Spanish themes, and criticises the first movement of his octet. St Petersburg début at a University concert on 12/24 February. Meets Dargomyzhsky and Cui. |
| 1857 | Death of Glinka at Berlin. Overture on a Spanish March theme composed. |
| 1858 | Illness (inflammation of the brain). Completes Overture on the themes of three Russian Songs (first performed on 21 December/2 January 1859). Starts composition of first group of twenty songs, and of incidental music to *King Lear*. |
| 1859 | Overture to *King Lear* first performed 15/27 November at a University Concert: much praised. |
| 1861 | *King Lear* music completed. Meets Rimsky-Korsakov (26 November/8 December). |

| | |
|---|---|
| 1862 | Foundation of Free School of Music, 18/30 March. Meets Borodin (November or December). |
| 1862–63 | Two summer holidays spent in the Caucasus. |
| 1863 | Balakirev first appears as conductor. Composition of 'A Song of Georgia'. |
| 1864 | First group of twenty songs completed. First performance of Second Overture on Russian themes (*Russia*) on 6/18 April at a Free School Concert. Contemplates opera *The Fire-Bird*. |
| 1866 | About 'one third' of the first movement of the C major symphony completed and scored. Adventurous visit to Prague and Vienna. First collection of Forty Russian Folk Songs published. |
| 1867 | Conducts Glinka's two operas in Prague. First performance of 'Czech' overture (*In Bohemia*) on 12/24 May. V. V. Stassov first uses phrase 'moguchaya kuchka' ('mighty handful'). Appointed conductor of Russian Music Society. Invites Berlioz to Russia. Starts work on *Tamara*. |
| 1868 | Appointed Director of Free School (28 January/ 9 February). Grand Duchess Helena Pavlovna and 'Conservatoire' party try to oust him from conductorship of Russian Music Society. Holiday in Caucasus. First performance of *Lohengrin* in Russia. |
| 1869 | Forced to resign from conductorship of Russian Music Society. Death of father. Visits Moscow and stays with Tchaikovsky. First performance of *Islamey* by Nicholas Rubinstein, at a Free School Concert on 30 November/12 December. |
| 1870 | Shaky financial position. Failure of concert at Nizhny-Novgorod (June). |
| 1871 | Consults soothsayer. Rumour of madness. |
| 1872 | Financial failure of Free School Concerts. Withdrawal from public life. Takes clerical post on the Warsaw railway. |

| | |
|---|---|
| 1874 | Resigns directorship of Free School. Rimsky-Korsakov takes over. |
| c. 1874–5 | Resigns post on Warsaw railway. |
| 1876 | Gradual reappearance. Work on *Tamara* started again. Starts editing Glinka's operas for publication. |
| 1881 | Takes over directorship of Free School from Rimsky-Korsakov. Death of Mussorgsky. |
| 1881–1906 | The four early overtures on folk themes (Spanish, two Russian and Czech) all revised and published. |
| 1882 | *Tamara* completed. |
| 1883 | First performance of *Tamara*, 7/19 March. Appointed Director of Music of the Imperial Chapel, with Rimsky-Korsakov as his assistant. |
| 1884 | Meets Lyapunov. Belyaev's influence increasing. |
| 1885 | Conducts concerts in connection with Glinka memorial at Smolensk. |
| 1887 | Death of Borodin. |
| 1891 & 1894 | Visits Warsaw. Last appearance in public as a pianist, 5/17 October 1894. |
| 1894 | Retires from Imperial Chapel. |
| 1895–96 | Group of ten songs composed. |
| 1898 | Symphony in C major first performed at a Free School Concert on 11/23 April: Balakirev's last appearance as conductor. Second collection of thirty folk-songs. |
| 1898–1910 | Composition of much pianoforte music, more songs, second symphony, E flat piano concerto. |
| 1899 | Meets J. H. Zimmermann, music publisher. |
| 1904 | Revised *King Lear* music published. |
| 1905 | Publication of pianoforte sonata. |
| 1906 | Cantata for the unveiling of the Glinka memorial in St Petersburg first performed in Russia on 3/16 February. |

# Appendixes

| | |
|---|---|
| 1908 | Second symphony completed. Death of Rimsky-Korsakov. |
| 1909 | Concert of his works planned for February could not take place for lack of support. |
| 1910 | Dies of a cold resulting in pleurisy, 16/29 May. |

## *Appendix III*

## CATALOGUE OF WORKS

---

## STAGE MUSIC

Overture and Incidental Music for Shakespeare's *King Lear* (1858–61, rev. and rescored 1902).

## ORIGINAL CHORAL WORKS

6 Anthems for unaccompanied mixed chorus:

> 'Rest with the holy ones' (Requiem).
> 'From Heaven the prophets'.
> 'Thy soul is regenerated'.
> 'Song of the Cherubim'.
> 'All flesh is silent'.
> 'It is worthy'.

Anthem for women's or children's voices (also arranged for mixed chorus):

> 'Christ is risen' (*c.* 1887, publ. 1906).

Hymn in honour of the Grand Duke of Vladimir, Georgi Vsevolodovich (V. Likhachev) for mixed chorus, S.S.A.T.T.B.B. with pianoforte accomp. (1889).
'Leaving song of the Pupils of the Polotsky Ecclesiastical Girls'

College' (A. Yasherova), 'The Golden Time has Flown
Away' for unaccomp. women's chorus of 3 voices (1891).

'Hymn in honour of the most august Patroness of the Polotsky
Girls' College, the Empress Maria Feodorovna' (A. Yasherova)
for women's chorus of 4 voices with pianoforte accomp.
(1898).

'Hymn for women's choir' (V. Likhachev), 'Beneath the shadow
of Thy overflowing mercy', unaccomp. (1899).

'Hymn for women's choir (4 voices)' unaccomp. (Pushkin), 'The
Prayer of the Russians' (also published in a version for unaccomp. mixed chorus), (1899).

Hymn—'Praise to Almighty God' (M. Samochernova) for unaccomp. women's chorus of 4 voices (1902).

'School Hymn for Women's or Children's Choir' (P. Lebedinsky), 'We sing you a hymn, O dear school' (1902).

Cantata for the Unveiling of the Glinka Memorial in St Petersburg (V. Glebov) for soprano, chorus and orchestra (1904).

'Second Leaving Song of the Pupils of the Polotsky Girls'
College' (N. Zabelina-Bekarevich), 'Farewell for ever, our
unforgettable haven . . .' for unaccompanied women's chorus
of 3 voices (1908).


## CHORAL TRANSCRIPTIONS

Balakirev: 'Cradle Song' (arranged from No. 4 of first twenty
songs for two-part women's or children's chorus with small
orchestra or pianoforte accompaniment (1898).

Chopin: 'Mazurka' for unaccomp. mixed chorus, S.A.T.T.B.B.,
(words by Khomyakov)—arranged from Mazurkas Op. 6, no.
4 in E flat minor, and Op. 11, No. 4 in A flat major (*c.* 1887,
publ. 1898).

Glinka:

    (1) 'Venetian Night' for S.A.T.B. unaccomp. arranged from
the song, No. 21 in Balakirev's list.

    (2) 'Cradle Song' for S.A.A.T.T.B.B. unaccomp. arranged

from the song, No. 40 in Balakirev's list (*c.* 1887; both publ. 1900).
Folk-songs: 'Two Legends' for S.A.T.B. unaccomp.
    (1) Nikita Romanovich (from Balakirev's 2nd coll., No. 6), (1902).
    (2) The King's Son from Cracow (from Balakirev's 2nd coll., No. 8) (1902).
and (3) 'Oh! my heart' for S.A.T.B. unaccomp. (from Balakirev's 2nd coll., No. 27) (unpubl.).


## ORCHESTRAL WORKS

Polonaise-Fantaisie (185?, unfinished).
Overture on a Spanish March Theme (1857; rev. and rescored 1886).
Overture on the Themes of three Russian Songs (1858; rev. and rescored 1881).[1]
Symphonic poem *Russia* (1884; revised and rescored version of Second Overture on Russian Themes, 1864, publ. 1869 as 'Musical Picture, *1000 years*').
Symphony No. 1 in C major (1864–66 and 1893–97).[2]
Symphonic poem *In Bohemia* (1906; rev. and rescored version of Overture on Czech Themes, 1867).
Symphonic poem *Tamara* (1867–82).
Symphony No. 2 in D minor (1900–08).
Suite for orchestra (1901–08): 'Préambule', 'Quasi Valse', 'Tarantella'.
Suite on pieces by Chopin (1910).
    1. Préambule (Étude).
    2. Mazurka.
    3. Intermezzo (Nocturne).
    4. Finale (Scherzo).

[1] Arranged for pianoforte duet by the composer.
[2] Arranged for two pianofortes by the composer.

Orchestrated by Balakirev.
  Chopin: Mazurka No. 7 for string orchestra (1904).
  Piano Concerto in E minor, Op. 11, re-orchestrated and
    partly rewritten (1910).
  Glinka: Eastern Dances from *Russlan and Ludmila* for one
    orchestra (*c.* 1868).
  Lvov: Overture to *Undine* (1900).
  Various works by Glinka, Dargomyzhsky and Cui.

## PIANOFORTE AND ORCHESTRA

'Grande Fantaisie' on Russian Folk-songs, op. 4 (1852).
Concerto-movement in F sharp minor, Op. 1 (1855–56).
Concerto in E flat major (begun 1861–62, resumed 1906–09;
  completed by S. Lyapunov).

## CHAMBER MUSIC

Septet for flute, clar., strings and pianoforte (1852).
Octet, op. 3, for flute, oboe, horn, strings and pianoforte (1855–
  1856).
String Quartet (op. 2? unfinished), 'Quatuor original russe',
  (1854–55).
Romance for Violoncello and pianoforte (1856).

## ORIGINAL WORKS FOR PIANOFORTE SOLO

Sonata in B flat minor (1905).
Mazurka No. 1, A flat ma. (1861).
Mazurka No. 2, C sharp mi. (1861).
Mazurka No. 3, B mi. (1886).
Mazurka No. 4, G flat ma. (1886).
Mazurka No. 5, D ma. (used in Sonata) (1900).
Mazurka No. 6, A flat ma. (F mi. in Soviet ed.) (1902).
Mazurka No. 7, E flat mi. (1906).

Nocturne No. 1, B flat mi. (1856, rev. 1898).
Nocturne No. 2, B mi. (1901).
Nocturne No. 3, D mi. (1902).
Scherzo No. 1, B mi. (1856, publ. *c.* 1860).
Scherzo No. 2, B flat mi. (1900).
Scherzo No. 3, F sharp ma. (1901).
*Valse di bravura* (No. 1), G ma. (1900).
*Valse mélancolique* (No. 2), F mi. (1900).
*Valse-Impromptu* (No. 3), D ma. (1901).
Waltz No. 4, B flat ma. (*Valse de Concert*) (1902).
Waltz No. 5, D flat ma. (1903).
Waltz No. 6, F sharp mi. (1903).
Waltz No. 7, G sharp mi. (1906).
Polka, F sharp mi. (*c.* 1859).
*Islamey*, Oriental Fantasy (1869, rev. 1902).
*Au jardin* D flat ma. (1884).
*Dumka*, E flat mi. (1900).
*Berceuse*, D flat ma. (1901).
*Gondellied*, A mi. (1901).
*Tarantella*, B ma. (1901).
*Capriccio*, D ma. (1902).
Toccata, C sharp mi. (1902).
*Tyrolienne*, F sharp ma. (1902).
*Chant du Pêcheur*, B mi. (1903).
*Rêverie*, F ma. (1903).
*Humoresque*, D ma. (1903).
*Phantasiestück*, D flat ma. (1903).
*La Fileuse*, B flat mi. (1906).
*Novellette*, A ma. (1906).
*Esquisses* (Sonatina), G. ma. (1909).

## ORIGINAL PIANOFORTE MUSIC BASED ON BORROWED THEMES

Fantasia on Themes from Glinka's opera, *A Life for the Tsar* (1854–5, rev. 1899).

Arr. of Glinka's song, 'The Lark' (*c.* 1862).
*Spanish Melody* (1902).
*Spanish Serenade* (1902; rev. version of 'Fandango-Étude', 1856).
Impromptu on the Themes of two Preludes by Chopin (E flat mi. and B ma.) (1907).

## PIANOFORTE DUETS

30 Russian Folk-songs (based on *Thirty Songs of the Russian People,* see Arrangements for Voice and Pianoforte) (1898).
Suite (1909; started in the 'fifties)
    1. Polonaise.
    2. Little Song without Words.
    3. Scherzo.
*On the Volga.*

## PIANOFORTE TRANSCRIPTIONS
(Pianoforte solo unless otherwise stated)

Beethoven:
    Cavatina from String Quartet, op. 130 (1859).
    Allegretto from String Quartet, op. 59, No. 2 (1862).
    String Quartet, op. 95 (2 pfs. 4 hands) (1862).
Berlioz:
    Introduction to *La Fuite en Égypte* (1864).
    *Harold en Italie* (pianoforte duet) (1876).
Chopin:
    Romance from Concerto, op. 11 (1905).
Dargomyzhsky:
    Two excerpts from "Rogdana" (pianoforte duet).
Glinka:
    Fantasia on themes from *A Life for the Tsar* (see above).
    Song, 'The Lark' (see above).
    Song, 'Do not speak' (1903).
    *Jota Aragonesa* (pianoforte solo and duet) (1864).
    *Night in Madrid* (pianoforte solo and duet) (1864).

*Kamarinskaya:* Fantasia on Two Russian folk-songs (1902).
Oriental March from *Russlan and Ludmila* (Liszt-Balakiriv).
*Prince Kholmsky* (pianoforte duet) (1864).
Lvov:
  Overture to *Undine* (pianoforte duet).
Taneyev:
  2 Valses-Caprices (A flat ma. and D flat ma.) (1900).
Zapolsky:
  *Rêverie.*
Edited by Balakirev:
Odoyevsky:
  Berceuse
Vyelgorsky–Liszt:
  Song, 'I loved him'.
Tausig:
  Selected pianoforte compositions.
I. F. Laskovsky:
  Pianoforte compositions.

## SONGS[1]

*Three Forgotten Songs* (1855)
  1. Thou art so captivating (A. Golovinsky).
  2. The Link (V. Tumansky).
  3. Spanish Song (M. Mikhailov).

20 Songs (1858–65).
  1. Brigand's Song (Koltsov) (1858).
  2. Embrace, kiss (Koltsov) (1858).
  3. Barcarolle (A. Arsenev, after Heine) (1858).
  4. Cradle Song (Arsenev) (1858).
  5. The Bright Moon (M. Yatsevich) (1858).
  6. When thou playest, carefree child (K. Vilde) (1858).
  7. The Knight (Vilde) 1858).

[1] Gerald Abraham's translations of the titles, as published in Grove's *Dictionary of Music and Musicians*, 5th edn. p. 368.

8. I'm a fine fellow (Koltsov) (1858).
9. My heart is torn (Koltsov) (1858).
10. Come to me (Koltsov) (1858).
11. Song of Selim (Lermontov) (1858).
12. Lead me, O night! (Maikov) (1859).
13. Hebrew Melody (Lermontov, after Byron) (1859).
14. Rapture (Koltsov) (1859).
15. Why? (Lermontov) (1860).
16. Song of the Golden Fish (Lermontov) (1860).
17. Old Man's Song (Koltsov) (1865).
18. When I hear thy voice (Lermontov) (1863).
19. Song of Georgia (Pushkin) (1863) (orchestrated in the 'sixties; orchestral version published in 1885).
20. Dream (M. Mikhailov, after Heine) (1864).

10 Songs (1895–96)

1. Over the Lake (Golenischev-Kutuzov).
2. The Wilderness (A. Zhemchuzhnikov).[1]
3. The sea does not foam (A. K. Tolstoy).
4. When the yellow cornfield waves (Lermontov).
5. I loved him (Koltsov).
6. The Pine-Tree (Lermontov, after Heine) (begun *c.* 1861).
7. Nachtstück (Khomyakov).
8. The Putting-Right (L. Mey) (orchestrated by Lyapunov).
9. 'Mid Autumn Flowers (I. Aksakov).
10. The rosy sunset fades (V. Kulchinsky).

10 Songs (1903–04)

1. Prologue (Mey) (also orchestrated).
2. Dream (Lermontov) (also orchestrated).
3. Starless midnight coldly breathed (Khomyakov).
4. 7th November (Khomyakov).
5. I came to thee with greeting (Fet).
6. Look, my friend (V. Krasov).

[1] Also arranged for piano solo (1898).

7. A whisper, a timid breath (Fet).
8. Song (Lermontov) (begun *c.* 1861).
9. Under the mysterious mask (Lermontov).
10. Sleep (Khomyakov).
'Dawn (Khomyakov) (1909).
'The Crag' (Lermontov) (1909).

## ARRANGEMENTS FOR VOICE AND PIANOFORTE

Collection of Russian Folk Songs (40) (1866).
*Thirty Songs of the Russian People* (1898).

*Appendix IV*

# ORIGINAL COMPOSITIONS OF M.I. GLINKA

edited by M. A. Balakirev and S. M. Lyapunov

---

## STAGE MUSIC AND CHORAL WORKS

1. *A Life for the Tsar*, opera in 4 acts with epilogue.
2. *Russlan and Ludmila*, a magic opera in 5 acts.
3. *Tarantella*, the poem of Myatlev, arranged for the stage (recitation, chorus, orchestra, dances).
4. *Prince Kholmsky*. Music for Kukolnik's tragedy (overture, 4 entr'actes and 3 vocal items).
5. 'Polsky' (E flat major) for chorus and orchestra.
6. 'Farewell song of the pupils of the Ekaterinsky Institute' (female chorus, solo and orchestra).
7. 'Farewell song of the pupils of the Smolny Institute' (female chorus, solo and orchestra).
8. 'Prayer—At a difficult time' (chorus, solo and orchestra).

## ORCHESTRAL MUSIC

1. Spanish Overtures:
    (a) *Capriccio brillante*—on a theme of an Aragonesa Jota.
    (b) *Night in Madrid*—fantasia on Spanish themes.
2. Fantasia on Russian Dance and Nuptial Folk-songs (*Kamarinskaya*).
3. Valse-Fantaisie.

339

*Appendixes*

## CHAMBER MUSIC

1. Sextet (Eb major) 'pour le piano, 2 violons, alto, violoncello et contrebasse'.
2. Quartet (F major) 'pour 2 violons, alto et violoncello'.

## PIANO MUSIC

*Piano duet:* 'Elementary Polka'.
*Piano solo:*
1. Fugue (A minor).
2. 'Thème écossais varié'.
3. 'Souvenir d'une Mazurka'.
4. 'Barcarolle'.
5. 'Tarantella'.
6. 'Petite Mazurka'.
7. 'Séparation'—Nocturne.
8. Arrangements made by the composer for his little niece Olga Shestakova:
   (a) Chorus of magic maidens from the opera *Russlan and Ludmila*.
   (b) Chorus 'Glory to thee' from the opera *A Life for the Tsar*.
9. 'Las Mollares'. Andalusian dance, written down for pianoforte.

## SONGS WITH PIANO ACCOMPANIMENT
### (*a*) for one voice

1. My harp.
2. Elegy.
3. The poor singer.
4. Consolation.
5. Ah! thou, dear love, art so fair.
6. 'Le baiser' (I love you).
7. Russian song.
8. 'Pour un moment'.

9. Memory of the heart.
10. Tell me why.
12. Disappointed.
13. Song (Ah! thou, dear night).
14. Song ('Grandpapa! one girl for me').
15. Georgian Melody.
16. 'Shall I forget?'
17. Song (Autumn night).
18. A voice from another world.
19. 'Il Desiderio'.
20. The conqueror.
21. Venetian night.
22. The leafy forest rustles.
23. Do not speak.
24. Do not call her divine.
25. 'I am here, Inezilya'.
26. Had I but known you.
27. Nightly vigil.
28. Where is our rose?
29. Zephyr of the night.
30. Duettino.
31. 'Doubt' (with an arrangement for two voices and with accompaniment for violin or violoncello).
32. 'Desire's flame is burning in the blood'.
33. First little Russian song.
34. Second little Russian song.
35. 'If I meet you'.
36. 'I remember the wonderful moment'.
37. 'Who is she and where is she?'
38. Bolero.
39. Cavatina.
40. Lullaby (with arrangement for two voices).
41. Russian song.
42. Fantasia.
43. Barcarolle.
44. 'Virtus antiqua'.
45. The Lark (with arrangement for two voices).

46. To Molly.
47. Song of Farewell.
48. 'How sweet it is to be with you'.
49. 'I love you, dear rose'.
50. To her.
51. Darling.
52. 'You will soon forget me'.
53. 'Do I hear your voice?'
54. The toasting-cup.
55. Marguerite's song.
56. 'Rozmova'.
57. Adela.
58. Mary.
59. The gulf of Finland.
60. (a) Prayer (at a difficult time).
    (b) the same with chorus.
61. 'Do not say that you are sick at heart'.

### (*b*) Arrangements by M. I. Glinka for two voices

1. Elegy 'When you asked your soul'—original music by M. Yakovlev.
2. Romance 'Forgive me, forgive me'—original music by P. Fedorov.

## CHURCH MUSIC

1. The Cherubim.
2. Ekteniya.
3. Reformation.

S. M. Lyapunov also made various arrangements included in a second list and the whole was in the form of a contract in the possession of the publisher Jurgenson. The contract was signed by Mily Alexeyevich Balakirev and Sergei Michaelovich Lyapunov on the 8 December 1905. The document is in the Glinka Museum in Moscow.

# GENERAL INDEX

Abaza, U. F., 84
Abraham, Gerald, 11, 12, 122, 145,
     193, 196, 206, *321*
Adamovsky, V., 39
Aksakov, I. S., 281
Albrecht, E. K., 58
d'Alheim, *see* Olenina, Maria
Allegri, 104
Araja, 28
Arensky, 124, 213
d'Argenteau, Countess, 134
Arsenev, A., 268, 271
Augener, 56, 247
Averkiev, D., 83–4, 106

Bach, J. S., 61, 104, 237
Bakhmetev, 119
Balakirev, A. K. (father), 22, 23, 26,
     37, 38, 40, 77, 87
Balakirev, Mily: as conductor, 24, 47,
     73–6, 78, 81–3, 85, 86, 98, 145
  as pianist, 15, 24, 31–2, 34, 38–9,
     131, 140–2, 155
  as teacher, 16, 29–30, 39–40, *60–8*,
     96, 101, 102, 105, 125–6
  his music: 'Arabesque' style, 248,
     257, 307
     'Fresco' construction, 210, 212,
     257, 309–11, 318
     'Mosaic' construction, 200, 237–9
     'Oriental' style, 44, 50, 90, 115,
     160, 188, 190, 196, 205, 220–2,
     273, 278, 306, 307
  influence and use of Czech folk
     music, 72, 181
     English folk music, 33, 164–5
     Russian church music, 55, 120,

195, 197, 254, 256–8, 264, 285,
     302, 310, 315
  Russian folk music, 25, 33, 41, 49,
     50, 51, 56–7, 89, 147, 162, 176,
     189, 205, 212, 213, 221–2, 251,
     253, 265–6, 283, 289, 293–301,
     302, 303, 309, 310, 314–5, 323
     Spanish folk music, 31, 245–6
  interest in folk music, 108, 136
Balakireva, Anna (sister), 23, 40, 122
Balakireva, E. I. (mother), 22, 23
Balakireva, Maria (sister), 23, 40, 77, 92,
     122
Balakireva, Varvara (sister), 23, 39, 40,
     45, 77, 92, 122
Batyushkov, 85
Beethoven, 23, 24, 36, 38, 43, 44, 56,
     58, 61, 62, 81, 141, 142, 169, 175,
     177, 220, 240, 254, 255, 311, 318
     (*see also* Index of Balakirev's
     works)
Bellini, 28
Belyaev, M. P., 57, 109, 114, 123, 124,
     125, 129, 133, 134, 142, 293
Berlioz, Hector, 27, 36, 41, 43, 48, 56,
     61, 65, 78, 79, 84, 85, 86, 91, 98,
     105, 113, 117, 118, 142, 148, 175,
     314 (*see also* Index of Balakirev's
     works)
Bernard, M., 129, 245, 293
Bessel, 51, 129, 159, 176, 249
Bizet, 42
Blumenfeld, F. M., 124, 150
Boborykin, P. D., 25, 26, 39, 132
Bobrinsky, Count, 78
Borodin, Alexander, 29, 33, 55, 62, 63–
     64, 66–7, 68, 96, 98, 105, 106, 110–
     111, 112, 122, 126, 133, 154, 170,

343

# General Index

# General Index

Lyapunov, S. M., 11, 15, 17, 30, 45, 82, 101, 106, 123, 126, 129, 130, 134, 144, 145, 151, 152, 153, 154, 156, 208, 237, 251, 253, 254, 259, 320, 322, *324*

Lyapunova, A. S., 12, 31, 46, 153, 251, 322, *324*

Maikov, A. N., 274
Malherbe, C., 148
Maria Feodorovna, Empress, 262, 263
Massenet, J., 116
Meck, Madame von, 17, 45, 105
Méhul, 47
Mendelssohn, F., 24, 47, 85, 91, 175
Mey, L. A., 281, 283
Meyer, 131
Mikhailov, M., 270, 277
Monsigny, 28
Mooser, R. A., 37
Moscow conservatoire, 60, 87, 90, 102, 109, 113, 129
Mozart, 23, 25, 42, 45, 47, 61, 66, 81, 95, 171, 254
Mussorgsky, F., 63
Mussorgsky, Modest Petrovich, ('Modinka'), 16, 17, 29, 30, 33, 40, 44, 48, 53, 55, 57, 60–4 *passim*, 67, 68, 83, 84, 98, 103, 105, 112–113, 126, 154, 166, 184, 214, 224, 235, 258–9, 264, 274, 281, 303, 321
Muzalevsky, V., 156, *324*

Napravnik, 87, 93, 95, 151, 156, 166, 265
Newmarch, Rosa, 141, 146, 156, 188, 194, *324*
Nizhny-Novgorod (Balakirev's birthplace), 21, 22, 23, 24, 26, 37, 42, 48, 51, 62, 95, 254, 263–4
Noskowski, 136, 137, 139, 140

Obolensky, D. A., 84
Odoyevsky, Prince, 32, 245 (*see also* Index of Balakirev's works)
Olenin, A. A., 30, 120, 121, 123, 124, 125, 130, 132, 133, 134, 137, 140, 145–6, 149, 155, 296, 322

Olenina, Maria, 123, 124, 149–50, 284
Orda, N., 135
Orlova, O., 261

de Pachmann, 141
Paderewski, 141
Paesiello, 28
Palestrina, 104
Pawlowski, 135, 136
Payevsky, V. E., 143
Pergolesi, 47
Petrov, A. A., 145–6
Piccini, 28
Polotsky College for Girls, 261–3, 269
Práč, 56, 293
Prague, Balakirev's visit to, 11, 55, 57–8, 70–9, 87, 154, 181, 245, 325
Pring, S. W., 137, 155, 156
Prohazka, 73
Pushkin, 28, 29, 49, 54, 261, 263, 277, 278
Pypin, A., 114, 143
Pypina, U. P., 139, 143

Rachmaninov, S., 317
Rahter, D., 243–4
Ravel, M., 146
Richter, Sviatoslav, 141
Rimsky-Korsakov, A., 68
Rimsky-Korsakov, Nicholas Andreyevich ('Korsinka'), 17, 29, 30, 33, 43, 48, 49, 55, 58, 61, 62, 64–6, 67, 68, 79, 82, 83, 84, 85, 88, 91, 97, 98, 101, 102, 104, 105, 106, 108, 110–15 *passim*, 117–21 *passim*, 123–6 *passim*, 131, 133–4, 142, 145–6, 152, 154, 166, 188, 189, 190, 204, 254, 258, 259, 264, 308, 312, 314, 316, 321, 324
autobiography, 15, 30, 54, 195–6
collection of folk music, 57, 212, 213, 297–8
correspondence with Balakirev, 49–50, 52, 55, 65–6, 69, 106, 107, 324
correspondence with Borodin, Cui, Stassov, 53, 56, 98, 106
Romanovsky, N., *324–5*

346

# INDEX OF BALAKIREV'S WORKS

# Index of Balakirev's Works